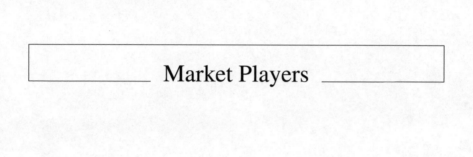

Market Players

Market Players

*A Guide to the Institutions
in Today's Financial Markets*

Gail Rolland

A John Wiley and Sons, Ltd., Publication

This edition first published 2011
© 2011 John Wiley & Sons, Ltd

Registered office
John Wiley & Sons Ltd, The Atrium, Southern Gate, Chichester, West Sussex, PO19 8SQ,
United Kingdom

For details of our global editorial offices, for customer services and for information about how to
apply for permission to reuse the copyright material in this book please see our website at
www.wiley.com.

Library of Congress Cataloging-in-Publication Data

Rolland, Gail.
    Market players : a guide to the institutions in today's financial markets / Gail Rolland.
        p. cm.
    Includes bibliographical references and index.
    ISBN 978-0-470-66555-8 (hardback)
  1. Financial institutions.   2. Banks and banking.   3. Financial services industry.
  4. Capital market. I. Title.
    HG173.R656 2011
    332.1–dc22

                                                                                    2010039913

A catalogue record for this book is available from the British Library.

ISBN 978-0-470-66555-8 (hardback), ISBN 978-0-470-97687-6 (ebk),
ISBN 978-1-119-99037-6 (ebk), ISBN 978-1-119-99038-3 (ebk)

Typeset in 11/13pt Times by Aptara Inc., New Delhi, India
Printed in Great Britain by TJ International Ltd, Padstow, Cornwall, UK

For Richard

Contents

Acknowledgements

The author wishes to thank the many market participants who gave up their time to offers insights and opinions to the author and to Lorraine Sarsfield Boulting for her assistance in the research.

Introduction

The international financial markets play a crucial role in the economy and it is large institutions that dominate and influence these markets; in this book we are going to take a look at these large players that yield so much influence on the markets and therefore on all our lives. All of us will have market exposure, whether it is through investing ourselves, or through our savings or pensions, or even just because of the incredible influence that financial markets today have on the global economy. It is easy to think of the markets as being the domain of the banks but this is too generic. In actual fact there are various different types of 'bank' that we will see active in different areas for different reasons along with many other non bank institutions, such as insurance companies, that also have an important role to play. The purpose of this book is to explain these institutions and why they are active in the markets. We will look at the sort of markets in which these firms are the key players and try to understand why they are involved, what the markets can do for them. This will mean that we have to think about their motivations and the cash flows coming into the firms that they will need to offset in the marketplace. Of course these are typically large, complex firms so we need to focus on the parts of their business that will be involved with these financial markets. We will not attempt to describe every part of their business, just those areas that will lead to the trades that we see on a daily basis. Today's markets are predominantly international and so we need to look at different sorts of international institutions but we will also look at some specifically national ones. Whilst we cannot look at every country in the world we can get a good perspective if we take a look at representative areas covering the US, Asia and Europe giving us a good overview of these global players.

The timing of this book comes on the heels of a major period of upheaval. The recent Financial Crisis has meant that the markets have become the focus of much attention, most of it unflattering. It can also be difficult to distinguish the different players and the impact they can have, despite its importance in understanding what is happening in this industry. So one of the main reasons for writing this book is to make these distinctions, to explain the role of these different firms for the benefit of anyone with an interest in learning more about them to increase their understanding of who are the major influences on the markets today. We must remember that to reach this point this industry had been through a period of two decades of pretty much sustained economic growth, and its own growth was in many cases quite breathtaking in the speed with which both the firms and the markets expanded. To give an example of this in 1998 the BIS[1] started to report figures on the OTC derivatives market, a market that has come under a lot of scrutiny since the Financial Crisis and one that we will discuss a little later in this chapter. In 1998 the estimated notional amount of these contracts outstanding was $70 trillion.[2] By June 2008 this had risen to $683.7 trillion.[3] If we look at the international debt in issue we see a similar rise:

June 1998 international debt in issue $3.6589 trillion[4]
June 2008 international debt in issue $25.2782 trillion[5]

These figures show a pretty phenomenal growth in the product available in the market, and it is not just the product range that has expanded but also the level of trading activity. If we look at the foreign exchange market we can get a feel for how daily turnover increased in this market by looking at the figures for three sorts of foreign exchange contract, FX spot deals, FX forwards and a product that is a combination of the two, the FX swap. We will look at just what these deals are a little later, but at the moment let's consider the increases in market turnover:[6]
So it is against this background of growth that we ran into the problems of 2007/2008.

---

[1] Bank for International Settlements.
[2] The Global OTC Derivatives Market at end-June 1998, BIS.
[3] The Global OTC Derivatives Market at end-June 2008, BIS.
[4] OTC Derivatives Market Activity in the first half of 1998, BIS.
[5] OTC Derivatives Market Activity in the first half of 2008, BIS.
[6] As before for 1998 and 2008.

Table 0.1 FX Market Turnover

	1998	2007
FX spot[1]	$577,737 billion	$1,004,889 billion
Outright Forwards[2]	$129,671 billion	$361,730 billion
FX swaps[3]	$734,122 billion	$1,714,370 billion

[1] A foreign exchange deal buying and selling currencies for immediate settlement, most commonly two days after trade.
[2] A foreign exchange deal buying and selling currencies for settlement on a given future date.
[3] This is a deal in which a currency is bought or sold for spot settlement and simultaneously reversed on a forward trade.

FINANCIAL CRISIS

What actually caused the crisis is a topic that will be researched and discussed for many years to come, but most agree that there were several key issues that were catalysts. These included inappropriate lending by banks. We saw over recent years a sharp increase in the banks lending money to borrowers who proved not to be able to manage the debt. To make matters worse they were sometimes even carrying out secured lending against insufficient collateral. This is the sort of thing we see with the infamous sub-prime mortgages – a dangerous mixture. A prime borrower is one that meets criteria of credit worthiness, such as having a good track record when it comes to making payments on loans and having a good income to borrowing ratio which would suggest they would be able to afford to service any debt. These are the borrowers who will be able to access the normal market rate, be that a mortgage rate for a retail customer or an interbank rate for a bank. The sub-prime borrowers are those that do not reach these criteria and therefore carry with them an additional credit risk. These borrowers therefore need to pay a higher rate of interest to cover this risk and this is where the problems lie. Quantifying just how much risk they bear is far from simple, particularly since this will be a moving dynamic. In a stronger economic scenario we are likely to see relatively few defaults and missed payments from sub-prime borrowers if, for example, they are able to stay in work. However if we have a weakening economic scenario, with increasing unemployment and falling asset values, this can have a particularly large impact on the sub-prime borrowers, probably the most vulnerable customers of the bank. As jobs are lost so payments may be missed. Then on top of this, if house prices fall the assets can end up being worth substantially less than the loan value, in other words the

borrowers have negative equity. This is exactly the scenario we have seen
not just in 2008 but into 2009 and beyond, causing an ongoing problem
for the markets. We should also not forget the prime borrowers. In a
weakening global economic situation they are not immune: a prime
borrower today could become a sub-prime borrower tomorrow. As an
example of this we only have to look at the situation with Dubai World,
the state-owned property company that took the markets by surprise in
November 2009 when it asked to delay payment on debt of nearly $60
billion. This was completely unexpected by most, particularly bearing
in mind the ownership of the company. Also the timing was a shock,
coming just before they unveiled their most famous piece of real estate,
the Khalifa Tower. So if we bear in mind these factors, unfortunately
the scene was set for the financial crisis that affected the markets from
2007.

This was a particularly difficult couple of years for financial markets
as we began to question not just the players but the whole infrastructure
of the industry. We saw a crisis of liquidity that brought about a series of
failures of financial firms and more banks to the brink of failure, which
resulted in unprecedented government intervention to prevent the whole
banking system from failing. These failures included AIG and Northern
Rock whom we will look at later in this book as examples of what can
go wrong within a financial firm.

As well as the problem of inappropriate lending there is also a belief
that there was a lack of understanding of both the risk and how to value
some of the structured products the banks were using to package and
pass on these underlying potentially dangerous exposures. Financial
markets in the 21st century pride themselves on their sophistication.
Starting from the core idea of moving money from one party to another
markets have grown in character to encompass many different ways
to achieve this. This is with the purpose of trying to match supply and
demand of participants' particular requirements for a sort of cash flow or
a return. An example of this might be if you were a potential borrower
but all of your income was linked to the price of gold: then to make
the best match between requirement and cash flow the market could
try and structure a deal whereby the interest you pay would be linked
to the movements in the gold price. For example, when the price rose
you might pay a higher interest rate to compensate for being able to
pay a lower interest rate when the price fell. This would match with
your cash flow and make the borrowing easier to manage. What we
should remember, though, is the impact on the other side of the fence,

the lender of the funds. Depending on how the deal was structured they could end up with a long period of receiving low returns if the price of gold remained low, maybe throughout the entire life of the deal. This is the risk they would take in return for the potential benefit of receiving high returns if the price of gold were high. The thing is we never know in advance what the price will be. We can model expected returns, which is how we will set the rates on this deal, but expectation and reality can prove to be far apart. This is the criticism being levelled at the market following the crisis, that their expectations were out of line with reality and, in retrospect, that they should have taken a more cautious view. That is easy to say from the perspective of an economic downturn and with the benefit of hindsight, but when the markets are operating in a strong economic scenario the perspective can be very different and this has an impact on the maths used by the market to calculate their values. Maybe this is an example of optimistic valuation.

Another reason often cited for the crisis is tied in with this, and that is that the market suffered from inadequate regulation which allowed this kind of anomaly to happen. The financial markets are regulated by central banks and market authorities whose purpose, with regard to the markets, is to set standards that participant firms must meet in order to protect end-users such as you and I. The past 25 years have seen great changes as the regulators have striven to keep pace with the fast-changing markets, in terms of both product and globalization. The overriding principle that has been applied in most countries is one of self-regulation. The firms should be given a series of guidelines, within a legal framework, and for the most part they are expected to find for themselves the best way to implement these. Now, again with the wisdom of hindsight, many market commentators are saying that this was not strong enough regulation and that the regulators should have been more prescriptive in telling the firms what to do. Of course there is no guarantee that this would have been any more effective. Looking at it starkly, if the firms themselves struggled with risk and valuation why should the regulators have been any better? After the crisis it was said that there was too much reliance on mathematical modelling but at the time it was believed that these models were using correct cash flow projections. So the problem may not be in the maths but again comes back to dealing with the unexpected and whether it really should have been expected. The net result is that the regulators have taken a close look at the markets and the participants and this is likely to result in greater micro-management of the firms, but whilst still balancing the need to allow the markets to trade and continue to develop, on the one hand, with prudency on the other. We will look at the central banks and other market regulators and the key role they play in the financial markets later in this book.

As we have said, the focus of this book is to look at the institutions in the financial markets but before we can continue to look at these different types of firm we should take just a little time to make sure we understand the products of the market, the instruments that are being traded. We need to do this to give ourselves the vocabulary that we will be using later as we explain the actions of the firms that we see in the marketplace. As we go through the sections looking at the various types of firm we will often have to focus on cash flow coming into the organization that can then be translated into a market exposure, so it makes sense to outline these financial market products.

OVERVIEW OF THE MARKETS

There are four key market areas that we will primarily be talking about:

Figure 0.1   Market segments

At the end of this section we will take a brief look at the commodities market, but we will see that this market tends to be less comprehensively covered by the full range of financial institutions, so to begin let's take a brief look at each of these four core areas.

Foreign exchange

This is the market for exchanging one currency against another. It tends to be regarded as the largest, particularly in terms of number of trades and value of tickets on a daily basis, and also the most truly global. With many parts of the financial markets we will see that a lot of the interest, and therefore a lot of the deals, tend to be quite regionally focused. As an example, if we look at the UK government bond market, the Gilt market, we will see that the bulk of the trading, and the bulk of the ownership of the securities, will be in the UK. Foreign exchange, though, the buying and selling of currencies, is the one that is likely to attract more natural interest all around the world. For example, someone in Malaysia importing from the US is going to need to buy US dollars to pay their invoices in the same way that someone in Germany will need to do the same, as will someone in Dubai. So, whilst the individual trades will be different, with the Malaysian importer selling Malaysian Ringgit (MYR) and buying US dollar (USD), whilst the German importer sells euro and buys USD and the importer in Dubai sells Emirati Dirham (AED) and buys USD, the common link in each of these cases is the buying of USD. In the foreign exchange market the USD is known as the market base as it is the currency involved in the majority of trades, so we can see it as a sort of benchmark against which the values of other currencies are set in the markets.

Earlier in this introduction we gave some figures on daily turnover of spot and forward trades, and these represent two of the core products traded in the foreign exchange market and actually also describe the two key ways of transacting our business, not just in this but in most other market sectors as well, with trades being executed for value immediately or for value sometime in the future. When we talk about the 'value date' of a trade we just mean when we actually have to make payments and legally exchange ownership. In this instance, a spot trade is one where the currencies are bought and sold for settlement as soon as possible, most commonly two days after the trade was executed, and a forward one is where they are bought and sold for settlement on a given future date. In both cases the deal is done (or struck) today; the difference between the two is when the actual transfer of monies will take place. With the forward market you are committing yourself to buy or sell at a price you agree today but you may not actually exchange monies until one month, three months, one year, maybe even longer, from today. In all markets the trades will be executed by dealers, either verbally or electronically, with the dealers being the individuals who are authorized to deal on behalf of the firms for whom they work. Then the money and/or instruments involved will literally need to be delivered between the counterparties. This is called the settlement process, and the deal is settled when these transfers have taken place. Today, most things are transferred electronically, both currencies and financial instruments, but still the transfer has to happen and until it does the parties in the deal have a risk that the trade will fail. In our statistics on market growth we saw a third type of FX deal, the FX swap. Swaps, in many forms, play an important part in financial markets and in every case the basic idea is to exchange something between two counterparties. This could be an interest rate or a currency, or even just a risk, and this deal will last for a finite amount of time. So if we look at the FX swap transaction, the actual deals we do are to buy/sell a currency in the spot market and then reverse this trade (sell/buy) the same currency in the forward market. The net result is that we are exchanging the currency for a finite amount of time and so are effectively borrowing and lending it. This begins to explain why FX swaps have become so popular. From a trading perspective they will be used if a trader has a view that interest rate differentials may change, for example, if a trader feels that the gap between interest rates in the US dollar and the euro will widen or become narrower. They can also have a very practical purpose in that they can allow for synthetic borrowing or lending. If we take an example it might be easier to understand this: let's say that a company wants to borrow British pounds, but does not have any access to a borrowing line in this currency, but they do have the possibility to borrow in US dollars. They can use this borrowing line to create a synthetic borrowing in British pounds by combining it with the FX swap. To do this the borrower would borrow the funds they need in USD and then immediately sell these dollars to buy British pounds (GBP) as a spot trade, whilst at the same time buying back the USD and selling the GBP as a three-month forward trade. The net result would be that during the three months between the spot and forward settlements they would be holding GBP, which is what they wanted, whilst the forward deal committed them to giving back the GBP on the forward date and getting back the US dollars they need to repay their loan. So all in all they managed to synthetically borrow GBP.

Foreign exchange plays a crucial role in the financial markets as it gives us the means to so effectively have international markets, by allowing us to transfer our holdings from one currency to another. So this market itself acts as a facilitator for other markets, although we should also remember that it is an actively traded market in its own right and as such is as likely to be affected by the actions of the market participants as any other. Indeed maybe more so, since the very size and liquidity of the market means that it can be extremely sensitive to market sentiment and forces which is why we can see prices move so much during the course of a trading day. You have only to look at how the currency market reacted to the very thought that there could be a hung parliament in the UK (selling GBP), several months before the

General Election, to see that this market does not need facts, it is happy to trade on fear and rumours – basically on market sentiment.

Debt Markets

The debt market is typically divided into two parts, the money market and the long-term debt market. Money market debt normally has a maturity of one year or less, often much less, with long-term debt being greater than a year. The debt market is the one in which investors lend money to borrowers. Sometimes this is done as a direct contract, with two parties agreeing to borrow and lend directly with one another, and sometimes this happens through the mechanism of creating a security. When an institution wants to borrow money rather than borrowing directly from a known lender they can instead issue a security that will be bought and sold in the market. At the time the security is issued the first (or primary) buyers will basically provide the money for the borrower, but then this initial buyer can sell on this security without the borrower knowing anything about it, or frankly even caring very much. This means the ultimate lender can change many times before maturity. This debt security is basically a promise to repay all the money lent under this deal, plus any interest due to whoever owns the security at maturity, in other words to an unknown lender. The security itself is a legal contract that sets out how much has been borrowed, the maturity of the loan, any interest rate due, the mechanics of how this will be paid and any special conditions that may apply. In the market we typically refer to this as 'paper' since originally these would have been physically printed and may even have physically changed hands when bought and sold, but in the 21st century we are more used to electronically transferring ownership of this 'paper' so it need not necessarily even exist in physical form. Bonds are a good example of this type of security, commonly used for issuing long-term debt that we will see used by a wide range of institutions, in fact most of the ones we will look at in this book.

In the money market we do not use the expression 'bond' for short-term debt but we can still find examples of these types of securities (treasury bills, commercial paper) and also a more direct borrowing and lending model such as we see in the deposit market. This is the market where funds are placed on deposit with banks by other banks, institutions and individuals and are then made available to be borrowed by those same groups of market participants. This part of the market is dominated by the commercial banks and so we will take more of a look at this in the section on commercial and retail banking where it is a foundation stone of how that whole part of the banking system can work efficiently.

As at 2008 the global debt market was estimated by the IMF[7] to stand at \$83,529.60 billion, or 352% of the global GDP,[8] but in character it is very different from the foreign exchange market. We tend to see a lot less daily turnover than we saw in the foreign exchange market as many of these instruments are bought by investors to hold to maturity, whether that is in one month or 10 years, in order to earn the interest rate. So, whilst this is not a market without speculative trading, it does have a very strong investor underpinning. It is also more fragmented which is why it is more difficult to find daily turnover figures. There are many different subdivisions of the market, such as domestic and international products, domestic being primarily debt being issued to target local investors, whilst the international market is broader in its reach. We have these differences to try and match funding and return needs, as we have said before, and we can see that there are some borrowers and lenders who are motivated by, say, wanting to avoid foreign exchange exposure or to gain tax advantages. Therefore we do not tend to see the same universality that we had in FX – there are distinct pockets of interest that are often regionally created. Nonetheless we definitely should not underestimate the importance of this part of the market in providing financing and investment products.

When we look at the debt market we tend to see it dominated by two distinct types of risk, interest rate risk and credit risk. Credit risk is the risk that the borrower will not make the expected payments, such as repaying the debt at maturity or the interest payments promised. Interest rate risk comes about from these interest payments. Whilst in many cases the interest rate is a known rate, what is not known is whether this will be a good rate all through the life of the instrument. If a debt instrument pays an interest rate of 5% this could be a good rate at the time it was set, but half way through the life of the deal interest rates could have doubled, so 10% might be a more appropriate rate, and this means the instrument becomes less valuable – this is interest rate risk. Lots of debt instruments carry both types of risk, but there is one group, debt issued by governments in their home markets and currencies, that carries only interest rate risk as we would not expect the governments to

---

[7] International Monetary Fund.
[8] Global Financial Stability Report, October 2009.

default. This is because we believe that governments could print money to redeem the debt if necessary. This is something we will speak of again a little later.

Equity Markets

Unlike debt, equity is not about borrowing and lending. Instead the equity market is about buying parts of a company. This means it has a completely different risk profile. When you buy a share of a company you are buying into its fortunes, without, normally, any guarantees being given to you by the company itself. In theory if the company does well then the value of your investment will grow and if it does badly the reverse should happen. Of course in real life we do not always see this happening as this is a market that trades a lot on expectation. So, we may see that a company produces fantastic results and yet its share price may fall because maybe the results were not quite as good as expected, or maybe the market does not see how the company can maintain this level of success. The whole idea of equity valuation is thus a very tricky area and will often differ from what a fundamental analysis of the company would suggest it should be. From the perspective of the company issuing equity they are selling partial ownership to raise funds without a commitment to repay. The trade-off, of course, is that control of the company could change, either with or without the management's approval, as has happened in the case of hostile takeovers when another company has taken a majority holding in the company through the purchase of shares. For the most part, though, we tend to say that ownership of equity represents ownership of the company but not necessarily control.

In the equity market there is both private and public equity. Public equity is about shares of publicly listed companies, those that have listed on a stock exchange and whose shares are publicly offered, normally via the exchange mechanism. This means that this market is very transparent as all deals are notified to the exchange, and most deals are actually carried out on the exchange. Private equity is buying and selling parts of an unlisted company. This is much less transparent and tends to be a highly negotiated process and typically for large parts, if not all, of the company. Public equity, by contrast, can be traded in lots as small as one share, which may be one of tens of millions available in that same company.

Public equity markets tend to be very transparent liquid markets, particularly for the larger companies. Transparency means that it is easy to see the prices of the securities and to track how much trading has taken place. Creating better transparency in the markets is a great aim of the regulators and so it is a key topic in the markets today. In recent times we have seen some problems in the equity markets to do with a lack of consistent transparency. Sometimes there will be groups of market participants who, by means of super-computers, can have access to information about orders and trades before the rest of the market, thereby giving them a potential competitive advantage if they trade on this information before the market becomes fully transparent. This is known as flash trading. Similarly there has also been a trend to fragment liquidity, taking trades away from the main market by offering these deals over private networks. Again this means that some participants have access to more information than others, so creating a less than equal playing field. These issues are particularly significant in the equity market as many people pay close attention to this market not only for the sake of monitoring individual companies listed but also as an overall view on the economy in which the markets are based. The strength, or otherwise, of an equity market can be a good barometer as to how well the economy is doing as it represents investors' willingness to risk their capital without any parachutes of guaranteed repayment or even interest, so must therefore reflect how well they feel the companies will be able to perform. Often this will be as a result of the strength of the economy in which these companies are trading.

Derivatives

Derivatives are not securities like the ones we have just been looking at because they are not financial instruments which can raise money. Instead they are instruments that derive their existence, and therefore their values, from the underlying markets that we have already looked at, and many more. The primary purpose of a derivative is to create a forward value for these underlying markets. In the section on foreign exchange we spoke about forward foreign exchange, and actually this is an example of a derivative, probably the simplest and easiest to understand, but they can quickly become much more complicated. Essentially, though, there are three core forms of derivative instrument: forwards, futures and options, which we will look at briefly below.

Forwards

As we saw in the section on FX, a forward is simply a contract between two parties to buy and sell a known amount of an underlying commodity of some sort, on a given date for a fixed price. The price for this will be the price that we can see in the market plus what we call the time value of money. Simply, that is what it would cost us to borrow the money to buy the underlying commodity today, and against that cost we take off any income we might gain from it. For example, if we were doing a forward deal for a money market product whilst we would have to borrow the money to buy the product against that we might receive an interest payment so this would be netted off against our borrowing cost. So we say that the forward price of any underlying is its cash price adjusted by this time value of money cost.

Futures

A future contract is like a packaged forward: again a contract to buy and sell the known amount of the commodity on a given date at a fixed price, but in this case the commodity, the amount and the delivery date are all defined not by the two parties in the trade but by an exchange. This gives a level of standardization that we do not always see in the forward markets. Because of this standardization futures tend to be very liquid and actively traded, which is why often we see that their prices are not what we would expect them to be. In theory we should expect to be able to price them in the same way as we did forwards, but in real life they will often trade at very different prices. This is because we will encounter supply and demand at work in the market. Since futures contracts are for deals to be concluded in the future at the time of making the deal very little money has to change hands. This, along with their liquidity, makes them efficient for trading on a view of a rising or falling market and so, as we saw in the FX market, they can be very open to sentiment-driven movements.

Options

An option is somewhat different from the previous two derivatives as this is a contract that will be bought by one party from another and that will give the buyer the right to do something, if they choose, whilst committing the seller to stand by this. In other words the buyer has a right but not an obligation. Once again the contract will be for a known commodity, amount, date and price. It is then up to the owner (or the buyer) of the option to decide whether or not to do the trade depending on the market conditions. This is very different from the purer forward contracts, and yet we can still see why it is a forward pricing mechanism. Essentially if the buyer has bought a right to buy something (a call option) if the price rises above that agreed on the option contract during the period of the option then they can use it to buy the underlying at a cheaper rate, therefore giving the option a positive value. If, though, the price falls they will not use the option and so it will not have this positive value. What the option did was to allow them to be locked into a price to carry out the underlying trade if they so choose. When someone buys an option they will have to pay a fee to the seller to cover them for the fact that whilst the buyer has the right to decide whether or not they exercise their option, the seller has the commitment. Remember that for the sellers this product has a completely different risk profile – they have no choice once they have sold the option but to stand by the trade, and so the fee needs to cover them for this risk. This fee is known as the premium, and calculating what this should be is much more problematic than calculating a forward price. There is a big variable in that you do not know if and when the deal will be made and since this depends on market conditions the price will have to consider how the market is likely to move, normally based on how it has moved in the past. However the option is a very well used derivative and often appears embedded in financial instruments that we buy, such as mortgages and savings products, without us, as consumers, even being aware of it.

We should also mention the difference between exchange-traded and OTC derivatives. Exchange-traded derivatives, such as futures contracts – as we have seen – are products that trade on an exchange that sets the terms and conditions of the contract, provides the trading environment and ensures transparency by publishing trade data. They also make use of central clearing counterparties (CCP) that act as a counterparty to all trades carried out on the exchanges, thereby ensuring consistency of credit. This reduces the trade risk of dealing in this market and given that derivatives can be very volatile any steps that can be taken to reduce risk are generally considered important. Over-the-counter (OTC) derivatives are contracts that are defined by the two parties involved in the deal. This gives them a great deal more flexibility but will also tend to mean that they are less liquid and less transparent. Following on from the market turmoil during the Financial Crisis there has been a shift towards creating a hybrid sort of market, where OTC derivatives may still be traded on a tailored basis but when it comes to settlement the contracts are settled through a CCP, again to reduce settlement risk. It is the OTC market that has come under the most scrutiny from regulators; indeed in the US both the Senate and House finance bills that we will discuss in the next section called for reforms, and in some cases prohibition, of trading on this market, so it is very likely that upcoming legislation will address this and we may see an increase in required use of CCPs and possibly restrictions on how and by whom these products can be used.

So we have looked at the four key market areas that the institutions in the financial markets are likely to be using on a daily basis. In the markets these basic ideas are greatly expanded and here we have just painted thumbnail sketches. The purpose of this, though, is so that we have a broad understanding of the types of markets in which the firms are involved and begin to get a feel for why they need to exist. Not every type of institution will be involved in every market, and even within the institutions there will be divisions amongst the different types of department. However as we go through the various types of firm and think about how and why they are involved in the markets we will be able to see various examples of how their business will lead them to having to be involved in these different market areas to fulfil both their needs and those of their clients.

There is one other market area that we should mention, and that is the commodities market, such as agricultural products, energy, metals etc. This market differs from the core money and capital markets we have just discussed as this is a market for the movement of physical commodities, although in financial market terms we are typically less concerned with the physical commodity and far more concerned with the value of the commodity. As we have seen with the other market sectors, we have both cash and derivative markets and for the most part the financial market institutions that we cover in this book will concern themselves more with derivatives than with cash. There are exceptions to this, such as gold, which certainly in recent times has had a massive increase in the level of interest in the physical commodity. So whilst there will be end-users involved in the actual commodities needing to access these markets for physical purposes or for risk management, for many of the financial institutions these commodity markets represent another trading and investment opportunity. They will be looking to buy oil not because they need it but because they believe the price will rise so we see both commodity trading desks in some of the major banks and commodity managers in the investment management companies. However it is fair to say that the coverage of this market is nowhere near as widespread as for the other market sectors. From an investment perspective it is the alternative investment funds that tend to look at this area and whilst there are a number of major banks and trading companies that run active trading desks this will not be the case universally. However it is worth noting that at many points during our coverage of these financial institutions we will mention the commodities market, so you will appreciate that it does certainly have a place as an element of financial markets.

Part I
Banks

1
Introduction

If we were to look at all the trades carried out in the international financial markets we would see that for the majority of them at least one of the counterparties involved in the trade would be a bank. This must say something about the importance of banks in the infrastructure of the markets. The role they play in these trades will differ: sometimes they will be acting as risk-taking principals, buying or selling the financial products for their own purpose, be it funding, investment or trading, and sometimes they will be acting as intermediary on behalf of their customers. When doing this they often take a very time-limited exposure, or even simply execute orders, meaning that whilst their name is on the ticket they never own the risk of the deal. So for these different reasons we will see bank names so prevalent in the market, which begins to explain why the banking crisis of 2007 onwards had such a major impact on all the financial markets.

The financial markets are really about moving money. A market that is working well is one in which those that need funds are matched by those that have funds. This may sound obvious but getting the balance right is not necessarily easy. Not only do the two sides have to find one another but the deal also has to show advantage to both sides to justify entering into it. If a company is looking to borrow money they will naturally want to do this at the best possible rate, but similarly the lender will want to achieve the best return on their funds. So, somehow, the market has to find the rate that achieves these aims for both sides. This is where the market intermediaries come into play. They use their expertise to make this match and to find this balancing rate, either by directing the flow of funds through their own balance sheets or by creating and placing the financial products. At least this is the case at the moment. Maybe as technology and understanding of the markets continue to improve we could ultimately see a market without intermediaries, where all potential buyers or lenders meet all potential sellers or borrowers directly, but the markets of today are not at this stage, at least not across the board. So, for now, we will continue to see the intermediaries fulfilling these functions,

Depositors
funds –
Lenders

Borrowing
requirements
– Borrowers

Figure 1.1   Credit Banking

facilitating the movement of money. And, of course, the dominant group of intermediaries are the banks.

There are two key models of raising wholesale money that we should take a look at to begin to understand the importance of banks in this world: the first a traditional model of credit banking and the second the disintermediated model.

Traditional credit banking is where banks take in funds from their depositors, paying them an interest rate, and then these funds are lent on to borrowers, who in turn pay the bank an interest rate (see Figure 1.1).

The bank's profit will be the spread between the deposit and the lending rate, but for this profit they must take on the credit risk that exists on both sides of the deal. The risk of a borrower defaulting is clear to see, but there is also a risk that the depositor will want their funds back, a liquidity risk for the bank. This is also a simplistic view of the model, implying that depositor and borrower funds perfectly match one another, when in fact this is very unlikely to happen. Most bank lending is on a leveraged model, whereby they lend out proportionately more than they take in from depositors, and fund shortfalls by borrowing themselves. They will also mismatch maturities, taking in money on, say, an overnight basis, that they will then lend out for longer periods of time, working on the assumption that there will be a steady flow of short-term funds. The failure of this was a major issue for the banks in 2007, and even more so in 2008, when liquidity was so tight that in many cases they simply were not seeing the flow of short-term funds either from their customer base or from their peers in the market. So they found themselves completely caught out in that they could not afford lending they had already made let alone making new loans available. This is one of the reasons the regulators have had to focus so much attention on the reserve balances of the banks as we have seen how vulnerable they can be to changes in liquidity patterns. These reserve balances will provide some sort of protection by essentially buying them time if cash dries up in the marketplace. We will look a little more at how the market provides this liquidity to the banks in the following sections.

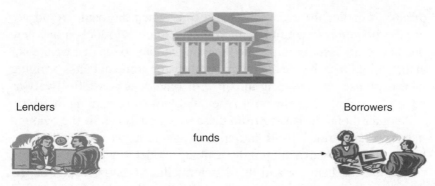

Figure 1.2   Disintermediation

The second model, disintermediated financing, shows us an alternative way of funds moving from those that have to those that need. In this model the bank does not stand in the middle of the deal taking on these credit risks, or at least not for the whole period of the loan or investment (see Figure 1.2).

This shows the bank as facilitator in the passing of funds, most commonly by creating the financial products that we outlined in the Introduction to this book. If the party that needed funds were happy to borrow then maybe this would be a bond, a public long-term debt; whilst if they were willing to sell partial ownership of themselves they would issue equity. The bank's role in this would be to create the product, in the name of the firm needing the funds, which they would then place in the market and try to sell to investors to raise the required cash. This is called the primary market, the market for initially raising funds. During this period the banks may find themselves exposed to some or all of the risk, but their intention would be to spread this as quickly as possible by placing the debt or equity in the market. The bank would then provide a route of liquidity by potentially trading these instruments throughout their lives in what is known as the secondary market. We cannot go too far with this statement because there is nothing in the model that obliges a bank to guarantee liquidity and we cannot always predict if the instruments will have any liquidity years after their initial issue, but more often than not we do tend to see that any liquidity that there is in the products will tend to centre around the firms involved in originally issuing the deal. In terms of cash flow the final net result is the same in both models, the matching of the two end counterparties and movement of funds between the two, but the process is totally different. As we discussed earlier there could come a time when the bank would not need to be in this diagram but all you have to do is to look at any new bond or equity issue coming into the market today to see that we are not at that point. In each case there will be a bank or group of banks bringing their expertise into ensuring this flow of funds works as effectively as possible. And of course in return they will look to be earning income.

Another thing we can see from these two models is how the banking industry has formed itself into reflecting these two ways of doing business. Put broadly, the credit banking model would be the world of commercial banking and the disintermediated model would be the world of investment banking. In the following chapters of this section we will look in more detail at these different types of banking, but a good way to distinguish them is to remember that commercial banking is embedded in core borrowing and lending, whilst investment banking is about raising funds without committing the bank's balance sheets long-term. In other words, without the bank being the ultimate lender.

In the UK and the US there has been a history of separating these two types of banking business by having different types of institution responsible for each, at least this was so up until the latter part of the 20th century, whilst this has not necessarily been the case in other countries. However over the past few decades the trend has been to integrate rather than to segregate, and so we have seen a series of high profile mergers of commercial and investment banking firms to form the large, dominant universal banks. These are banks that are active in both sides of the industry offering a full range of services to their customers, both wholesale and retail. However having said this we can still see a tendency to internally separate the business, often using different names for the different parts of the firm. A good example of this is JPMorgan Chase & Co. The bank that we see today was formed from a series of mergers beginning back in 1991 with the merger of Manufacturers Hanover Corporation and Chemical Banking Corporation, two of the largest commercial banks in the US. The bank then merged with JPMorgan in 2000, which whilst also a commercial bank, and again one of the largest in the US, was a firm that had spent its recent years, following the beginning of the process to repeal the Glass-Steagall Act, building its strength on the investment banking side. The Glass-Steagall Act was the financial Act that forced legal separation of commercial and investment banking in the US, and we will discuss this further later on. Since this merger, the bank has continued to acquire other banks, notably in 2004

Banc One, and then in 2008 Bear Stearns. All these acquisitions serve to add more strength to the bank's coverage of the market.

Today the bank divides itself into two business names, JPMorgan and Chase. Under the name of JPMorgan the firm undertakes investment banking business, along with asset management, securities services and private banking, which are all areas involved in financial markets and financial market products. Under the name of Chase they undertake commercial and retail banking. This will include wholesale corporate banking, and the sheer size of their customer base will create for the firm wholesale exposures typical of the credit banking model from numerous smaller size deals. This includes things such as mortgage lending, credit cards as well as the most traditional bank business of borrowing and lending (overdrafts, cheque accounts etc.). So the firm has divided itself to draw some distinction between the two different parts of their business and yet the firm as a whole is JPMorgan Chase, so their customers can benefit from the full range of services. This kind of modelling is mirrored in many firms around the world, often as a result of deregulation that we will examine further in the coming sections.

Following the Financial Crisis there has been a lot of debate over whether the idea of legally separating commercial and investment banks should be reintroduced, with many countries considering this as a solution to the banking crisis and as a preventative measure for the future. Part of this discussion has come about because of the creation of banks such as JPMorgan Chase, which by their sheer size and scope in the market are deemed to be 'too big to fail'. By this we mean that should these banks find themselves in difficulty, the governments, via the central banks, would really seem to have no choice but to bail them out. Whilst it is to be hoped that these banks should hold enough capital and reserves that they would be able to carry out their business and weather any storms and fluctuations of liquidity, in practice this has not proved to be the case. Instead we have had a situation where widespread intervention has been needed to shore up these banks, which has involved using taxpayers' money, as we have seen in 2008, as it was felt that the impact of their failure would be catastrophic for the global banking infrastructure and thus for the global economic situation. However, despite the many supporters of this change to the segregated model of banking no country has so far decided to introduce this into their banking reforms as at the end of the first decade of the 21st century. In large part this is down to the influence of the banks who would be faced with the task of having to separate these businesses and, potentially, give up lucrative sources of income, and we have often seen over the past few years that losses in one side of the business can to a certain extent be offset by profits in another, helping to support the value of the firm as a whole. It is highly likely, though, that legislation will be introduced in all the major centres focusing on several key issues, amongst which would be ensuring that regulators can efficiently take control of failing banks, limiting the amount of speculative risk taken by banks, particularly those which have received or would be likely to receive taxpayer bailout funds – in particular commercial banks – and providing funding for any bailouts from within the industry so as to reduce the cost to the taxpayer, including looking again at the capital and reserve requirements that should be imposed on the banks by the regulators. In the US 2010 saw finance bills passing through both the Senate and House of Representatives that will need to be merged into a new Finance Act, drawing on parts of both bills, that will incorporate measures to try and address these issues. Similarly in the EU regulators are looking to address the same issues, including the idea of imposing a bank tax to raise bailout contingency funds, but finding pan-European, or indeed international, solutions is never easy. This is particularly so when set against the backdrop at the time of weakness in the credit of key sovereign European borrowers such as Greece, Spain and Portugal, and fears that weakness in these countries could lead to yet more bank failures. So, as of the beginning of the second decade of the 21st century we find ourselves still sitting with a very uncertain picture, despite the return to profitability experienced by many banks. Potentially there is still a ticking time bomb as there is a strong feeling that the Financial Crisis is not yet over and the coming years may see more difficulties including, possibly, the collapse of one of the powerhouse banks that by their size and influence have been identified by many as being a major source of concern for the whole infrastructure of the industry.

In the following chapters of this section we will look some more at both commercial and investment banking so that we can see how the type of business undertaken by these banks will lead them to take particular roles in the financial markets. We will also look at other sorts of banks which we will encounter both as market participant and regulator, and again we can see how they have their own roles to play and influence on the markets.

2
Commercial and Retail Banking

This area of the business of banking is what most of us would think of as traditional banking. This is the part of the business where the bank receives in funds and then makes loans to its customers both individual and corporate. The sizes of deals can range from small amounts, say, less than $100, or pounds, or euros, to large, wholesale amounts in the tens or hundreds of millions, maybe even billions, although actually lending this amount of money in one go would be rare, but a series of loans to a large borrower can all too easily amount to this. So we should not jump to the conclusion that investment banking is for large sums of money whilst commercial banking is for smaller sums – the difference between the two lies far more in the way in which funds flow through the firm.

In the previous section we looked at the two core models of moving funds and now we need to develop that further to see how they translate into businesses. Commercial banking, as we said, sits on the model of credit banking. The bank receives money from depositors that they then on-lend. One thing we have seen clearly in 2008 and 2009 is how highly valued this is in both economic and political terms, with governments being obliged to commit public funds to bailing out these financial institutions during the financial crisis. The amount of funds committed was, in many cases, quite staggering to the public, with the USA's costs representing 6.3% of GDP, although this pales in comparison with the UK's 19.8%[1] (as at February 2009). Protecting the integrity of the financial system was all-important, though, to ensure that the market would still be there promoting and enabling the flow of capital. In order to get a feeling for the size of this industry we can look at the BIS[2] quarterly banking statistics, in which the BIS collects data from banks in 42 countries on their on-balance sheet asset and liability positions. Clearly this will include the major banking centres such as the US and

---

[1] Source: IMF Report: The State of Public Finances: Outlook and Medium-Term Policies After the 2008 Crisis.

[2] BIS – the Bank for International Settlement. We will look further at this organization in the section on central banks.

the UK, but also smaller locations such as Chile and Cyprus. For the banks their assets would be loans they have made either directly, as in lending to an individual, a company, another bank etc., or indirectly by lending via the capital markets, buying bonds etc. In June 2009 this report showed the total assets of these respondents to stand at \$34.1017 trillion, equivalent. Imagine if these loans could not be made because the banks were no longer there. Just think about the impact this would have on the global economy. Of course these assets are not exclusively direct lending to end borrowers. This figure will include securities, although less than 25%, and importantly many of these assets come from the banks trading within the banking community. Banks regularly borrow from and lend to one another, thereby making the international flow of funds required to finance trade, international investment and so on. In other words, the banks are not operating as isolated islands; they are interlinked with one another on many different levels. This is what we call the interbank system, a system that has many advantages but also many risks. This, again, has been highlighted to us in recent years and contributed to the political pressure on countries to support their banking systems not only for the sake of their own economy but to prevent international fallout. Banking is very susceptible to systemic risk: in a nutshell, the risk that a bank failing could cause the failure of other banks, both domestically and internationally. Following the Financial Crisis the G20 asked the BIS, the IMF and the Secretariat of the Financial Stability Board [3] to undertake a survey to measure the systemic importance of financial institutions both before and after the crisis, and to highlight some of the factors causing this systemic risk. In October 2009 they produced their initial findings.[4] In their survey sent to central banks and market regulators, banks were identified by all as being the most vulnerable of all financial institutions to systemic risk, with size and interconnectedness being the two major factors contributing to this risk. So, it should not surprise us that during the recent crisis the governments felt that it was necessary to take whatever steps were required to support the system and protect these banks that fulfil such an important function.

---

[3] The FSB was established in April 2009 to address issues of financial stability. It comprises representatives from national banking authorities, such as central banks, and representatives from financial organizations such as the SEC and the FSA.

[4] Guidance to Assess the Importance of Financial Institutions, Markets and Instruments: Initial Considerations Background Paper, October 2009.

However this has led to a lot of debate about the banks that are deemed 'too big to fail', those banks which by their size would cause unacceptable economic damage if they were to become insolvent. These banks are also known as 'systemically significant', as we have discussed above. It is ironic that the governments' having poured billions of dollars into these very institutions is a factor that has actually increased their size by inflating their balance sheets, which in turn may well increase their significance and importance in the financial markets. Governments, and government agencies, have also been involved in helping to broker deals, such as the sale of Bear Stearns to JPMorgan Chase and Merrill Lynch to Bank of America, which in both cases has substantially increased the size of these already large firms. However determining the size of a bank is not straightforward as there are many different measures we can apply. When we look at the largest bank in the world by asset size in 2009 we discover that it is Royal Bank of Scotland which is the largest, with assets totalling approximately $3.5 billion equivalent.[5] As we will see in a later section, this is a bank that has seen a lot of support from the UK government to shore up its balance sheets. However asset size is not necessarily the most common way of looking at a bank, since the unknown factor here is the quality of the assets. This is why we often look at a bank's Tier 1 capital or their market value. A bank's capital is divided into two parts, Tier 1 and Tier 2. Tier 1 capital is considered the most important measure of a bank's strength by the regulators because it looks at the core capital of the bank, its equity and its known reserves, and is reasonably transparent. Tier 2 is what is called supplementary capital comprising such things as loan provisions and less secure debt like subordinated debt.[6] It is Tier 1 capital that the regulators require the banks to hold to protect them against failure, as we discussed in the previous section. So, looking at this measure we would see that in 2009 the largest bank in the world would not be Royal Bank of Scotland but instead JPMorgan Chase & Co., with Tier 1 capital of approximately $1.36 billion equivalent, whilst the Royal Bank of Scotland on this basis would now be coming in 4th, with capital of just over $1.01 billion.[7] We can see another measure, though, if we look at market value. In June 2009 the Dow Jones Banks Titans 30 index, an index comprised

---

[5] *The Banker*, 2009.

[6] Subordinated debt is a class of debt that cedes precedence to senior paper in the event of a default, so therefore carries a greater risk premium.

[7] *The Banker*, 2009.

of the 30 largest banks as at June each year, was according the greatest weighting to HSBC, meaning that this bank had the highest market capitalization.[8] However this index does not include Chinese banks and many consider that at this time Industrial & Commercial Bank of China was the largest bank in the world, and also, according to them, the largest bank by deposits. Whilst not intending to confuse, this is really all about how you measure things. One thing that is consistent, though, is that whilst the absolute rankings may differ according to how size is measured the group remains consistent. What we see is a group of very large commercial banks who are the major institutions and in each case these will be the largest banks in their respective countries.

So, let's think about the business of these banks. Most commercial banks will divide their business into two parts, retail and corporate. The corporate side is then normally subdivided according to the size of the company and thus the amount of exposure it presents to the bank. Grouping the customers in this way performs two functions. On the one hand it helps to ensure that they are offered the right products, and secondly, for the bank, it helps to identify the type of exposures they will see coming from these customers. If we look at the retail banking side the bank will offer a range of ways in which the customers can basically place funds with them or borrow money. Since each deal is with an individual the sums of money involved are very small in banking terms, per deal. However it is when all these small deals are put together that the bank finds itself facing large exposures, but we will look at this in a little while. On the corporate side, the same basic idea applies but the size of the deals can vary enormously. If one of your corporate customers is a large multinational firm, conducting business internationally, and regularly requiring large-scale funding, then this customer cannot be compared to a small enterprise, maybe something like a shop, which would typically want very similar services to the retail customer, maybe on just a slightly larger scale. This is why it makes sense to subdivide the business area, again so that the bank can tailor the service it offers. Size of transaction is important as this will affect how the bank handles the transaction as well as its risk analysis and, of course, its profit potential per deal or per customer. Banks typically have invested large sums in technology to find the most efficient way to deal with various types of customer flow in order to maximize their profit potential.

---

[8] Market capitalization is the market value of the firm, broadly the share price multiplied by the number of shares.

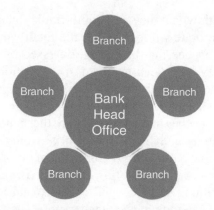

Figure 2.1   Bank-Branch networks

If we look at the model of how a bank sets itself up to reach its customers we can start to get a feel for how the money flows through the organization. If we start with the most classic view of banking that most of us will see, we will have a picture something like the one in Figure 2.1.

Here we have the bank's Head Office at the centre and its branches out in its "universe" where they will interact with the customers. Straightaway, we can change this, though, to represent the fact that we are looking at banking in the 21st century, where commercial banks are often international in character and so many operate regional head offices as well having their main one. However, this idea of internationalism is actually a tricky one when we look at the whole business of commercial banking. What we tend to see is that this business is a curious mixture of internationalism and nationalism. If you are in a major financial centre and you go out to look for bank branches you are likely to see a fair range of international names, although the market will be dominated by domestic ones. Some banks, such as HSBC, have spent many years building up international presence on pretty much all levels, so we are likely to see branches of HSBC in all our major financial centres, and beyond. However it is what happens beyond these centres that really shows this distinction. Straightaway you will see far, far fewer international names on the bank branches. Obviously this will be partly a density issue – there will naturally be fewer branches of banks outside the financial centres so logically we should see fewer branches of non-domestic banks, and yet this also ties in with a core truth of retail banking: most customers prefer to bank with the domestic names that they know and with which they feel comfortable. Interestingly we also see this in the corporate world, not just the retail world. This issue of familiarity has been one that has been addressed by several banks in recent years as they have been involved in international takeovers and mergers. Take, for example, the acquisition by Banco Santander of Spain of the UK building society[9] turned bank, Abbey National, back in 2004. Even in 2009 the branches in the UK still bore the name Abbey, although finally signed alongside Santander, and it was only in January 2010 that they finally removed the word Abbey from all branding. This was partly as they were now incorporating other brands, such as Bradford & Bingley, and the timing seemed right to finally make this move. Note, though, that the new branding is Santander, not Banco Santander. Using the Spanish word for bank may well have been a step too far in integrating this into the British corporate culture! This is, though, a successful acquisition, giving great shareholder value and allowing the Spanish bank good exposure to the UK savings and, especially, retail mortgage market, so it seems to have fulfilled its objectives. Yet to retain and build on the market share the bank has had to tread carefully with its existing and potential customers, hence maintaining the familiarity of the name and the branding. Probably the best compliment that could be paid to the bank in the initial stages was if the customers could barely discern the difference, ironic as that may be.

Another thing about this diagram of Head Office and branches is that if we think back to the 1980s there were many people in the banking world who thought that by now branches would be obsolete. There was a trend at the time towards automating bank-to-customer business flows with a push towards the use of ATM machines and eventually moving toward full internet banking. Whilst use of these channels has definitely increased, business thinking seems to have changed. What has become clear is that the customer base is not yet ready to give up on branch banking and the banks themselves have had to respond to this need. So whilst they are happy to offer automated services they have also had to remain happy to offer physical locations, if that is what the customers demand.

So, returning to our diagram, we need to make another adjustment. In the diagram we have branches and we have a Head Office. Now we need to connect them (see Figure 2.2).

---

[9] For an explanation of what a building society is see Part Two, Section 1, Banks in UK.

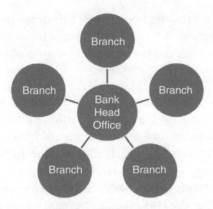

Figure 2.2   Bank-Branch connectivity

This may seem obvious but actually it is crucial for understanding the risk and cash flow through the bank. On an individual branch level the transactions are carried out either by physical or automated means. However all of those flows belong not to the branch but to the bank. So whether a retail customer wants to borrow a small amount of money or a corporate customer wants to borrow a large sum of money, in both cases the branch is just the link between the customer and the bank, which in the diagram is evidenced by the Head Office. Rather than just thinking generically about Head Office it is now time for us to start thinking about how the bank manages these cash flows and so we should take a look at the treasury department where we will begin to see how and why these commercial banks have to be so active in the financial markets.

THE IMPORTANCE OF THE TREASURY DEPARTMENT

The bank's treasury department will typically have three main purposes:

1. To fund the bank and manage exposures on its balance sheets – to borrow any money the bank needs and invest any excess cash they may be holding on a daily basis, often with many trades during the course of the day, and then to manage any resultant risks, such as interest rate risk that these deals create.
2. To execute customer deals – so if, for example, a corporate customer wants to buy a large amount of a foreign currency they might give an order to the bank to execute on their behalf.

3. To run proprietary trading books on behalf of the bank – this is where the bank's dealers will buy and sell financial products on behalf of the bank purely with the purpose of making profit over a short time horizon.

We will look at the business of trading and the different trading models a little later, but for now it is enough to differentiate between the bank executing a deal on behalf of a customer and the bank taking positions as the result of making a conscious, short-term investment decision which is proprietary trading. The first two of these points tie in with everything we have been discussing so far, that link between borrowers and lenders and the bank acting as the intermediary through which the cash will flow. The third builds on the knowledge and expertise that the bank gains by being in the market for the first reasons. Since they are so immersed in the cash flows they are well positioned to be able to determine in which direction markets are likely to move, at least in theory, and it is from this that they will build their trading capabilities. This then becomes a symbiotic relationship because often the customers, particularly the large corporate customers, will want to build relationships with banks that have a strong presence and understanding of the markets so that they can be confident that they will be given good advice and execution of trades. We will talk more about this relationship aspect to banking a little later on. First, though, let's take a look at the role of the treasury department, both in the bank and their corporate customer, and the sort of activities that we are likely to see in this area.

Generic Role of Treasury

The treasury department is the area of a firm that deals with ensuring the firm is liquid, that it has enough money to cover its obligations and requirements, both within the bank and also within its corporate customer. This basic function can and will lead to many other tasks as we consider the full implications of keeping the firm liquid. Firstly, in order to know how much a firm would need to borrow they would first need to know how they stand in financial terms, so the treasury department has got to be embedded within the real financial business flow of the company. This can mean different things, looking at the long-term strategy of the firm and also the short-term cash flow. For example, if the company is planning an acquisition this will have a cash implication and it will be the job of the treasury department to find financing solutions. So it is important that it should be involved in the corporate strategy decision-making process, at some level, and in the valuation of investment to ensure that the funding cost does not dwarf the investment value. On a more day-to-day basis they will need to be aware of cash flow through the firm, both actual and expected, so cash flow forecasting, trying to model how this will be in whatever currencies the firm needs, is likely to be an important part of this job. Then taking this modelling into the real world, their next task will be to manage the physical cash flow. Typically the aim will be to use cash flow as efficiently as possible, to minimize borrowing costs, which may well involve planning future foreign exchange deals, allocating cash across different business unit accounts, taking credit balances from one part of a business and allocating them against debits within another – whilst still maintaining records and accounts. The purpose of doing this is to avoid going outside to borrow money, and therefore paying an interest rate, when the money can be efficiently moved within the organization. Normally speaking excess money that is placed with a bank will earn less interest than money borrowed from a bank will cost, so operating an internal flow of cash would seem to make sense. Similarly they will likely be looking at foreign exchange markets, buying and selling whatever currencies the company needs to perform its business operations. Again, we will see many treasury departments trying to manage this internally as well; allocating currencies where needed to once again avoid selling currencies at the lower bid rates and buying at the higher offer. Although, of course there will be many occasions when they will need to go outside to the banks to make their foreign exchange deals and this will be a large part of the business flows between corporate treasury and bank.

These two areas of financial planning for corporate strategy and cash management within the firm will, in turn, give rise to a couple of other tasks that the treasury will need to manage. Thinking back to a firm potentially making an acquisition, to raise this wholesale financing the firm will typically need to issue debt or equity. This will mean interacting with a bank, although in this case it will be the investment banking side rather than the commercial banking side, but nonetheless it is something that must involve treasury. There may well be reports and projections that will need to be prepared for presentation to the bank, listing authorities, credit rating agencies or any other interested parties. However the money is raised there will be a cost involved, maybe in an interest rate but also in fees to be paid to the bank, auditors, advisers, etc. This cost needs to be quantified and evaluated. So, the treasury will have to take a very hands-on role in this project. Sometimes, though, things do not go according to plan. Maybe the acquisition does not take place or maybe there is a market situation that means plans for the financing need to be shelved; these are the sort of risks for which the treasury will need to have made contingency plans. Even if the funding goes ahead, let's say the company issued a bond to raise the money over a five-year period, perhaps it turns out that this may not have been the best way to fund the deal due to a change in the interest rate environment, and again the treasury should be looking to manage this. In other words, these exposures will bring about risks and these risks need to be managed, so risk management would also be a core feature of the treasury department, which will typically include using financial derivatives for managing financial exposures as well as dealing with insurance and disaster recovery planning. So, we can see that these core functions in treasury can be very broad-based yet the theme that ties them all together is the financial wellbeing of the firm, ensuring that it has enough money, that funds are raised and managed as efficiently as possible and that any excess funds are well invested, and that the risks of this process have been identified and a management strategy defined.

Bank vs Corporate Treasury

Everything we have said above about the functions of treasury will be pretty much true for most treasury departments. Obviously the larger firms are more likely to have larger and more active treasury departments where we can see deals coming from them on a daily basis. Smaller companies will not need to carry out so many trades, or indeed large-scale trades, so we may only see the results of their treasury management by going through their core banking products such as their cheque accounts and overdrafts. Nonetheless, regardless of scale, their motivations must be the same. Managing the finances of the firm must be paramount. If we look at a bank treasury department it can be easy to forget this as the bank model of treasury management contains the additional twist of having many dealers within the department carrying out not only funding-related jobs, but also traders making prices in financial products to customers, often via other dealers known as salespeople, as well as making prices and dealing with other market counterparties, all of which may lead to them choosing to run proprietary trading positions. When we spoke about the generic treasury function we spoke about the firm interacting with the bank to raise money or manage risks, and this means we need to find the bank counterparts, and for the most part they will be here in the treasury dealing room. We will exclude from this the large-scale, long-term debt or equity funding which we will pick up in the section on investment banks, but for the shorter maturity, day-to-day requirements we will normally find the counterparts here in the commercial bank area, specifically in treasury. So automatically we can determine that the bank treasury has to perform a dual function: to act as the corporate treasury for the firm and to service the customer cash flow. Remember, though, that the two sides are not mutually exclusive. The customer cash flow is a very important source of liquidity for the bank, whether it comes from the corporate or the retail market and we have seen too often over recent years what can happen when a bank loses this cash flow. However what will often happen is that the flows and exposures that come from the customers will not naturally match the requirements of the bank so the whole process tends to mushroom with the customer deals becoming yet another flow to be managed, and so on. This goes a long way to explaining the importance of the interbank market as the banks try to match up their cash flows within the bank community, thereby spreading liquidity and risk. This is why when in 2008 the banks started to lose confidence in one another it had such an immediate and strong reaction on the market, with the liquidity in the interbank market starting to dry up as banks were unwilling to commit funds to each other or to let go of precious cash balances for fear they would not be able to replace them. This being the case it is even more important that a bank is seen to be managing its own treasury cash flows as efficiently as possible and to perform this they tend to rely strongly on internal systems to monitor and assess the risks as they appear within the books of the bank.

ROLE OF TRADING AND SALES

It would probably be useful for us to take a look at the organization of the bank treasury department so that we can see how the exposures arise. As with a corporate treasury the bank will have a treasurer, someone who takes responsibility for all the functions of treasury. Clearly this can be a very high ranking position, particularly if we think of banks with hundreds of employees within their treasury department. The second we say this, though, we can also begin to appreciate that it can be a very hands-off position. In many banks the treasurer will not be the person who executes deals or even makes day-to-day decisions; instead their role is more strategic. However ultimate responsibility must lie with them. The treasury department will then be further peopled with dealers, both traders and salespeople. These dealers will cover the markets that the bank and its customers need to access. Given what we have already said about the corporate treasury and its requirements we can expect to see foreign exchange (FX) traders, along with dealers working with short-term borrowing and lending, the money markets. Since we have said that the customers will need to manage the risks of their FX and money market exposures we will also see derivative traders for these areas trading forwards, futures and options on foreign exchange and short-term interest rates.

Traders are dealers whose job is, most commonly, to make prices to customers and other counterparties of the bank, and to run positions, hopefully for profit. They have a short-term view on the markets, looking to hold positions for only days or weeks – or in some markets even less time – which is why they are often accused of creating market volatility. They will be allocated trading books, groups of related instruments in specific markets, and they then take responsibility for these instruments on behalf of the bank. For example, you might have a trader in FX that looks after Latin American currencies, or a trader in money markets that trades US treasury bills. There are some traders that do not make prices, whose role is purely to take risk positions on behalf of the firm. These are known as proprietary traders, and whilst they will work in specific market areas they often take a broader view as in perhaps being able to take positions in any currency if they can see an opportunity to make a trading profit rather than being restricted to a smaller group of currencies for which they take responsibility. So we can see we have various different types of trader sitting in our dealing rooms and we will look at some more models of trading in the chapter on Investment Banking.

So at the centre of the relationship we have the treasurer, surrounded by the traders, carrying out trades under their direction, as in Figure 2.3. Since the treasurer ultimately takes responsibility for all the cash flows it is important that the bank should keep careful track of these, so whilst each individual trader will take responsibility for their own positions, the bank will generally use a position keeping system that can produce reports showing positions by dealer, currency, product, maturity, in short any view that can enable management to see the various exposures that the firm is holding at any given time.

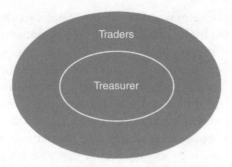

Figure 2.3   Treasury-Bank Tradeflow

As we have said these positions that are being run by traders will come from two sources. One, from trades with other market counterparties, such as interbank trades, and two, from the customers. This is where we bring the salespeople into the picture (see Figure 2.4).

So now we have added a third ring with the sales channels. This ring sits beyond the traders because all the flows that the sales channels bring into the bank will pass to the trading books, meaning that once the deals have been executed it is the traders that take responsibility for managing them. The salespeople are one of these channels and will talk to the larger customers of the bank, typically those with more than a certain amount of cash flow. The actual amount will depend on the bank, but there has to be enough profit potential to justify hiring a human intermediary, and this profit potential will come from both the size and number of deals the customer is likely to make. Over the past 20 years the number of salespeople working in this area has fallen sharply. This is

Figure 2.4   Treasury-Bank Workflow

due to an increased use of bank-to-customer trading systems which have eliminated the need for human intervention. Therefore those salespeople that can still be found in the treasury department will normally be servicing the larger institutional customers, such as the multinationals, that will tend to be more active and deal in larger sizes. Or they will be dealing with the more complex products such as derivatives that might require more explanation before a deal can be struck. We will talk a little more about the use of trading systems shortly, but first we should understand what the salesperson has to offer to the customer. Their job is not simply to relay prices from the traders, but more to build this relationship between bank and customer that we have already referred to. We said that often customers choose to deal with banks who they feel have a good understanding of the markets and it is through the salespeople that they can perceive this. The salesperson will give commentary on what is happening in the markets, the type of trade flows the bank is seeing (although they must always protect the anonymity of their other customers) and offer advice on the best products to match the client's needs and views on where the markets are moving. Then when a customer wants to actually deal the trade will be executed by the salesperson although, as we said, the risk will belong to the trader. This means that it is the trader's responsibility to manage the position, to cover it by doing the opposite trade in the market, if necessary, and to generally try and make the maximum profit from the deal. Of course, in the money market area, the trader has to remember that part of the responsibility of the treasury department is to fund the bank, so if the customer deal is to place money with the bank then they may want to keep these funds to offset against their own bank's loans, but if the customer is looking to borrow money then this will be added to the totals that they will need to borrow to maintain their liquidity balance.

Customer deals do not all come into the treasury department via the salespeople. We will also see them arriving through automated dealing systems and through the branch network. These are the other sales channels that we referred to in our diagram. In order to be cost-efficient the banks have invested heavily in the technology that will allow their customers to deal with them electronically. These dealing systems will mimic the role of the salesperson in that they relay prices, but there is not one single price for each market participant. Prices can vary according to the credit risk of the counterparty and also to the size of the deal. So these dealing systems have to be sufficiently flexible to allow for these differences, applying spreads to lower bids, and raise offers according to preset criteria, whilst taking a feed from the trading desk of the more generic market rate. The customer will then see a rate that is good for them to deal on and the first the trader will know of the deal will be when the exposure appears on their book. There is no need for them to intervene any earlier. This means that the smaller deals are automatically being aggregated on the bank's books to become part of their overall market exposures. Similarly this will be the case with the deals coming in from the branches. Again these transactions will be too small to need direct access to the bank's treasury department but as they are accepted through the branch network they will be passed through to the head office system. In this part of the banking world we are dealing with rates that are not as sensitive as those seen in the wholesale market. Rates for most of the retail and small corporate transactions will change irregularly. The basis will be the wholesale rate but this will be adjusted by a spread for risk and size and so will not need to reset with the frequency with which the wholesale market moves.

KEY BANK PRODUCTS

The last thing we need to do is to look at the products that banks offer their customers and see how they can translate into the exposures the banks need to manage in the financial markets. If we take a look at some of the typical products offered to the retail sector (Table 2.1) we can see how they could translate to equivalent financial market positions.

Table 2.1 Retail-Financial Market Product Equivalents

Retail Product	Equivalent Financial Market Product
Placement products	
Current & Cheque accounts	Overnight or call[a] deposits
Savings accounts	Overnight or term[b] deposits
Borrowing products	
Overdrafts	Overnight or call[c] borrowing
Personal & Consumer loans	Term[d] loans
Mortgages	Long-term[e] loans

[a] Call deposits are placements that roll over on a daily basis until one or other party decides they no longer want to be in the deal.
[b] Term deposits are placements left for a given amount of time, be it one day, one year or whatever maturity is agreed between the two parties.
[c] As with call deposits these are rolling loans.
[d] As with term deposits these are fixed maturity loans.
[e] Long-term loans are for periods of greater than a year and in the case of mortgages considerably longer.

If we look at the placement products they will be bringing money into the bank, but most commonly for uncertain periods of time. However these accounts provide a lot of the liquidity required by the banks to finance their lending, even on a mismatched maturity basis such as when this short-term money is used to finance long-term lending. Any excess money, or liquidity, that the bank finds itself holding can easily be offered to other banks in the interbank market. When we look at the customer borrowing products we can see that they cover a far broader range of maturities. Overdrafts are borrowing facilities that can change on a daily basis so they could lead to the bank having to use overnight (or call[10]) borrowing in the markets to finance them. Personal and consumer loans will normally have longer, fixed maturities to them and mortgages will generally be the longest. Banks will also often offer loans through credit cards and again these will have variable maturities to them but with the added complication that they have variable principal amounts as the loans taken out on the cards will differ from month to month. Nonetheless these will still be loans that will need to be funded in the markets.

Sometimes these products will not just be straightforward, vanilla transactions, they may include additional features such as capped mortgages with maximum interest rates included in them or savings accounts that guarantee to pay the investors the greater of a fixed interest rate or the value of a movement in another market such as a stock market index. These products basically have embedded derivatives; the derivatives will affect the risk and payout of the products and so the bank will need to use the market equivalents of these products to cover the exposures. All in all the various parts of the financial markets are necessary to match and manage the exposures that come from the banks offering the products that you and I use on a daily basis. The skill of the banks comes in presenting what can sometimes be complex financial products to their customers in the most straightforward way, so that when we use our credit card we do not need to think about the liquidity implications of what we are doing; instead that is the responsibility of the bank, and this is what drives so much of their activity in the markets.

---

[10] Call money is when funds are made available until the lender decides otherwise and they call back their loan. Similarly the borrower is not locked into borrowing the funds for any set time, they can decide to pay back the funds whenever they wish.

Finally, in Text Box 2.1 is a summary of some of the key things we can observe about commercial banking and the financial markets.

Box 2.1 Summary of Commercial Banking Activity in the Financial Markets

Their role in the markets:

- The commercial banking part of a bank can be seen in the markets as an issuer in the debt markets, particularly the money markets that they will access daily, raising funds to cover the cash requirements of the bank.
- They can be seen as investors placing in the market any excess cash balances they may have, and also looking after the reserve investments of the bank.
- They are also intermediaries as they transact business on behalf of their clients and run trading books.

The markets in which they are most active:

- Commercial banking has a strong presence in FX and money markets where they will normally be active traders.
- They are often to be seen as market makers in government debt, both long and short-term.
- The equity market is the market they are least likely to be involved in as this is more closely allied to the investment banking model.
- They will be users of derivative products to cover the exposures they create in the products they sell to their customers.
- They are also likely to trade derivatives, particularly FX and money market ones.

3
Investment Banking

In the previous chapter we looked at the business of commercial and retail banking which is generally intuitive and easy to understand, in concept. This is because it embodies the basic idea of borrowing and lending: you need funds, I have them, I lend them to you, you repay to me plus any interest due and so we have made a bilateral contract between the two of us. Investment banking can seem more complicated because the firm that creates the deal will not intend to be either the borrower or the lender. Instead they are the facilitator in the transaction, bringing together those that need funds with those that have funds to still complete the flow of funds that, as we have said, underlies the business of finance, but in this case the intention is to limit the exposure of the bank. This is what we saw illustrated in the Introduction to this part of the book, in the diagram of disintermediated financing (see Figure 3.1).

Investment banking, or merchant banking, has been around for centuries and in fact many of its roots lie in the commodity trading taking place within Europe, then across the Atlantic once the Atlantic trading routes had been established, and beyond. In the section on Banking in the UK we will talk some more about merchant banking versus investment banking to highlight some of the differences that evolved in the structure of these two types of organization as the banks themselves evolved, but in principle they are there to perform the same function. Going back to the trading roots, this kind of international trading brought problems beyond the scope of a merchant selling their produce for cash in a local market. Whilst it could be hard enough to ensure payment and liquidity in this local environment just think how much more problematic it would have been to ensure payment in, say, a transatlantic deal with limits on not only transport but basic communications. Of course, this meant that, without guarantees of payment, we had problems of liquidity for the producers. This created a market opportunity and we saw from the 18th century a corporate securities market opening up to try and manage these exposures, along with raising finance for governments and supporting key infrastructure developments such as the development of railroads and other transport and communication links. Not

Lenders   Borrowers

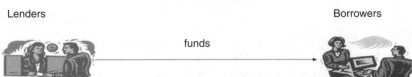

funds

Figure 3.1 Disintermediation

surprisingly, the bankers of the 18th century often had strong links with this transatlantic trade itself, such as the sons of Alexander Brown the linen merchant from Northern Ireland, who formed Brown Brothers & Co. in 1810 in Liverpool, before opening branches in Philadelphia and New York within the following 10 years. Just as an interesting sideline to this piece of market history, Brown Brothers started out in the business of investment banking but following the creation of Brown Brothers Harriman the bank shifted its emphasis from investment banking to commercial banking, back in 1931, just before the passing of the Glass-Steagall Act.[1] Brown Brothers was ultimately bought by Bankers Trust, one of the largest US commercial banks, which in turn was bought by Deutsche Bank. One of the earliest investment banks was Baring Brothers, founded on Christmas Day in 1762 and then named John & Francis Baring & Co., merchants. Barings is a name renowned in recent times for the trading scandal that brought the bank to its knees, leading the bulk of the business that was then contained within Barings PLC to be sold to ING Bank of the Netherlands for the sum of £1. How interesting that this prestigious and influential bank in the history of investment banking should be brought down through one of the core activities of 20th century investment banking – trading.

Today there are relatively few pure investment banks left, particularly following the events of September 2008 when both Goldman Sachs and Morgan Stanley, the last two major US investment banks, changed status to become bank holding companies. This was to allow them access

---

[1] We will talk about the Glass-Steagall Act a little later as it has had an important impact on the markets by segregating business models.

to funding from the Federal Reserve Bank, including preferred stock investment from the US Treasury Troubled Asset Relief Programme (TARP). Having said this, though, Goldman Sachs continues to operate very much as a traditional investment bank, running three core business divisions: investment management; trading and principal investments and asset management and securities services. Embedded within these three divisions are the three core businesses of investment banking: advisory, origination and trading. Asset management is something we will consider later in this book, and we will look at securities services later in this chapter. So whilst we may not have so many dedicated independent investment banks today, as we have said, the investment banking function will still be found in the investment banking divisions of the full-service banks such as JPMorgan Chase, Citigroup etc. For now, though, let's take a look at these three core businesses.

ADVISORY

This is the area of investment banking that probably has the closest connection to the investment banks of the 18th and 19th century. Looking at the history of the banks we have already mentioned, such as Barings and Brown Brothers, we see that they were often cited as advisors to governments and corporations and it was these key relationships that gave rise to their ability to raise money such as by creating securities and placing them successfully in the markets. This theme of strong relationships is one that we see still today as we look at the names of the firms advising, again, governments and corporations on a continuous basis, and this can lead to follow-on business in terms of origination and trading. As an example of this, if we look at the firms that are primary dealers to the US government, we see a list of 19 banks. These primary dealers are the banks that deal with the Federal Reserve Bank (the Fed), in terms of advising them on market conditions and how best to raise funds, through to committing to underwrite new issues for the government brought to the market by the Fed, and trading with them on these securities in open market operations whereby the Fed manages monetary policy. We will talk more of this in the chapter on Central Banks and Market Regulators. At the moment there are 19 primary dealers, but in 1988 there were 46, with the fall being accounted for primarily by consolidation in the market. The Table 3.1 lists these primary dealers as at December 2009:

Table 3.1   US Primary Dealers

BNP Paribas Securities Corp.
Banc of America Securities LLC
Barclays Capital Inc.
Cantor Fitzgerald & Co.
Citigroup Global Markets Inc.
Credit Suisse Securities (USA) LLC
Daiwa Securities America Inc.
Deutsche Bank Securities Inc.
Goldman, Sachs & Co.
HSBC Securities (USA) Inc.
Jefferies & Company, Inc.
J.P. Morgan Securities Inc.
Mizuho Securities USA Inc.
Morgan Stanley & Co. Incorporated
Nomura Securities International, Inc.
RBC Capital Markets Corporation
RBS Securities Inc.
UBS Securities LLC.

If we now look at the equivalent in the UK market (Table 3.2), the Gilt-Edged Market Makers (GEMMs) we find a list of 16 firms, many of whose names are familiar:

Table 3.2   UK GEMMs

Barclays Capital
BNP Paribas (London Branch)
Citigroup Global Markets Limited
Credit Suisse Securities
Deutsche Bank AG (London Branch)
Goldman Sachs International Limited
HSBC Bank PLC
Jefferies International Limited
J.P. Morgan Securities Limited
Merrill Lynch International
Morgan Stanley & Co. International plc
Nomura International plc
Royal Bank of Canada Europe Limited
Royal Bank of Scotland
The Toronto-Dominion Bank (London Branch
UBS Limited
Winterflood Securities Limited

and again if we look at the French equivalent (Table 3.3), the Spécialistes en Valeurs de Trésors (SVTs) we find yet more examples of the same names:

Table 3.3   France SVTs

Barclays Capital
BNP Paribas
Calyon
Citigroup
Commerzbank
Credit Suisse
Deutsche Bank
Goldman Sachs
HSBC
J.P. Morgan Securities Ltd
Merrill Lynch
Morgan Stanley
NATIXIS
Nomura
Royal Bank of Scotland
Santander
Société Générale
UBS

and so on. Again and again we will see the names Morgan Stanley (US bank), Barclays Capital (UK bank), BNP Paribas (French bank) etc. as these are the firms who have worked to build up the reputation, skills and customer base to work efficiently on behalf of not just their "own" governments but also internationally.

We can also see more evidence of the strength of these relationships if we look at the UK government's advisory bill for the bailout of UK banks in 2008, with, amongst others, Deutsche Bank receiving £5.3 million, Goldman Sachs £4.5 million and Morgan Stanley £1.5 million. Advisory business is an important source of revenue for these investment banking divisions. In its third quarter 2009 figures Goldman Sachs reported net revenue of $325 million,[2] 36% of the total revenues of its investment banking, with the rest being revenues from their underwriting commitments. Whilst $325 million sounds like a lot of money this is actually 47% below the third quarter of 2008! If we then add this to their first and second quarter figures ($527 million and $368 million, respectively) we come to a very impressive $1.22 billion for the year to date. Interestingly a very similar figure to JPMorgan's $1.26 billion reported advisory revenues for the same period. However one of the key things about advisory income is that it is fee income that does not depend on the firm taking risk positions on its balance sheets, unlike

---

[2] Goldman Sachs Group Inc, October 2009.

underwriting which gives the bank a risk that is not easily quantifiable. This commitment may or may not require the bank to put funds against a deal depending on circumstances, and as such is a risk transaction for them. The bank's advisory income comes from advising the firm's customers on how to raise wholesale funds, as we described in the chapter on commercial banking, including funds for specific purpose such as project finance, along with other corporate issues such as restructuring and mergers and acquisitions (M&A). Sometimes this will result in public deals coming to the market, such as when a company decides to list on a stock exchange and makes its Initial Public Offering (IPO) of stock, other times it may result in a private deal such as when they negotiate a sale of part or all of a privately owned company, a private equity deal. Sometimes it may result in nothing, and it is for this reason that the trend has grown towards charging customers for the time spent on trying to arrange a deal, rather in the manner of a law or accountancy firm, even if no transaction ultimately occurs. Individual fees will not be routinely published as these are negotiated between the bank and its customers, although when figures such as the reported $450 million costs incurred by BHP Billiton in its yearlong attempt to take over Rio Tinto in 2008–9 are put into the public arena this is the sort of figure that causes discomfort amongst the corporate world. We should remember, though, that this is a total cost figure, including extensive legal fees and not just the fees paid to the advising financial institutions.

The department of the bank that deals with these areas of business is the Corporate Finance department. This area deals with potentially very sensitive and confidential information. If, for example, a major multinational was seeking advice on how to raise £5 billion this could affect various things such as: the company's share price, as the market speculates on why the funds are needed; its competitor's share prices, as, for example, the market considers whether a hostile takeover could be being planned; and the rate at which the company can raise money as the market has had time to consider whether they would be willing to commit funds and if so for what return. In other words the whole success and timing of the issue can be taken out of the hands of the bank and its potential customer if information were leaked before time. This is why Corporate Finance departments are said to be surrounded by "Chinese walls": metaphorical walls which are internal barriers to prevent the sharing of sensitive information between departments. These barriers are made with internal rules and controls, often using software firewalls and sometimes physical barriers distancing those parts of the bank that may have interest in the same customers for different purpose. A classic example of this would be Corporate Finance advising a customer on how to raise funds and the trading desk dealing in existing securities of the name for profit, so these worlds are kept as separate as possible.

From the Corporate Finance department we can ultimately end up with four possibilities for the client:

- They issue equity in the capital market.
- They issue debt in the capital market.
- A loan of some sort is arranged for them by the bank without going to the public markets.
- A corporate event such as merger, takeover, de-merger, is arranged.

Of these four the most commonly seen event is a debt capital market issue, although there were periods in 2008 when announced M&A activity exceeded debt issue, but this was due to the market conditions which were particularly difficult for corporate bond issuance, with equity issuance at all times being by far the smallest part of their business. In the year to date up to December 2009 M&A activity had fallen by 33%, whilst debt capital market issuance had risen by 31% and equity issuance by 23%.[3]

However for these debt and equity transactions the Corporate Finance department cannot work in isolation. Their job involves winning the mandate from the customer to bring a deal to the market, but the actual origination of the security will involve a different area whose expertise will lie in how to create the securities, in terms of structure and pricing. So whilst Corporate Finance will continue to be involved in the deal right up to the point of issue, ensuring all necessary legal work, administration etc. has been properly completed, the business responsibility will pass to another area.

ORIGINATION

The process of successfully creating a security is the rather like walking a tightrope. As long as the needs of both issuers and investors are kept in balance the originating firm should be able to bring a successful deal to the market, but as soon as they lean too far towards one or the other the whole deal can fail – and in this case it is often the originating bank

---

[3] Thomson Reuters, Investment Banking Scorecard, December 2009.

that is the one to suffer, either financially or in reputation or both. As we have said origination is about bringing deals to the market. In order for these deals to be successful they have to raise the funds needed by the issuer, at the best possible rate, and yet have to look sufficiently attractive to tempt investors' funds. In the Introduction we spoke about the two ways of raising money – via the equity and debt markets – so it is through the origination process that we will first see the investment banking divisions in the markets. The processes used for these two types of instrument will be different so we will look at each in turn.

Equity Issuance

When a company decides they want to list on a stock exchange and publicly offer shares for the first time they will need to make an Initial Public Offering (IPO). The investment bank will have to prepare the company for issue, ensuring that the company can meet the listing requirements of the particular exchange, which may mean making sure that it has sufficient turnover, records and value, all on an audited basis. Different exchanges have different requirements, and even within a single exchange there are different levels of listing, so one of the reasons for using the investment bank is to ensure a good fit. It is not uncommon for a company to apply for listing and be refused in the first instance, so the more diligent the preparation process the better. Assuming this is all going to be in order, the bank has to come up with the physical structure. In the equity market the basic structure of ordinary shares is a security that represents partial ownership of a company and gives the investor a voting right and a dividend payment, if the company chooses to make one. From this basic structure the bank may decide to create a variation, such as a voting right deferred share, one in which the company will not issue voting rights before a given period of time in order to protect the company from hostile takeovers, or a preference share, which carries a guaranteed dividend rate, again assuming the company chooses to pay a dividend. The reason for using these variations may be to make the offering appeal to a particular type of investor, or just to make the offering sufficiently attractive to investors in general. Again, it is the bank's responsibility to ensure that the structure would be acceptable to the exchange and also to the issuer and that it would be saleable. Ultimately, though, what is most likely to prove attractive to both issuers and investors is the pricing. The bank will try to determine the best possible value for both sides and it will do this by using its position in the market. It will look at values for similar issues and companies, and try to gauge potential demand, whilst, of course, respecting any confidentiality issues. Most commonly the bank will determine a price at which the shares will be issued, but sometimes a firm will use a Dutch auction process whereby the investors will bid for the shares. In either case a prospectus will have to be prepared to give potential investors all relevant information about the company and the issue.

2008 and 2009 saw a raft of equity follow-on issues, secondary issues of shares by firms already listed on an exchange. This can be by a mechanism such as a rights issue, where the shares are offered to existing shareholders on a pro rata basis according to how many shares are held, or they could be offered in the general market on either a public issue or an invitation placement. Again the mechanism chosen should be the one likely to produce the best result. In 2009 we saw an increase of 37% in the global issue of follow-on equity as compared to an increase of just 9% in the IPO market,[4] although we should say that a 9% increase in most years would be seen as very good. In both initial and follow-on equity deals if the bank underwrites the issue they will be committing to provide the issuing company with the funds they need, either by committing to buy the issued shares themselves or, sometimes, by providing an alternative financing agreement if all or some of the shares cannot be issued or sold. So, there is a clear vested interest in making sure the deal is successful. Interestingly, in 2009 JPMorgan made an estimated $2.2 billion in underwriting fees, 50% more than in previous years, leaving them as number one in the league table for equity issuance having brought 383 deals to the market.[5] The league tables are an important tool for the markets to measure the relative strength of the banks in origination. Another interesting thing to be seen from the issuance of 2009 is that much of the growth in this part of the market came from Asia, particularly Japan and China for IPOs and India for follow-on equity issue, whilst the league table shows us only one Asian firm, Nomura, appearing at number 9, with only 3.9% of the market share against JPMorgan's 12.3%.[6] In Text Box 3.1 we take a look at what happened when Google came to the market in 2005 as an example of how things sometimes do not go according to plan.

---

[4] Thomson Reuters, December 2009.
[5] Ibid.
[6] Ibid.

Box 3.1 Google IPO

In 1985 Google came to the market, with Morgan Stanley and Credit Suisse First Boston as the originating banks and underwriters of the deal. They decided to use the Dutch auction method with potential investors being given an expected share price range of $108–$135. It was thought that since the auction meant that the buyers, who had first to pre-register with either of the issuing banks, would be stating the price at which they would be happy to buy, this should represent the fairest possible price. At the time Google estimated its share price to be above $100 but they were looking to raise money in a volatile market, with an IPO scheduled for August, a notoriously difficult month to bring an IPO. This is why just before the auction the price range was reduced to $85–$95, and then after the auction closed the price was set at $85 per share, and the number of shares to be issued was reduced by 5 million. The story could end there with us believing that the process had worked well, the shares were not as keenly sought as had been originally believed and a difficult task had been well executed, if it were not for the fact that bidders found themselves scaled down, owing to the lack of supply and excess of bids, and the price then jumping 17% on the first day of trading. Theoretically movements like this should be avoided by the Dutch auction process so it is probable that in this case the process was not effective, and the net 'losers' were Google. Interestingly, though, an initial price of even $135 would still look a bargain in November 2007 when the shares reached their all-time high of $747.24!

Fixed Income

As with equity origination, on the fixed income side of the market we are concerned with creating debt securities such as corporate bonds. Again if we hark back to history, we find that the roots of one of our most famous investment banks, Goldman Sachs, lie in promoting the use of commercial paper in the second half of the 19th century. Commercial paper is a form of short-term corporate debt, although classified as a money market product as its maturity will be below one year, and so we can see once more how investment banking business being carried out today reflects the model that we saw in the industry's very beginnings. In the Introduction to this book we spoke about the difference between money market and long-term debt instruments, and traditionally investment banking concerns itself more with long-term debt, although there are exceptions such as commercial paper and short-term government securities. Some of the processes we saw in equity issuance will be the same as in fixed income, but the end product is completely different so the means of coming to the result will differ. Unlike equity, fixed income will pay a known return, usually an interest rate, to the investors, and make a promise to repay the loan, so the whole process of pricing will be about pricing this income flow relative to the risk of not receiving it due to credit problems. Again, unlike equity, it is normal for a borrower to come to the market many times, either to increase their borrowing or to refinance existing borrowings, so the process of comparison can be a bit easier as the banks can often look at the returns investors are already receiving for this issuer and use this as a starting point for pricing the new debt. Alongside this the banks are again going to have to look at peer group comparators and gauge investor appetite to make sure the pricing is accurate.

Earlier in this chapter we spoke about primary dealers for government securities and as we said these firms are the ones that will be the originators of government debt. The process most commonly used is once more the Dutch auction method. All the primary dealers are expected to provide the central banks with competitive bids for the government's issues, and the securities will then be issued at the best (lowest) rate, or cost, for the government to issue their securities. Unlike the story of Google this method does generally work very well for the governments. Since most of the major countries tend to issue paper on a regular basis we tend to find that the auction process allows this paper to be absorbed as seamlessly as possible into the market without any of the pops, either up or down, that we saw with Google. Obviously it is not flawless, but we have only to look at the US government's cumulative sale of $2.109 trillion of notes and bonds (debt of more than one year in maturity) in 2009 that attracted an average bid-to-cover ratio of 2.60 at the 74 auctions. The bid-to-cover ratio measures by how much the auction is over bid and obviously the higher the figure the greater demand. For comparison, the average bid-to-cover in 2008 was 2.19 over 50 auctions.[7] Of course this method does not always work as we saw in March 2009 when the UK government only achieved a bid-to-cover ratio of 0.93 on its auction of 40-year bonds, the first time it had achieved

---

[7] Bloomberg, 23 December 2009.

a cover of less than 1.0 since 2002. However, subsequent auctions achieved ratios closer to the average for the maturities of around 1.90.

In the corporate bond market banks normally get involved in competitive bidding not to buy the issue but to win the mandate to bring the issue. Corporate finance will use their relationships to encourage potential borrowers to ask the bank to bid for the right to issue the bond. These bids will be based on the rates at which the banks think they can sell the paper and also their ability to bring a successful deal. Sometimes borrowers will choose not to go with the lowest bid given to them, but instead to go for the house with the greatest expertise in the market area, even if they have to pay a small amount more. Once the bids have been received the borrower will decide which bank or banks should receive the mandate and they will then launch the deal, typically as quickly as they can. As with the equity market there will have to be a prospectus produced, but unlike equity this is not quite as crucial to the decision-making of the investors since the issuers will be listed companies and so the credit will often be known to the investors. To help further, the issuers are often rated by a credit rating agency that will give the investors some guidance on how safe the credit is, although these ratings agencies have themselves come under a lot of criticism in the past couple of years. Nonetheless a core function of the ratings system is that it allows market users access to what are believed to be impartial opinions on the credit. Clearly they are free to carry out their research but for many it speeds up the decision-making process by removing the absolute need to do this. Once the mandate has been awarded to the bank that will be the lead manager on the deal, they will typically syndicate the issue. This means that they will contact other banks to offer them a share of the underwriting commitment for the deal, in return for which they receive some of the securities to sell, at a preferential rate by giving them a portion of the fees charged to the issuer of the deal. This will not guarantee that they will make a profit but if the issue is well received the fact that they are effectively receiving the securities at a discount will be the means by which they can make their underwriting fee and emphasizes why it is important that the lead bank has done all it can to price the deal well.

TRADING

The third core business of the investment banks has always been trading and this follows naturally on in the chain from advisory to origination and so on to trading, dealing in the securities once they have been issued. One of the basic of ideas of creating financial market securities is that they will be tradable, that the holders should be able to sell them on if they need to liquidate their positions. This is why it is natural for the investment banks to run trading operations, to offer this facility. Of course this is not the only reason – making a profit is always going to be a big motivator. In the chapter on Commercial Banks we introduced the idea of the dealing room, peopled with traders and salespeople. Again in the investment banking division we will find the same idea. In some of the full-service institutions it will be physically the same room, in others the two worlds are separated, with the FX and money market flows that we saw in commercial banking being covered by the Treasury dealing room whilst the debt and equity flows that we have met in this chapter are covered in a separate dealing operation for Capital Markets.

When we look at how these capital market products are traded we come across a few very distinct models that have an impact on this. First of all there is a distinction in the two marketplaces for the equity and fixed income products in which the products are traded: equity is traded on exchanges and fixed income is more commonly an over-the-counter (OTC) market. This has little to do with physical locations as most exchanges are screen-based today, but there is a difference in the actual trading model. With the exchange-traded model the exchanges operate a membership system and deals need to be executed through these members. Therefore it is natural that the investment banking divisions need to be members of these exchanges in order to access the market and be able to trade on it for their customers and themselves. Lists of members are publicly available and so it is easy for clients to identify possible counterparties in any given exchange, and so again we see the same names as before appearing as members of all the major stock exchanges. The OTC market is a little different as there is no formal marketplace, either physical or electronic. There are trading systems that are commonly used in various market areas, which almost create a de facto exchange but with a crucial difference: use of these trading systems is not exclusive so the systems, whilst they may be seeing the bulk of the trades, will not be seeing all of them. So for a customer wanting to trade in say, corporate bonds, it is more difficult to identify who would be the natural market counterparties.

A second difference lies in the actual trading of the securities. Most equities today are traded on an order book system. This is where orders to buy and sell are input to the exchange and as buyers and sellers meet on a price level so the deal is executed. This is not the typical model for bond trades, which are generally either market-maker or price-maker driven. When we spoke of the primary dealers for government securities we were speaking of market-makers whose responsibility was to make two-way prices to the market, both customers and other professional counterparties, in order to promote liquidity. When they make these prices they are committing to either buy at the bid or sell at the offer should the counterparty choose to deal. The downside to this is the risk that the banks take on board by committing to always make these two-way prices. If the counterparty chooses to deal they will give the trader a risk position that they will then need to trade out. This is why the market-makers have increasingly used Inter-Dealer Brokers to deal with one another,[8] and also why in many markets the model has changed to price-making. There is a subtle distinction here that makes a big difference in risk. As a market-maker you are obliged to make a price, as a price-maker you choose to. In practice if you are a client of the bank you are unlikely to see any difference as the bank will want to do your business if they possibly can, but if you are another professional counterparty, such as another bank which may be a potential rival, then the firm may choose not to make you a price. Or alternatively they may decide to show one side only, a bid or an offer. This means the trader will not be obliged to deal unless they are happy to do so. Technology has helped a lot in this as there are many trading systems actively used in the market whereby the dealers can input one-sided prices and the system creates two-sided prices by taking the best bids and offers, just as we saw in the description of order-driven markets.

Whilst we are talking about models of trading there is one more that we should mention and this is proprietary trading. We touched on this in the section on commercial banking and this is when the trader is not expected to make prices but instead is only intended to take risk positions on behalf of the bank. Proprietary trading is a key part of the whole trading world but is also the riskiest part, as the bank ends up running a risk position for an amount of time. How long will depend on market conditions and internal controls, but it will be short-term, as we said earlier. This is an element of all trading; traders, be they market-makers, price-makers or pure proprietary traders, will generally be expected to run positions as well as passing deals straight through their books, in other words undertake an element of proprietary trading.

---

[8] See Part 5, Chapter 27.

For some of these traders the positions will sometimes come about as a result of carrying out a customer trade, for example, when a price-maker has made a price to a customer on which the customer has chosen to deal, and sometimes as a result of the trader taking a view on the market and dealing on this view, the trader choosing to take a position. In either case for the trader to choose to run the position they must take a view that the position will make a greater profit if they deal to unwind the position at some point in the future rather than straightaway. On the whole the trader will generally have greater profit potential on these risk positions over the put-through trades,[9] but against this profit potential they must face greater risks. However, a trader that is exclusively a proprietary trader will be focused on taking these views and making these decisions on running positions; although their counterparties could well be other banks or customers, they will always deal only at their choice. So this is the trader that is likely to carry the most risk on their trading book. These three key trading models are the ones that we are likely to find in the capital markets dealing room, depending on the markets in which the firm is trading and represent the different types of risk involved in running a trading operation.

So whilst advisory, origination and trading are the three key core businesses of investment banking, and the areas in which we will see these firms in the market in the most high-profile way, there are also two other parts of the business that we should mention: research and securities services.

RESEARCH

The research department provides research and analysis for the various departments of the bank, along with information that can be sent to the customers. Once again the banks have to be careful with the interaction between this department and others, and again this is as a result of various market scandals. One such involved Merrill Lynch and analysis of high tech companies during the boom period for this sort of firm, back in 2002. They were given a $100 million fine after admitting that some reports from their analysts had overstated the company's expectations on some companies to attract new investment banking business. This came about after the New York State Attorney at the time, Eliot Spitzer, came across e-mails from Merrill Lynch staff members working in the

---

[9] Trades where the trader immediately unwinds a position as soon as they have received it.

department saying that they had overstated things and famously one by the internet analyst Henry Blodget in which he said that he devoted the bulk of his time to projects that would bring in investment banking business to the company. Underlying all this was the fact that the salary and bonuses of research staff were linked to their contribution to the profits of investment banking. This was a massive conflict of interest and along with the fine Merrill Lynch agreed to overhaul their internal procedures, instituting firewalls and disengaging these two activities financially. Merrill Lynch was probably not the only house guilty of these sorts of actions and reforms in this part of the corporate infrastructure followed around the market. The point is that investors receive research that they believe to be true opinions on companies, markets, economies and if they cannot trust that this is the case then it is worthless to them. This is one of the reasons we have thriving independent research companies, but nonetheless research remains a core banking activity.

The research department will typically be divided by currencies, markets, sectors, with individual analysts concentrating their research on limited parts of the market to enable them to specialize and gain the depth of understanding that can translate into not just an invaluable internal resource but also a marketable commodity. The economists and chief analysts of the major firms will make regular appearances on financial media, some of them gaining almost cult-like status, such as Henry Kaufman who whilst working for Salomon Brothers in the 1970s and 80s was widely believed to have an enormous influence on markets with his pronouncements on interest rates being said to trigger market movements. Such is the power of a well-respected analyst.

SECURITIES SERVICES AND CUSTODY

Everything we have spoken about in this chapter, the core workflow of investment banking, leads to the existence of securities that are then bought and sold in the marketplace. This buying and selling has given rise to another part of our industry that the banks have recently started to really appreciate and to promote as another core business area. The business of Securities Services and Custody deals with looking after the securities after a trade has happened. Going back in time, and not even too far back – and in some countries this will still happen – if you bought an equity instrument you would receive a share certificate. If you bought a bond the same thing would apply and when the bond was due to mature you would surrender this certificate to receive back the money due. Also this bond certificate would have detachable parts at the bottom; these were the coupons that would need to be detached and presented to receive the interest payments. This would all be fine if we were working in small, physically confined markets such as we would have seen in, say, the 19th century, but by the 20th century it was clear that the markets had expanded beyond making this practical, and so the business of custody began. Instead of each individual certificate being transferred between buyers and sellers after each trade the certificates began to be held in custody by either a bank or, ultimately, a central custodial organization such as Euroclear or Clearstream (originally known as Cedel) that were set up in the 1960s. Today it is common for securities to be held by these central custodians, and rather than being in paper format they are now electronic, as we saw in the Introduction. In Text Box 3.2 we look a little more at these two institutions.

Box 3.2 Euroclear and Clearstream

Euroclear

The Euroclear System was first established in 1968 by Morgan Guaranty Trust Company and was the first International Securities Depository. At the time it was working in the world of paper securities and so its intention was to provide a central location where the securities could be held and ownership transferred by book entry accounting, without having to physically move the paper. This is known as immobilization as the securities still exist in physical form but would not require physical transfer. Following the creation of Cedel in 1970 by a consortium of banks, Euroclear was also taken out of single bank ownership when it was sold to the market-owned Euroclear Clearance System PLC. This independence was further consolidated in 2000 when Euroclear Bank was created so that the system itself could offer the banking services that it had previously had to source from external banks thereby further consolidating the whole offering package for transfer of securities and payments (the settlement process), along with an expanding list of services such including providing intra-day liquidity to its users, securities lending, collateral management and more. Today Euroclear's focus is on European securities and as of Q3 2009 the value of securities in the Euroclear system was €19.9 trillion, with the system seeing a turnover, year to date, of €379.8 trillion.

Clearstream

Clearstream was formed in 2000 after a merger between Cedel and Deutsche Börse Clearing. Like Euroclear it offers settlement and custody, with a bias for fixed income products over equity, and it has also held a banking licence since 1996. Alongside the classic custody and settlement product Clearstream has also been developing a range of value-added services such as order routing within their investment fund services, to provide more of a securities services offering. As of November 2009 the value of assets under custody was €10.7 trillion.

The downside to using a central depository is the need to have accounts that cost money and time to maintain, but these accounts are the way in which central depositories can ensure that all monies due on the securities within their system, such as dividends on equities and interest payments on debt, are allocated to the owners. Since the banks are inherently involved in these securities markets themselves, and need to have not only the custodial accounts but also the staff to manage them it became a logical progression to offer to carry out this service to their clients, looking after their assets within the bank's accounts, passing through cash flow and providing them with accounts, and from this has been spawned an increasingly sophisticated industry in its own right. As well as custody the banks offer a whole range of services to their customers, who are typically the investment firms, services which include settlement; fund administration, accounting and valuation; collateral management; securities lending and cash management. Having good technology is often the key to being able to offer these services and this is an area in which the banks have to invest and therefore their securities services customer can leverage off this investment. For these services the banks charge a fee, which again is risk-free in terms of market risk and balance sheet use, although there are other business risks that the bank has to consider in committing to this kind of contract. This area of the business sounds much distanced from the model of disintermediation that we identified as being the main reason for the existence of investment banking, but we must remember that we are looking at a moving industry. It is important for the banks as business units to maximize the potential profits from the marketplace, as we are about to see, and if we go back to Goldman Sachs' 3rd quarter earnings for 2009 we can see that they achieved revenues of $325 million for advisory services, a traditional investment banking core business, whilst over the same period revenues for securities services were $ 472 million. This shows, relatively, how much this business stream can mean to the banks.

INVESTMENT BANKING IN THE 21ST CENTURY

Back in the 1980s the investment banks were like the A-list celebrities. Names like Salomon Brothers, Merrill Lynch, Goldman Sachs were the banks everyone was talking about, everyone wanted to work for them and they were seen as all-powerful in the markets. In 2009 only one of these three still exists in an independent form. Salomon Brothers was merged into the Citigroup family in 1998, following its acquisition by Travelers Group insurance company, and Merrill Lynch became a wholly owned subsidiary of Bank of America in 2009. So it would be easy to think that the era of investment banks is over but that would be completely wrong and we only have to look at debt and equity issuance to see that volumes have increased manifold. So what has changed is the structure of the market, as we have been seeing throughout this chapter. Rather than talking about investment banks we have been talking about investment banking divisions, parts of those full-service banks we identified in the chapter on Commercial and Retail Banking, and whilst we still have a few independent ones they are in the minority. This in turn has brought about problems of its own, which came to prominence after the Financial Crisis. At a time when RBS reported a net operating loss in 2009 of £6.232 billion, £3.607 billion attributable to shareholders, they also announced an operating profit in their Global Banking and Markets division of £5.709[10] billion. This, of course, brought the issue of bonuses into the public arena as the bank announced its plans for its bonus pool. The fact that the bank had received £45.4 billion of taxpayers' funding, making it 70% state-owned, rising to 84% after shareholder approval to join the government's Asset Protection Scheme, led many to say that just because this area of the business was profitable that profit should not be distilled by the payment of bonuses. This is the core of the problem that will be facing the market and its regulators for many years, not just at RBS. Could the Global Markets and Banking division have made those profits if the bank had not been bailed out by the government but allowed to fail? Should profits in one area not be used to offset losses in another? How much of the profit made in capital markets issuance was made because the banks were unable or unwilling to lend directly?

---

[10] RBS Annual Report 2009.

And let's not forget to ask how much of the profit in this same area has come from the banks refinancing themselves since $262.5 billion was raised in 2009 in the equity capital markets for the financial sector, and $2.2816 trillion[11] in the debt capital markets? In other words is the industry making profits from the industry? These are questions where there will be many willing to argue on either side but the fact remains that they highlight key issues facing banking, and specifically this area of banking. In the past there had been differences between the regulation of commercial banks and investment banks, but there will undoubtedly be changes in the regulatory system in the light of the recent Financial Crisis. The regulators are faced with a tricky task of trying to protect the banking system without stifling it, and also without putting national money at risk. They will be watching the flow of deals very carefully to monitor the real strength of the markets, looking beyond profit numbers that often demand greater scrutiny to determine just how profits were made, such as looking at profitability against turnover to give an idea of the sort of risk the banks may be taking on board, whereby profits today could become losses tomorrow. The sort of reforms we can expect will need not just to look at the classic issues of capital and liquidity for these banks but should also look at the infrastructure of how the market works to ensure the firms are measuring and accounting for risk that is actually in line with the potential losses in the markets, as well as the regulators looking at themselves and how they have performed in the past and how they will need to reshape in the future. So the whole future of the regulators is as much in question as the future of the banking industry and we will look a little more at the market regulators in a later chapter.

Finally, though, in Text Box 3.3 we have a summary of the key points we notice about investment banking in the financial markets.

Box 3.3 Summary of Investment Banking Activity in the Financial Markets

Their role in the markets:

- The investment banking side of the business is far more rarely seen as an issuer in the markets than the commercial banking side. If we are speaking of independent investment banks then they will have to fund their positions so they will need to use the money markets

---

[11] Thomson Reuters Investment Banking Scorecard, December 2009.

to raise these funds, but if they are part of a full-service bank then they will often be 'customers 'of their commercial banking side.

- Similarly whilst they may be investors of excess liquidity and reserves this is likely to be less than the commercial banking side.
- It is as an intermediary that they will be at their most visible, actively advising clients, originating deals and running trading books.
- They are likely to run the most number of active trading books as this is a core part of their business model.

The markets in which they are most active:

- The securities markets are the natural home of investment banking, and they are likely to be very active in long-term debt and equity.
- Whilst they may sometimes be seen in FX and money markets this is likely to be a smaller part of their business.
- They will tend to be very active in derivatives, running trading books but also embedding derivatives in the structures they create to fulfil the funding and investment needs of their clients.
- This group is probably the most innovative in terms of creating financial market products and they are likely to be the most active in markets such as structured securities.

4
Private Banking

This area of banking is unusual in that what defines it is not the product being offered but the customer base. Private banking services high net worth individuals (HNWIs), most commonly defined as those with a minimum of $1,000,000 of investable assets, with a sub-group known as the ultra-high net worth individuals (UHNWIs) who have at least $30,000,000. However if we look at the policy of individual private banks we will see some variation on this in terms of their target audience. Some banks are happy to offer private banking services to individuals with as (relatively) little as $250,000 of investable assets, whilst others are more interested in the higher end of the spectrum and so will be targeting individuals with $5,000,000 or more. When we talk about private banks we should be using the term private banking divisions as, once more, when we look at the top 10 private banks, ranked by assets under management (AUM),[1] we see the same names that we have seen before in our league tables, along with some new names of course, but none are companies that exclusively offer this service (see Table 4.1). The first of these specialist banks, Banque Pictet & Cie, comes in ranked at 13 with $165 billion AUM.

In Switzerland the standalone private banks, such as Pictet & Cie, have an interesting legal status. They are known as *private bankers* to distinguish them from other private banks and date back to the 1800s, with some of them still in the hands of the original families. Set up as partnerships, the partners have collective and unlimited liability for the bank's commitments and as of 2009 there are 14 such firms in Switzerland, the smallest of which, Mourgue d'Algue & Cie has only 18 employees.[2] Table 4.2 lists these companies.

Whilst the market for HNWIs is an international one there are pockets of concentration for the clients, such as the US, where in 2008 we would find 2.5 million of these individuals, which represents 28.7% of the global total. Europe and Asia-Pacific follow the US, and then with a

---

[1] The International Private Banking Study, 2009.
[2] Swiss Private Bankers Association.

Table 4.1   10 Largest Private Banks

	AUM $BN
UBS Wealth Management	1391
Bank of America Private Bank	979
Morgan Stanley Smith Barney	678
Credit Suisse Private Bank	607
HSBC Private Bank	352
Deutsche Bank Private Wealth Management	228
Goldman Sachs	215
Barclays Wealth Management	212
Wells Fargo Private Bank	204
Citigroup Private Bank	200

large percentage drop we come to Latin America, the Middle East and
Africa. This total number stood at 8.6 million in 2008 but this was down
by 14.9%[3] on the previous year which is a testament to the impact of the
Financial Crisis, and an indicator of a particular issue affecting this part
of banking. In mass retail banking a customer can remain 'eligible' with
a bank for pretty much as long as they choose. Clearly their patterns
and levels of activity may change; they may move from being net savers
to net borrowers, and vice versa, but in most cases they can still be
customers of the retail bank in some form so the bank can gain from
the customer whatever business is available. In private banking this is
not the case. Market movements such as we saw in 2008 have severely
affected the net worth of many of the HNWIs, hence the 14.95% fall,
and this in turn impacts on the private banks. Of course loss of wealth

Table 4.2   Swiss Private Bankers

Baumann & Cie
Bordier & Cie
E. Gutzwiller & Cie
Gonet & Cie
Hottinger & Cie
Landolt & Cie
La Roche & Co. Banquiers
Lombard Odier Darier Hentsch & Cie.
Mirabeau & Cie
Mourgue d'Algue & Cie
Pictet & Cie
Rahn & Bodmer Cie
Wegelin & Co.

[3] Cap Gemini 2009 World Wealth Report.

is not the only reason for a firm to lose customers – these days the wealth of this group of investors is actually quite mobile and the industry has become increasingly competitive over recent years, hence the changes we have seen in strategy amongst some of the market participants.

PRIVATE BANKING SERVICES

As we look at the services offered through private banking to their customers we are going to see many of the same sorts of product that we identified earlier when we were looking at retail banking. The key difference, then, comes in how they are presented to the client. Private banking is very much about relationships and this is the dominant theme in how these services are differentiated from those of other parts of the bank. Private banking customers will have their own advisor, whose job is to know and understand the cash flows and investment requirements of their customers. At a time when much of the IT budget within banks has been used to automate services and reduce the amount of physical interaction between the bank and its customers, this may seem something of an anachronism. In practice this will often translate to the advisor speaking personally and regularly to their clients by phone, particularly at the lower end of the wealth spectrum. Of course, at the higher end there will generally be a lot more time-consuming face-to-face contact. Clearly this needs to be paid for, and so in return for this premium service the private banking customers will pay fees. These fees will act as an important cushion as we will see that for many of the services offered by the bank they will once again need to access wholesale financial markets to offset the resultant exposures.

One of the reasons that we see so many full-service banks becoming very active in this industry sector is because of the range of services offered to the customers. Whilst the core definition of private banking remains focused on investment services for HNWIs today when we look at the full range of products offered by most of the banks we see many which emulate those offered through the retail banking side. This will include services such as typical banking facilities like cheque accounts, overdrafts and savings accounts. The difference between these offerings through private banking and the mass market offering lies in the service attached. Often the banks will offer these customers multicurrency accounts, guaranteed high overdraft limits, preferential interest rates, all designed to match the customers' cash flows and needs. Of course all of these products will give the firms the same market exposures that we identified in the chapter on Commercial and Retail Banking but do remember that in this world we can be looking at very different balance sizes. To illustrate this in the chapter on Commercial and Retail Banking we used an example of a customer with £100 but if we were talking about a private banking customer we would expect to add several noughts to this figure per customer, and since these customers are normally net investors, or at the very least tend to carry quite large deposit balances and income flows, this can be an important source of liquidity to the banks. In terms of loans, again the product offering matches the clients. If these clients require mortgages they are again likely to be for substantial sums, meaning more principal on which interest is payable and these are the clients who are likely to need services such as the marine and aircraft financing offered by some banks. Again, if we think about scale, these will represent significant exposures to be managed by the bank. So whilst the products look the same the cash flow for the bank is more concentrated than we see in the retail banking sector, which in turn can potentially mean more vulnerability as it gives a different risk profile from diffuse individual retail flows. There is also the elite band of the Mega-Wealthy, those with $100 million or more who are another class of client. In many cases these will be business entrepreneurs, and their importance to the business flow of the firm can go beyond that of the more traditional private banking client. Often these individuals hold a lot of their wealth in stock of their own companies and in real estate, so this opens classic commercial and investment banking opportunities such as wholesale financing and corporate advisory, as well as their core private banking business.

As we have said the customer base here is normally a net investor, and so of course private banking has to focus heavily on providing investment solutions. This group of investors tends to be quite conservative, on the whole, with the bulk of their investment in equity and fixed income. Market conditions have caused some to change the composition of their portfolios, notably reducing their holding in equity and increasing fixed income, and the chart in Figure 4.1 shows the typical asset allocation for HNWIs for 2008.[4]

There are two ways in which the private bank tries to manage their customers' funds, either on an advisory or a discretionary basis. If a client opts for advisory services they receive recommendations on how to invest, backed up by the bank's research and analytical products, though

---

[4] Cap Gemini 2009 World Wealth Report.

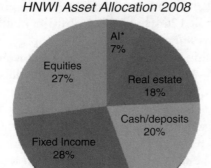

HNWI Asset Allocation 2008

Figure 4.1   High Net Worth Asset Allocation

*AI – Alternative investments, including investment in derivatives, FX, commodities, hedge funds, venture capital, private equity, structured products.

they take responsibility for making the actual investment decision. In other words the advisor performs the same function that we saw when we looked at salespeople in the dealing room. One crucial difference, though, is that the advisor will not be located in a dealing room, and whilst they may well have access to the same market data technology they will not be in the same environment as the traders, nor witness the institutional trade flows into the firm. When the customer decides to act the trade will be executed through the advisor and then routed through to the appropriate dealing room, normally by the private banker dealing with a salesperson or through an electronic trading system. Discretionary management is where the funds are managed on the clients' behalf by the bank, an investment management service. Depending on the customer and the size of their funds, there are a number of investment possibilities. They could have a discretionary portfolio created for them or, quite often, the funds will be placed in an investment account. Much of the investment made for the private banking customers will actually not be direct investment, outright purchase of securities, but rather this sort of indirect investment with investment being made into funds. Whilst these funds are not necessarily those run by the bank through its investment management divisions a lot of banks do run funds that they specifically target at this group of customers, bearing in mind their normal patterns of investment. An example of this would be Barclays Multi-Manager Wealth Funds, where their private banking customers can place their funds in one or more of a limited number of funds covering different market sectors. This gives the customers the benefits of pooled investment but also the ability to spread their exposure, but all within one vehicle.

This idea of using one vehicle is actually crucial to the model of private banking. As we have seen private banking has elements that are akin to retail banking and also to investment management. If we split this up we could see that the role of the private bank could, in fact, be replaced by a retail bank account and investment services such as advisory and execution, of the sort they would receive from a stockbroker. Or their funds could be managed for them either on a discretionary basis or within a pooled investment vehicle, both of which can be provided by investment management. In other words the business model is not unique. However the advantage offered through the private banking service is that all these elements are brought together under one umbrella, giving the customers a seamless management of their wealth. Obviously from the bank's point of view they then have the possibility to maximize the business opportunities from this customer by keeping all the strands in-house.

ONSHORE AND OFFSHORE WEALTH MANAGEMENT

One area of private banking that has provoked a lot of interest in recent times is onshore and offshore private banking. Onshore banking is when the services are offered to clients in the same country as the bank, and with all assets being booked in that country, which will be defined as the domicile of the investor. Offshore banking is the opposite of this. Most commonly the bank and the client are in different countries and the assets are booked in the location of the bank. This is one of the reasons why Switzerland has played such an important role in private banking. There has been a long history of offering offshore services out of Switzerland along with their famous laws regarding the anonymity of funds within their banking system. In 2008 Switzerland ranked third in terms of leaders in wealth management with 9% of the market equating to around $5 billion AUM.[5] However Switzerland has recently been the subject of much scrutiny and, it must be said, much criticism. As we said historically funds held in Swiss banks were protected by strict rules of confidentiality, which is in contrast to the trend for transparency and

---

[5] The Economic Significance of the Swiss Financial Centre, Swiss Bankers Association, November 2009.

accountability that we see in today's markets, but was a cornerstone of their offshore banking model. A landmark event took place in February 2009 when UBS finally agreed to pass to the US authorities relevant client data on about 250 US clients believed to be trying to evade tax by placing funds within this Swiss bank, and by doing so UBS was obliged to break this code of silence. This, however, was the tip of the iceberg as far as the US authorities were concerned, although for the Swiss authorities the decision for a Swiss bank to hand over any information was not taken lightly. Banking confidentiality has been embedded in Swiss law since 1934 but the concept is far older and it was only after much persuasion and to avoid punitive criminal charges being brought against UBS that the authorities agreed to persuade the bank to make this compromise. The problem is that some believe that the famous Swiss secrecy of banking allows tax evasion, or worse, and whilst the Swiss Financial Markets Supervisory Authority (FINMA) believes this not to be the case the reputation of Swiss banking took a heavy hit in 2009. UBS in particular saw not only damage to its reputation but also a large fall in its AUM. We also saw a marked division occurring between the large foreign-owned, more full-service banks operating private banking out of Switzerland, and the purer, traditional Swiss private bank. The former pretty much ceased to market offshore services, preferring to focus their Swiss business on domestic, onshore clients, whilst the latter opted to stay within the letter of Swiss law and continue business as normal. Nevertheless further changes in regulation are bound to affect this sector of Swiss banking and we are likely to see more changes in the future. There are also other centres that would like to make inroads into Switzerland's share of this market, such as Liechtenstein, which in 2008 accounted for just 1% of this private banking market but which, in March 2009, accepted the OECD standards on cooperation in tax. This commits them to sharing specified information on justified grounds with the tax authorities of other countries, and yet at the same time reinforced their commitment to banking confidentiality.[6] So they hope that by publicly agreeing to these international standards they will be successful in attracting funds, particularly those leaving Switzerland.

So as we have seen, private banking is a hybrid business, combining elements of different parts of the universal banking model. Its value to a bank is twofold: first, it brings in another source of fee-based income, and secondly – and maybe more importantly – it brings a substantial cash

---

[6] The Liechtenstein Banking Centre, Liechtenstein Bankers Association 2009.

flow into the firm, with the accompanying implications for liquidity. It is, though, yet another very competitive business and many banks have recently been actively increasing their exposure in this market as they identify not just the size of the market today but the potential growth. This is especially true of some parts of Asia where significant growth is already being seen and is expected to continue, so for many banks this is now regarded as a prime target.

Finally, to summarize, we have listed in Text Box 4.1 the key points to note about private banking in the financial markets.

Box 4.1 Summary of Private Banking Activity in the Financial Markets

Their role in the markets:

- Private banking departments are not really seen as issuers in the market as more than anything they work with an investment cash flow rather than a borrowing one. The only time we may see them will be to fund the everyday needs of the independent institutions in the same way as any other business would need to raise money in the markets for this purpose.
- They can be seen as investors, placing their clients' funds. On their behalf they may make direct and indirect investments by buying funds. They can also create funds themselves for their customers.
- The basic role of private banking is to be an intermediary, forming the link between their customers and the market.

The markets in which they are most active:

- Private banking will be seen in FX and money markets placing funds and managing their clients' liquidity.
- Since most of their customers are long-term investors they are active investors in long-term debt and equity.
- Similarly they will be seen in the derivative markets, again as their client demands require, but given that for the most part private bank customers tend to be quite conservative we are not likely to see this as being a major part of their business.

5

Central Banks and Market Regulators

This final chapter of this section on banks looks at the role of central banks within the financial markets. Once again we are writing this at a time when central banks are very much in the news. This is for several reasons. Firstly, one of the main roles of a central bank is to be the banker to the government. So in a period such as this when the governments have had to take many actions relating to financial market bailouts and the subsequent cost of this, not to mention the sovereign crises affecting European countries such as Greece which led to the need for international intervention to support the eurozone, we are seeing the central banks very actively carrying out the necessary transactions to raise these funds. Secondly, we have also been looking at a global recession and it is the central banks that carry out the monetary policy transactions to try and guide us through this, stimulate economies and yet avoid inflationary actions, so once again a lot of attention has been focused not just on what they are actually doing, but also on what we believe they are planning to do.

In the second part of this book we will look at banking in a number of key geographical areas and so for now we will concentrate on speaking generically about the functions of most central banks. We also need to look at the other market regulators, and some key trade associations that influence the international markets so that we can gain a clear idea of who paints the background against which the banks and other institutions that we are discussing will transact business. As we will see this will clearly influence not just how business is carried out but even what type of business they can do. We also need to think about the future – again – and consider how this landscape might change in the light of recent events.

Whilst the concept of a central bank is firmly embedded in history the interesting thing is that before 1900 there were actually only 14 of them, and it was only in the middle of the 20th century that we saw a sudden spurt of these central banking authorities being created. So the majority of the central banks that we see today are very much modern day institutions. Let's look firstly at their key functions to gain an overall view of how and why we will see them in the markets.

FUNCTIONS OF A CENTRAL BANK

Currency Issue

Whenever we think of central banks probably the first thing that comes to mind is seeing their names on banknotes as the official issuers of the legal tender. This is certainly a key part of what they do today but it was not necessarily easy to introduce this into the market. It was back in 1604 that we saw the first central bank, Amsterdamsch Wisselbank (Bank of Amsterdam), starting to fulfil this function, at least after a fashion. At the time the Dutch Republic was using a metal coin-based system of currency, which made for difficulties in an expanding, and increasingly international, economy. This included an increasing requirement for more monetary coinage, but also the economy seeing an increasing amount of foreign coins appearing within their financial system. This led to a problem with debasement, which in turn meant that the actual values of the coins themselves were uncertain. There were many mints producing the coins and whilst laws were passed setting out values to them, these laws were slow to enact, and actually did not solve the problem of debasement. Over time the amount of silver in a coin could fall significantly, for example falling by some 40% in the 50 years from 1550 to 1600 in the Dutch Republic.[1] So, as part of the solution to this we saw the creation of an exchange bank. This exchange bank would only accept coins for deposit if they met certain quality criteria, thereby setting a standard. So if debts were settled within this exchange bank system it meant that lenders did not run the risk of receiving coins of less intrinsic value. This idea was expanded further in 1609 when the municipality of Amsterdam picked up on the fact that most of the international borrowing and lending between merchants was happening with the use of bills of exchange, which was debt of less than three months in maturity, and that this enabled trade to take place more efficiently. The municipality then dictated that these bills had to be settled within the exchange bank system, meaning that the merchants had to open accounts with the bank and thus they started to

---

[1] *Geld, Währung und Preisentwicklung: Der Niederrheinraum im europäischen Vergleich 1350–1800*, R Metz, 1990.

create a centralized system. Of course this is not the end of the story and there continued to be problems with coinage, a lot of which came from all the foreign coin within the commercial system that we have already mentioned, and the fact that there was no central mint. Ultimately, though, in 1659 an ordinance was passed to create a more uniform currency and the Wisselbank was given the task of maintaining stability, much as central banks do today. We should also mention banknotes and how they came into the picture. Originally these were receipts for deposits with the central banks. Again, looking at Amsterdam we saw the first of these being issued in 1683, although in their initial structure they had fixed maturities to them, making them like debt. However at maturity the holder of the receipt could either repurchase their deposits of coin or receive another receipt so from this we started to see the beginnings of the banknote system, as it became clear that more and more people were happy to leave their bullion deposited and just accept receipts instead.

If we look at the UK, we see another old-established central bank that played an important role in the creation of banknotes. The Bank of England was established in 1694 and almost immediately started to issue notes against deposit that bore the words that they promised to pay the bearer on demand. In other words they had no fixed maturities. Initially they were made out by hand and individually signed by one of the bank's cashiers, for the precise sum deposited, but in 1696 it was decided not to write them for amounts less than £50. In the next hundred years this changed with notes being created in round amounts for firstly, £20, then £5 and this was followed by £2 and £1 notes, and so we had a range of notes in circulation. Unfortunately we should not think that these central banks were the only ones to issue banknotes as we can clearly see in the US. For example, in 1836 in the US there were 1600 private banks each with a state charter to issue banknotes, all of which differed in colour and design, causing confusion and eases of counterfeit – not to mention the problem of credit risk coming from bank failure. However just 25 years later we saw the issue of the United States notes, notes that became known as greenbacks, that carried various security features embedded within them such as the incorporation of the seal and the use of linen paper with coloured fibres, and these then became the pre-eminent notes. This meant that by the time of the Federal Reserve Act in 1913, the Act that created the Federal Reserve Bank that we will discuss in the next part of this book, these Federal Reserve notes that we still use today became the only currency produced and represented

99% of all the currency in circulation at the time. Going back to the UK, though, we do come across a strange anomaly. As in the US, some private banks in the UK had been allowed to issue banknotes under certain constrictions. The last of these being Fox, Fowler & Co. a bank that ceased to issue notes in 1921, but the UK is unusual in that today in the 21st century the banknotes that are legal tender throughout the whole of the kingdom are issued not just by the Bank of England but also by three banks in Scotland:

- Bank of Scotland
- Clydesdale Bank
- and Royal Bank of Scotland,

and four banks in Northern Ireland:

- Bank of Ireland
- First Trust Bank
- Northern Bank
- and Ulster Bank.

We should know though that under the Banking Act of 2009 the Bank of England took over responsibility for regulating this note issuance and ensuring the level of protection behind their notes is equivalent to that behind notes issued by the Bank of England itself, particularly as we may recognize some of these bank names from our discussions relating to the financial crisis!

Whilst the UK is a country with multiple issuers of the currency, we find a similar model with the euro. When the euro was first introduced in 1999 there were no physical notes or coins as the countries joining the system kept their original currencies as hard currencies and ran a parallel book-value system with the euro. Then in January 2002 the legacy currencies were replaced with euro notes and coins, and these are issued in the name of the European Central Bank (ECB) although physically issued by the individual national banks according to the quantity assigned to each member. This means that there is a variety of different coins available, all with the same values but designed and minted in the different countries.

Central banks have two key customers: the government and the banks, most specifically the commercial banks. Since the 1990s the trend has been towards making central banks independent, particularly of political influence. For most of the major countries their central banks are certainly more independent, even if not fully, but even for the most independent within their statutes there is often a provision for re-nationalization should that be necessary. However, today's central banks, regardless of legal status, do tend to exhibit a high level of transparency, sharing with the market details of their objectives and targets so that the market has a good idea of what to expect. Continuing this theme following the 2010 election in the UK one of the first acts of the new Chancellor of the Exchequer,[2] George Osborne, was to set up a new department, the Office of Budget Responsibility, which would take responsibility for economic forecasting away from the government to further enhance its independence. This would mean that there would be a greater distance between the government and the central bank in terms of the actions the bank would take to protect and improve the economic situation of the country, since an independent central bank would now be acting on independently defined views on the economic situation, that could not be accused of any political bias.

Next we will take a look at the sorts of functions these central banks will actually carry out for their customers, particularly the governments, and see how this fits in with the discussions we have already had about banks and the impact of their actions on the markets.

IMPLEMENTING MONETARY POLICY

Government Debt Issuance

As we have said, one of the key roles of the central bank is banker to the government and as part of this one of the things a central bank will often do is to issue debt on their behalf. This is not always the function of the central bank: for example in the UK this task was passed to another agency, the Debt Management Office, but the process that they use is the same as that employed by central banks in other countries. In the section on Investment Banks we spoke about primary dealers, the groups of banks that will underwrite and trade government securities. The central bank or other issuing authority looks after the mechanics of this, setting the criteria for becoming one of these dealers and managing the actual issuance of the debt. This will involve consulting with the banks on how best to access the market, which is when the banks act in their advisory role, and then seeing the process on through to physically pricing and issuing the debt. Pricing is most commonly done by the Dutch auction

---

[2] This is the British minister in charge of economic and financial matters, equivalent to Finance Minister or Treasury Secretary in other countries.

method, but sometimes the central banks will decide to re-open existing issues, or in some cases to simply dictate the characteristics of the debt and the level at which it will be issued. The latter is seen most often in the smaller, less developed markets, but as a market becomes more sophisticated and has higher levels of issuance it is normally better to use a mechanism that brings the paper at the closest levels to market demand. However, this is a decision that the central bank or issuing agency will make, along with the final decision on what structure of debt to use, the maturity and any other material point. The decision on how much debt to issue, though, is normally dictated by the government's borrowing requirement but to make the process work efficiently this debt will have to be scheduled to ensure that it will be well accepted within the market. This government debt plays an important role in the relationship between the central bank and the banks as it will be used as collateral for some of the open market operations as we will see a little later. A lot of discussion has centred on the amount of debt that the major economies have had to issue in recent times, to stimulate economic growth, pay for the Financial Crisis and support other economies. The fear is that if the countries over-borrow the market will not be able to absorb the volume of issue, which is why we need to pay such close attention not only to the rates that are achieved but the cover level that we discussed in the section on Investment Banks. It is rather ironic that the UK is one of the largest issuers of debt having spent much time in the last few decades being one of the smallest issuers among the large economies, so much so that on many occasions the market has actually seen a lack of UK government securities and has wanted the government to issue more, in contrast to today.

Interest Rates

As part of its requirement to implement monetary policy, the central bank has to set the key interest rates for the market. These will typically be very short-term rates, usually overnight, and actually apply to the direct relationship between the central bank and the country's commercial banks, as it will represent ways in which money is lent to the banks, therefore affecting money supply, which has a knock-on effect on bank lending to its customers. This is why these interest rates are so important and will be used as a guide by the market for setting rates themselves for longer maturity deals. Again, most of the major countries have rate setting committees that meet on a regular basis to determine what the interest rate should be and then announce this to the market, an announcement that is eagerly awaited. Looking at recent times it would be quite easy to get the impression that central banks regularly make sweeping changes to the interest rates. In fact this is not really the case. The preference is for as few movements as possible and those that happen should then be subtle so as not to unduly upset the balance of the market. It is just that the economic and market conditions in the first decade of the 21st century have meant that the central banks have sometimes had to take very reactive, and sometimes even proactive preventative, actions that have resulted in large rate swings. Rate setting should always be a delicate balancing act as these interest rates will have such an impact on the relative strength of the economy. In a period of recession such as we have recently seen the banks have been trying to stimulate economic growth, whilst at the same time being wary of causing inflation, so much consideration has gone into each meeting of the rate setting committees (see Text Box 5.1).

Box 5.1 Interest Rates within the Eurozone

The ECB has two key interest rates with which it influences the markets. The first is a rate that comes from the Main Refinancing Operations. This is when money is lent to commercial banks, and some other financial institutions, on a collateralized basis for a weekly term. Each week the banks submit bids for money to their national central banks, between Monday afternoon and early Tuesday morning. These bids are subject to a Minimum Bid Rate that is set by the ECB's Governing Council, the highest governing board of the ECB. This rate is set on a monthly basis. The bids coming in from the banks are initially analysed by a Liquidity Committee of the ECB who will then put forward a proposal to the Executive Board that meets every Tuesday and who will make the final decision on how much money should be made available to the market. This proposal needs to take into account the liquidity position of the banks to try and ensure they are able to efficiently carry out their core business, whilst not compromising the position of the central bank itself. Since the national central banks will have daily contact with the markets they should be well placed to achieve this balance. The Executive Board allocates funds on a sliding basis, fulfilling the highest bids first then working downwards until all funds have been allocated. Any bank that is not successful in bidding for funds from the central bank will need to cover their requirements in the money market, and so the procedure continues on a weekly basis.

There is also a lending and deposit facility available to all banks within the eurosystem that they can use whenever required. These are known as the Standing Facilities and comprise a Marginal Lending Facility (MLF) and a Deposit Facility. Both of these will be for overnight periods and the rates are again set by the ECB on a monthly basis, with the rate for the MLF being set at a higher level than the Minimum Bid Rate for the Main Refinancing Operation, and the rate on the deposit facility being lower. Once again the ECB will carefully monitor the use of these facilities to inform their understanding of money supply within the markets, along with monitoring flows through TARGET2, the euro payment system.

Open Market Operations

As well as directly setting and changing interest rates another way in which the central bank influences money supply and the rates of the market is through other open market operations. An example of this is where the central bank will carry out either buying or selling of securities, typically government securities because of their safety, with the banks. There are various ways in which they can do this, one of which is by outright purchases and sales. If the bank purchases securities they will be putting money into the system, if they sell them they are taking money out. If they put money into the system then the banks should have the liquidity they need and so be easily able to lend money to their customers. If this is so there should be no reason for interest rates to rise and maybe they will fall, depending on the market conditions. Obviously if money is taken out of the system it becomes a more valuable commodity and rates will probably rise to attract more funds into the bank, which in turn leads to higher borrowing rates for customers. If the central bank wants to make a temporary change to the market, maybe to cover it over a short-term cash shortage or surplus, they can do this with repurchase agreements. This is where they still buy or sell securities but this time they also agree, at the same time, to reverse the deal on a future date, be that the next day, week, month or sometimes even longer. This changes the money supply for a limited time to allow for gentle easing or tightening, depending on conditions and timescale. Once again it will be the bank itself that decides when and how these operations will take place in order to implement the monetary policy in keeping with their stated objectives.

Quantitative Easing

Also on the government's behalf the central bank will have to carry out various exceptional functions that are going to have a direct impact on the market. The topic of issuance of currency in circulation has become particularly relevant recently as we look at the amount of borrowing some governments have had to do to finance their bank bailouts. One of the key reasons that investors are confident about buying this debt is the belief that, if necessary, governments can issue more currency to redeem their obligations, thereby making the debt credit risk-free. Indeed we have seen this in action with some of the quantitative easing strategies that have taken place in 2009, but it is important that we understand how this works, as it is a key bridge between the central bank's two customers. If we take as an example the quantitative easing in the UK it is easy to read the headlines and think that the Bank of England is printing money. In fact it is not quite this. Instead, the Bank will buy predominantly government securities, but also some corporate debt, which they buy, mainly from the banks, but also from some other institutions. The Bank then puts these assets on their balance sheets. This makes the balance sheets look healthier as the country now owns more assets. To pay for these purchases the Bank of England credited the banks' reserve accounts, therefore freeing them from some of their obligation to place money on reserve, meaning that they had more cash to lend into the economy. The net result should be that there is now more currency available for the economy which is the purpose of the exercise. All of this happens without the need to actually print more money, because the creation has happened electronically. A core issue, though, is whether the banks do make this money available to their customers, which is by no means certain as the central bank cannot order them to do this. If, instead, they choose to hold the balances to shore up their own positions, as we have seen to a certain extent in the UK in 2009, then this is something that the central bank can only counter by target setting and negotiation. It is also one of the reasons why the Bank of England decided to buy the securities not only from banks but other institutions such as insurance companies and pension funds to try and ensure that some of the funds filter through into the broader economy. Of course quantitative easing can lead to hyper-inflation, as we have seen in

Zimbabwe, but it is to be hoped that this is a case of extremes and will not be mimicked in the UK, although quantitative easing is never without risks, and is also a strategy that will generally look to be reversed, which again can cause future difficulties.

Managing Reserve Accounts

Central banks will also be seen in the foreign exchange markets supporting the currency when required and managing the country's currency reserves. In this respect the central banks act as a type of investment manager, managing the monies and gold held as reserves for the country, including any foreign currency reserves they may hold. These reserves will be held for various reasons including as the means to maintain exchange rate and monetary policy, in a similar way to the transactions we have just seen above, but also to service transactions such as overseas purchases, such as buying defence items from overseas suppliers, or to repay foreign currency debt that is due for redemption. We should not confuse these reserves with the funds managed by the Sovereign Wealth Funds, that we will look at in Part Three of this book, even though some of these funds will be comprised of currency surpluses but the way in which the funds are invested will differ between these two models owing to their different purposes. Managing normal currency reserves will involve dealing with the market as a customer, buying and selling acceptable securities, doing FX deals to change the balance of the funds and generally managing the portfolio on behalf of the government and the country. The key criteria tend to be liquidity and security so the funds are generally invested in the best quality assets available and whilst not normally seen as running market trading accounts many central banks will adopt an active policy to manage these assets and so will monitor the markets looking to maximize returns without compromising risk. For most central banks today the use of derivatives to hedge the funds is, to a certain extent, acceptable, but again bearing in mind the requirement to maintain some liquidity so that the funds can always be available to be used for their core purpose.

All of the above illustrate how central banks interact in the markets on behalf of the government, so we now need to look at their relationship with the commercial banks. We have already seen a trading relationship but the bank also takes on a supervisory and regulatory role, as well as continuing the role we saw them playing when we discussed the open market operations of ensuring that the market is well funded, by taking on the role of ultimate lender, and ensuring the infrastructure to allow money to move within the banking system.

THE CENTRAL BANK AS REGULATOR

As we have said another role of the central banks is to regulate the banking sector, and try to ensure that they do not find themselves with liquidity problems, or at the very least that if these happens they will not be wholly unexpected as everything possible will have been done to prevent them getting to this stage. Whilst this is not a traditional function of a central bank in historical terms it was the founding of the US Federal Reserve Bank that was given explicit regulatory obligations that started to formalize the role of central banks as regulators. This was followed after the Second World War by a number of European banks also embedding these principles in their central bank legislation. In a 2008 BIS survey 90% of the central banks said that they had full or shared responsibility for oversight of the financial system, with banks being traditionally the main focus of their attention. In central banks which do not have this regulatory function there is usually a financial stability unit that to some extent at least will monitor the financial landscape in order to ensure stability in the financial markets. In many countries the central bank is only one regulator and in the next section we will look at some examples of the other regulators involved in some of the key market areas. On the whole, although the focus of the central bank regulation will be on commercial banks, there may be a trend developing to increase this scope.

There are four core elements to bank regulation: supervision, setting reserve requirements, acting as lender of last resort and ensuring supply of deposit insurance. Let's take a look at each of these.

Supervision

Supervision is about understanding what the banks are doing and the risks they are running, and then ensuring they themselves understand this. It may sound simplistic but in practice is far from this. This is where the potential problems that come from supervision being divided between more than one set of regulatory bodies can arise. This is the situation that happens in many countries, where, for example, commercial banks come under the responsibility of a central bank, whilst investment banks would be the responsibility of another agency whose focus may be on securities markets. Whilst these regulators should be working in concert there are many who feel that the division means that the central banks do not have the full picture of the exposures facing the banks. This is partly due to the systemic nature of the markets, as we saw illustrated very clearly following the collapse of Lehman Brothers and the impact it had on so many of the other banks, and so if the bank is working with an incomplete picture this can compromise not only their supervision but also their role as lenders of last resort and put pressure on deposit insurance. This model of dividing regulation by type of institution is one that is bound to be reconsidered many times in the coming years.

There are also two main approaches to supervision, principle-based and rules-based. A rules-based system, such as is seen in the US, at least at the moment, is one where the regulators and the legislators create detailed rules and requirements that will dictate in the greatest detail exactly what the banks must and must not do. The purpose of the regulator, then, is to ensure that these rules are adhered to. In a principles-based system, such as is seen in the UK and other parts of Europe, there are still copious rules but the emphasis on the regulator is to ensure that the banks adhere not to the minutiae but to the broader principles. Sometimes these principles will be broadly expressed allowing leeway for the supervisors to determine what constitutes acceptable behaviour on – if necessary – a case-by-case basis, so allowing them to exercise discretion in evaluating the behaviour and performance of a bank. US Treasury Secretary Henry Paulson has for several years lobbied for a move to principles-based regulation in the US, with Italy often being cited as an example of how Italian bank regulators were able to dissuade Italian banks from involvement in the sub-prime mortgage market, despite the fact that it was not explicitly prohibited in Italy. This is an example of the advantage of the flexibility of the system. It is dependent, though, on good regulators, in terms of funding, diligence and scope of supervision. This is why the Finance Bill, which passed through the Senate in May 2010, included the creation of the Council of Regulators, to bring together the various different regulatory agencies to provide this broad oversight. As we have said earlier in this book the ultimate changes to regulation in the US will be a combination of the finance bills approved by the Senate and the House of Representatives and is likely to produce a watered down version of the two, but it seems highly likely that we could see a sea-change in this area in the near future.

Reserve Requirements

One of the ways in which the central banks try to ensure the security of the other banks is through the imposition of reserve requirements. We have mentioned these earlier but we should specifically define what they are and their purpose. These reserves are sums the banks have to lodge with the central bank to try and cover them for potential losses. This is to try and prevent them failing and therefore putting depositors' funds at risk. These reserve requirements are normally set by the central banks and will be dictated by the different levels of risk attached to the exposures the banks take on their balance sheets: the riskier the deals the higher the reserve level. Again it is not difficult to discover that these reserves will not necessarily cover the banks for the extent of losses, such as we saw with the sub-prime mortgage market, but determining the levels that provide safety without compromising the banks' ability to carry out its business is a difficult task. This is particularly true when we do not understand fully the extent of the risk as will happen as the markets continue to develop. Changing reserve levels is another tool that the central bank has to manage money supply, but it is not one that they would lightly use. For example increasing reserve requirements would cause interest rates to rise as banks need to put away more of the funds coming onto the balance sheets, so leaving less available for market liquidity. Changes to the formulae for determining reserve requirements would normally occur very infrequently although in 2009 the US Federal Reserve Bank made two adjustments, one in January and the second December that gave the net effect of lowering reserve requirements by about $1.5 billion[3] in response to the market's ongoing need for more liquidity. It does have to be said, though, that lowering reserve requirements is far less traumatic for the market than raising them. This latter can have far-reaching effects on the balance sheets of the weaker banks, potentially even pushing them towards a crisis point.

Lender of Last Resort

If the market is working efficiently then the banks should be able to raise any funds they need from their customers or from the interbank market so the role of lender of last resort should be a formality, a parachute that will hopefully not be used. However if for some reason the banks cannot

---

[3] Aggregate Reserves of Depository Institutions and the Monetary Base, Federal Reserve Statistics Release, November 2009.

fund themselves in the market the central bank will stand there and lend them funds directly. We saw an example of this earlier when we looked at interest rate setting in the eurozone. This process is not intended to bail out failing banks, but rather just to provide another source of liquidity. Generally these loans will be short-term, often overnight, and will normally be collateralized by good quality assets. As a rule of thumb we would have tended to see these facilities being rarely used, although recent times have proved an exception, showing us that this is driven by the overall liquidity of the markets. The fact that some central banks have had to set up special liquidity schemes in order to provide funding for the banks, therefore acting as lenders of last resort but doing so to prevent bank failure, actually takes us into new territory and again is a symptom of these particular times and market conditions.

Deposit Insurance

At the heart of the relationship between central banks and commercial banks lies the need to protect the banks' customers, particularly the retail customers, and this is why deposit insurance systems exist. As of June 2009 104 countries have explicit schemes in place, with another 17 considering the structure.[4] In most countries the system will be run by the central bank, typically with government backing, but in a number of countries there is more than one scheme, some of which are run by private companies, often focusing on particular types of bank such as cooperative banks such as we see in Japan, Cyprus, Poland and elsewhere. These deposit insurance systems will guarantee depositor funds up to a certain limit. This limit will be made publicly known so that depositors can manage their funds accordingly, spreading them amongst a number of banks if their totals exceed the deposit guarantee limit of any individual bank. In 2008 we saw a wave of increases in the level of protection offered in the light of the failure of a number of banks, to offer reassurance and prevent yet more money being taken away from the banking system. Still, though, the level of coverage differs quite substantially from country to country. For example, the US in 2009 was offering Federal Deposit Insurance Corporation (FDIC) deposit protection on deposits of up to $250,000 whilst the Albanian Deposit Insurance Agency was offering protection on LEK 2,500,000 (about $26,000). For these insurance systems to be effective there needs

---

[4] International Association of Deposit Insurers.

to be compulsory membership, but given the international nature of the markets there may be banks operating in a country that are covered not by that country's system but by their home country's system. So if we had an Albanian bank operating in the US and not covered by the US deposit scheme, in other words operating as a foreign bank, then the risk in the event of failure of this bank would be that it was covered by the Albanian insurance. In other words it would be a riskier enterprise than its domestic competitors. As well as including all banks within the system, the system itself has got to be financially viable. The deposit insurance needs to repay the depositors as soon as possible in order to maintain customer confidence and if the funding mechanisms have not been pre-arranged this may not be viable. We have seen problems of this sort with some Icelandic bank failures with the government then finding it difficult to raise the funds to make payments on the deposit insurance scheme. A similar situation loomed in Greece as the market anticipated failure of some of the Greek banks at the same time as they feared default on the sovereign debt of the country itself. In the chapter on Commercial and Retail Banking we mentioned the idea of banks becoming 'too big to fail', and this is a serious issue for the regulators and their deposit protection systems. Were one, or even worse more than one, of these institutions to fail it is highly unlikely that the insurance systems would be able to cover the claims. We have had examples of this is in the US where in the late 1980s the bank deposit fund became technically insolvent by $7 billion, and in Japan in the 1990s we saw Japan's Deposit Insurance Corporation exhausting its funds and both this and another smaller system again becoming technically insolvent. This is why it is important for all the elements of regulation to work together to try and prevent this insurance being called into play. However we will see in the chapter on Banking in the US just how many bank failures there were in 2009 and we will get a good sense of how important this insurance is to the industry and its consumers.

Payment Systems

As well as overseeing the market participants the central banks also have to oversee the actual infrastructure that enables the markets to work efficiently, specifically the payment systems that allow the movement of funds. This concept dates right back to the roots of central banking that we identified earlier with notes being written against deposits and then being transferred between accounts of banks belonging to the system.

Obviously in the 21st century this is far more sophisticated, and all movements will be electronic. Each country (or currency block) will have a national payment system and these are now predominantly real-time systems allowing for real-time transfer of fund ownership. A lot of effort has been made to ensure that these national systems can integrate to allow international transfers.

So these are the main functions that we will see being carried out to a greater or lesser extent by the central banks of most countries. We should now take a look at some of the other regulators we will find in the markets.

Bank for International Settlements – BIS

The BIS is often called the central bank of the central banks. It was established in 1930 in Basel, Switzerland and the BIS state its aims as being:

- a forum to promote discussion and policy analysis among central banks and within the international financial community;
- a centre for economic and monetary research;
- prime counterparty for central banks in their financial transactions;
- an agent or trustee in connection with international financial operations.[5]

Fifty-five central banks are members of the BIS and it is representatives from these banks, along with representatives from the BIS itself, that will sit on the various committees looking at key issues affecting banks and the market economy. They produce a large body of research and statistics along with organizing conferences and seminars at which the central banks can share experience. This is a core purpose of the BIS but it also offers banking services to its customers, hence being known as the central banker to the central banks. They provide the central banks with a range of deposit products with maturities from overnight out to 10 years, as well as foreign exchange and asset management services. They will sometimes advance money, normally on a short-term collateralized basis, but their mandate is not to lend to governments so this should not be considered a normal part of their business and all of their deals will be carried out through the central bank mechanism. They have, on occasion, made loans to countries in economic

---

[5] BIS website.

crisis, but this aid is more normally provided by the BIS coordinating a mechanism of combined guarantees from other central banks. The BIS is very well-known for the work it has done on promoting financial stability, in particular probably the Basel Frameworks for minimum capital adequacy standards, setting the level of reserves required by the banks. Basel I (the 1988 Basel Accord) and Basel II are the key frameworks that national legislators have used as the standard for their domestic legislation, and the documents themselves are the subject of regular review, once again particularly in the light of the Financial Crisis. Basel I focused on credit risk, classifying risk into one of five categories for which different risk weightings were assigned. Basel II, published in 2004, set up a framework to go beyond the credit risk considerations to encompass a range of financial and operational risks, The logic being still that the greater the risk to which the bank is exposed, but now on a more overall basis, the greater the reserve requirements should be. As of now a third document, Basel III, is under development to build further on this, and in December 2009 the Basel Committee on Banking Supervision produced two consultative documents as part of this process.[6]

MARKET ASSOCIATIONS

So far we have focused on banks, but we will now take a quick a look at some of the international associations covering the markets in which these banks, and the rest of the firms we will look at in the remainder of this book, find themselves operating. We have spoken about foreign exchange, capital markets and derivatives, and so we find that there is an international organization for the FX and money markets (ACI), the capital markets (ICMA) and the derivatives market (ISDA). We should say, though, that ICMA focuses on the fixed income market, rather than the full definition of capital markets, including equities, and this is because the public equity markets are exchange-traded and so it is the exchanges that regulate membership, trading practice and the sort of industry support offered by the other associations. The equity market is overall very fragmented, still drawn on national lines, despite the advances that have been made in trying to create pan-European and international exchanges, so does not as easily lend itself to a single, international trade association as the other markets do.

---

[6] These are *Strengthening the Resilience of the Banking Sector* and *International Framework for Liquidity Risk Measurement, Standards and Monitoring*.

ACI

The Association Cambiste International (ACI) was founded in 1955 and is the association for FX and money markets. Since it covers a very broad market it has about 13,000 members[7] who belong to national associations that are affiliated to the main body of the ACI, whilst all being autonomous. The focus of the association is predominantly on those involved in trading and sales in these markets, including setting recommended standards to cover the dealing operations, as well as acting as mediator and arbiter in the case of disputes. They publish The Model Code which is the document setting out these recommended standards and whilst not having legal authority to compel the market to adhere to them most of their members will use them as the basis for their internal systems.

ICMA

The ICMA (formerly International Securities Market Association, and prior to that Association of International Bond Dealers) was created in 1968 and has been representing the fixed income market since then. It is not structured in the same way as the ACI, instead the 375 institutional members in 45 countries[8] belong directly to the central organization. However, in common with the ACI, its intention is to represent this part of the market and promote good practice, so again it produces a set of standards, arbitration and mediation for its members. Following its merger with the International Primary Markets Association it now covers both primary and secondary markets, the markets for origination of securities and then for trading, covering the markets through from origination to placement and secondary trading. It also produces market data and encourages transparency of pricing in the OTC bond markets by publishing values on securities from a group of reporting dealers.

ISDA

The International Swaps and Derivatives Association, the newest of these trade associations yet arguably the most influential, was founded in 1984. Its purpose is to increase understanding and management of the risks of OTC derivatives and has 810 institutional members from

---

[7] ACI website.
[8] ICMA website.

58 countries.[9] As well as producing best practice reports ISDA has made a major contribution to its market sector with the creation of standardized documentation that is widely used when trading these products. This documentation has focused participants on the key information they need to agree both before and at the point of execution, as well as producing a list of standardized definitions to give people a common language when dealing with a market that by its very definition is always transforming. All of these actions have had a major effect on the market in helping to focus attention on the key risks of these transactions. ISDA covers a particularly complex area so the impact of its efforts at standardizing an essentially nonstandardized market have raised its status to a highly respected level.

All of these trade associations will work with national regulators, one another and other interested parties, such as the BIS, to provide the most comprehensive view of the markets and provide input on proposed changes in legislation that may affect the markets and its members.

Market regulation is very likely to undergo some substantial change over the next few years as we come to grips with recent events. It is important that the markets are well regulated but this needs to be done in a way that does not overly restrict the banks and other financial institutions, but allows them to operate in a controlled environment. They must never lose sight of the reason that the banks and the financial markets exist, to allow the flow of funds, so the regulators' job is to find the balance that allows this to take place and, certainly at the moment, to prevent another Financial Crisis.

In the next section of the book we will take a look at the banking systems in some major countries and we will see how they have set up their regulatory systems to cope with their specific banking environments, but finally we will make a last summary in Text Box 5.2 of how this part of the banking system is seen in the financial markets:

Box 5.2 Summary of Central Banking Activity in the Financial Markets

Their role in the markets:

- Central banks will not normally be issuers in the market in their own right, but rather on behalf of governments.

---

[9] ISDA website.

- They are seen as investors in the long-term debt and money markets.
- One of their primary purposes is to be an intermediary between the government and the market.

The markets in which they are most active:

- FX and money markets are where they are most commonly seen.
- They will use these markets to implement monetary policy.
- They regularly buy and sell with the commercial banks to achieve these aims.
- They will sometimes use the long-term debt markets, particularly in recent times, but traditionally their market activity is normally with the shorter maturities.
- The big exception to this is their role as issuing house for government debt.
- Equity is a market in which they are rarely involved and then only in very unusual circumstances.
- Their use of derivatives will normally typically be limited to forward products, like FX forwards and interest rate swaps.

Part II
International Comparisons

6
Introduction

So far we have looked at the various major types of banking model that we will come across in the financial markets and have been making the distinction between the sorts of business flows that come into these models leading to different types of involvement in the financial markets. Now we are going to consider some specific geographical areas, so that we can familiarize ourselves with how these generic institutions will look in these regions, as well as looking at some types of bank which are particular to them. The variety of institutions can be daunting when we first come into contact with the markets, so it helps to understand the similarities as well as the differences between them.

We are going to look at some of the major centres in Europe and Asia, as well as the US. In Europe we will focus on the UK, Germany and France as these countries represent the largest concentration of banks that we see actively in the markets. We have already seen the names of some of these banks in the league tables that have illustrated banks' involvement in different markets in the earlier chapters, but there are many other structures which make up an important part of their financial presence. So we are now going to take a closer look at some of these structures as well and so broaden our view on the different types of banking institution.

In Asia we will focus on Japan and China, but we will also talk about Islamic finance institutions from the Middle East and microfinance banks that we find particularly, though certainly not exclusively, in South Asia. Japanese banks have long been major players in the financial markets, although there have been a lot of changes to the banking landscape in Japan over the past couple of decades. We will look at how these changes have altered the business of Japanese banking in terms of how we see these banks in both the international market and the domestic markets.

In the section on the US we will again come across many of the names we have already encountered, particularly when we have been talking about investment banks and the 'too big to fail' banks, but we will also see examples of other types of bank in the US and understand why we may not have heard of these firms owing to their particular business models. We will also look a bit more at the Glass-Steagall Act in Box 11.1 on page 126 since it has been so influential on the markets and is so relevant to our situation today. We will try and see why some people now feel that in the 21st century we should return to this model of banking segregation. Another piece of legislation that has impacted the market is the repeal of the restriction on interstate banking in the US that happened at the end of the 20th century. This was part of the reason that the largest banks in the US were able to become so large, and we know how important this has turned out to be. Finally, on a negative note, we will also have to look at the number of bank failures that have occurred since the Financial Crisis and consider the impact this will have had on the US banking system, not just in terms of pure reduction in the number of banks but also what effect this will have had on people's confidence in the banking system.

7

Banking in Europe

When we look at banking in Europe we will see a mixture of conformity and individuality. There needs to be a level of conformity as one of the basic ideas of European regulation is to make a level playing field for European banks – this is where the idea of the European passport for banking comes in. This means that if a bank is authorized in its home country (the home state) and wants to carry out business in other European member states they can do so under a single passport which is granted by their home regulator, just as long as the regulators of the proposed new location (the host state) have no objection. To make this work there must be some conformity of regulation as the host state will be responsible for making sure that the systems and controls are in good order and to ensure the financial stability of the bank. Once the bank sets up its new operations it will then come under the jurisdiction of the host state regulator, so if we have too much disparity we can find ourselves with a very unbalanced European banking market.

In real life, though, there are disparities between the countries and in 2007 and 2008 this did cause a few concerns. We particularly saw this as people started to fear for the strength of some of the banks, and therefore began to look at the financial compensation schemes that we spoke of in the last chapter of Part I. What they saw was some quite substantial differences in the different schemes covering European banks, and this was made all the more significant by the fact that it is the home state, not the host state, that is responsible for covering the banks operating as foreign banks under the European passport. As an example along the lines of the one that we have already used, but this time focused on Europe, at the beginning of October 2008 the deposit guarantee scheme in Spain covered deposits up to €20,000 whilst at the same time in Ireland it had already been raised to €100,000. So a Spanish bank operating as a foreign bank in Dublin was far riskier than a domestic Irish bank. This is the same logic as we applied in the chapter on Central Banks when we used the US and Albania as our examples but here in this European context it is even more significant because the passport scheme was intended to make it bureaucratically easier for European banks to move around the member states, therefore promoting the idea of an integrated banking system. Therefore to counter this problem in October the European finance ministers decided to agree a minimum level for deposit cover of €50,000 to try and create some uniformity. However following this Spain actually increased its cover to €100,000 and some countries, such as Austria and Denmark, introduced 100% cover which whilst it may not remain in place permanently was intended to protect customers and customer confidence in the difficult period after the Financial Crisis. This is great, but unfortunately it does not help to build the uniformity that we were seeking.

When we look at the European banks we will always tend to see some national individuality to reflect the different economies of Europe. Some of the structures and relationships we will look at are firmly embedded in history, and many of the firms are very domestic, with little or no overseas presence, but are there purely to service parts of the domestic market, both retail and institutional. In this part of our book we are first going to consider some of the major European areas, focusing on the UK, France and Germany. We have chosen these as they represent the biggest banking areas in Europe and within these countries we are going to see examples of most types of banks, and their business flows, that we can see more broadly across Europe.

8

UK

HISTORY

The UK has a long tradition in the business of banking, generally said to date back to the dissolution of the monasteries in the 1530s which until then had been the keepers of money. This was followed by the creation of the goldsmith banks in London that stored gold and valuables for their customers and started to issue receipts against this. Whilst originally these receipts were against specific assets they move in time to being redeemable against a specific value of gold, although not necessarily the original assets deposited. Barclays Bank, for example, traces its roots back to one of these goldsmith banks, Freame & Gould. At the same time as the goldsmith banks were operating in London we started to see the creation of the county banks since clearly there were strict limits to how far the business of the goldsmiths could extend due to transport and communication issues. These banks were all personal liability institutions, meaning that the owners were personally and individually responsible for any losses the bank incurred, and so because of the risk involved this was likely to limit their growth and so create a very fragmented market. In 1826, though, a change in the law allowed joint stock banking, where banks could be formed by groups of partners, albeit limited to six, but still enabling the bankers to spread risk. This is the same idea that we saw in the chapter on Private Banking when we looked at the Swiss *private bankers*. For more than 50 years the joint stock banking model flourished but then in the 1880s we saw a series of mergers leading to the evolution of a two-tier banking system, with the top tier consisting of the key players who were the five largest banks, known as the Big Five, and six smaller but not insignificant ones, and then the second tier consisting of the other 250 or so banks that were in the market. The Big Five were Barclays, Lloyds, Midland, National Provincial and Westminster Bank. These banks, maybe with slightly different names, are still the dominant ones in the UK banking system today.

From the middle of the 19th century we could also see the three strands that make up banking in the UK. Along with the commercial banks that we have mentioned above there were also merchant banks that we introduced in the chapter on Investment Banking, and other financial institutions that carried out bank-like activities, such as building societies and friendly societies. This, then, is pretty much the structure the UK has kept since that time, although, of course, with changes to the types of business the banks are allowed to undertake and, importantly for London, the arrival of many international banks. Of course there have also been lots of mergers. Before 1833 the focus of banks had been very local, but 1833 saw the creation of National Provincial Bank of England which was the first bank with the stated aim of being a national bank. National Provincial formed part of the National Westminster Bank which is now part of RBS. These three types of banking institution covered very distinct areas of the whole business of banking. The commercial banks were basically deposit-takers, the merchant banks financed business, and so were really the corporate bankers and the building societies provided financing for homes and, in time, savings accounts. The 20th century saw some significant changes with, after the Second World War, a relaxation in the kind of banking services that could be offered, and also liberalization of merger rules. This is what really set the scene for the dominance that we see in the UK market today by the five largest banks.

In the early part of the 21st century these five largest banks are still Barclays, HSBC, Lloyds, Royal Bank of Scotland and Standard & Chartered. In 2009 these banks have combined assets of some £6.1 trillion, which is four times the GDP of the UK.[1] The financial markets account for around 8% of GDP and the industry employs more than a million people[2] so it carries great importance to the UK economy as a whole.

2008 was something of a landmark year for UK banking as we saw the forced nationalization and part-nationalization of some of the most important financial institutions. The first of these was the bank's 100% nationalization of Northern Rock, a former building society in February 2008. This is looked at in Appendix B as it was such an important precedent for the UK banking industry.

Following on from Northern Rock the government took partial stakes in RBS and Lloyds Group, giving them a majority interest in the former,

---

[1] European Banks Growing Bigger Sowing the Seeds of the Next Crisis, Bloomberg December 2009.

[2] Reforming Financial Markets, HM Treasury, July 2009.

and a large minority in the latter. It also fully nationalized another former building society, Bradford & Bingley, but with this one a deal was quickly brokered to sell parts of the business to the Santander Group. This included the savings division and branch network, whilst the bank's mortgage business transferred to public ownership meaning the bank ended up part-nationalized. A similar transaction happened with the Dunfermline Building Society in March 2009, when the retail and wholesale deposit business, branches, head office and residential mortgages were transferred to Nationwide, another building society turned bank, and the Bank of England took ownership of the society's social housing loans and associated deposits.

The UK government set up an agency to manage these bank investments, UK Financial Investments Ltd. This agency's purpose is to manage the government's bank holdings in a responsible fashion and to maximize shareholder value for the taxpayers. This may mean the need to intervene with the boards of the banks if they have concerns about its strategy or operations, and again, this is where they have been publicly seen in the markets in the discussion of bank bonuses. We will look more at this agency in Appendix C as an example of how governments have dealt with the problems that can arise from nationalizing the banking industry. The government has always made clear its intention to sell these bank shares and in November 2009 it confirmed that, as it intends to do with Northern Rock, it would break up its holdings in RBS and Lloyds and potentially sell them to new market entrants, therefore creating greater competition in the sector. As of the beginning of 2010 there were reputed to be as many as 35 organizations that had approached the FSA about setting up banking operations in the UK, notably amongst them Virgin Money, who in January bought a small regional bank, Church House Trust Plc, in order to gain access to its banking licence and speed its path to be able to open a branch network in the UK. Also 2010 has seen the opening of the first brand new high street branch-based commercial bank in more than 100 years as the US financier Vernon Hill brings Metro Bank to the UK. Their focus will be on retail and the small to medium-sized corporate market, and whilst offering the typical banking products their intention is to differentiate by service, including extended opening hours and dates, and a plan to open 10 branches in the London area by September 2011. It will be interesting to see the impact on the competitive market, where opening hours have gradually extended over the past decade, but not to the radical extent proposed by Metro, although its focused geographic presence could mean that this impact will actually be diluted. Another new bank name to enter the UK market is the supermarket Tesco, with ambitious plans to develop their Tesco Bank brand having bought out RBS' 50% stake in Tesco Personal Finance, and plans to offer bank accounts and mortgages under its own banking licence.

REGULATION

Financial markets in the UK are, at the moment, regulated by the Bank of England and The Financial Services Authority (FSA). Since 1997 the bulk of the individual supervisory function has fallen to the FSA whilst the Bank of England concerns itself with the broad picture. We have to add the caveat 'at the moment', since as we have seen before in our discussion of rules and principle-based regulation, the UK regulatory system is very likely to be the subject of substantial change. Following the General election of 2010 it was announced that the FSA would be scrapped with a lot of the regulatory function being returned to the Bank of England, along with the establishment of a new Banking Commission that would broadly oversee the banking industry to try and create policy to deal with issues such as the systemic risk within the industry. However one important regulatory function that for now remains firmly with the Bank of England is its responsibility as lender of last resort, and it is in this vein that special measures were introduced to deal with the very real prospect of failing banks and to help prevent the market from getting to this point. Amongst these was the passing of the Banking Act 2009 which set out procedures and safeguards for transferral of ownership into state hands for the protection of consumers. Whilst this Act allows for banks to pass into state hands – and as we have said this has already been the case and the government has set up an agency to manage these investments – it is the Bank of England that will be the most directly aware of any problems arising in the market with any of the licensed banks. They will be the ones who will see the banks' need for funds in their central bank returns and their reaction to open market operations. They will be able to identify whether any banks are having difficulties meeting their reserve requirements, and, of course, if any banks have to approach them to borrow directly, as we discussed in the chapter on Central Banks. In April 2008 the Bank of England set up a Special Liquidity Scheme which allowed banks to exchange illiquid assets such as mortgage-backed securities for liquid, tradable debt such as government bonds that they were allowed to hold for up to three years.

The scheme was originally intended to last for six months but was extended to January 2009, during which time 32 financial institutions took advantage of the scheme giving the bank assets valued at £287 billion against borrowing £185 billion.[3] In October 2008 the Bank of England also created a new discount window lending facility, the means by which they could lend directly to the banks against a wider range of collateral. This expression 'discount window' is one most commonly heard in the US where it actually referred to a window at the Federal Reserve Bank in New York that was the physical location to which the banks would go to borrow from the Fed. In the UK, though, the Bank of England also increased maximum maturities on these loans to banks to 364 days, an unusually long period for a central bank to make funds available to the market, so all in all they were doing everything they could to provide liquidity to the markets. Obviously all of this needed to be funded, resulting in the sharp increase in the amount of government debt issued. In the chapter on Central Banks we discussed quantitative easing, using the Bank of England as an example. To carry this out the Bank of England set up a subsidiary, the Bank of England Asset Protection Facility Fund, to ensure that all the various elements of the bank interacting with the markets were separated. This was to make sure that they could have the clearest overview on how the markets were conducting themselves, which, as we said, is their primary regulatory purpose.

So, if the Bank of England manages the big picture it must be the FSA that looks at the detail. The FSA regulates not just financial market firms, but also markets and exchanges, along with individuals working in the markets. They set out the standards and requirements for carrying out business and then monitor and take action against any participants either not abiding by these standards or failing to cooperate with them. The FSA runs a programme of supervision that is allied to the size and the risk of the firm. Obviously they will study the financial returns and the firm's compliance with the FSA rules and regulations, but for the larger firms, such as the banks, they operate a closer contact model, where they meet regularly with the bank's management and control departments. This concept of regular contact is crucial to the FSA understanding what the banks are doing, and yet as we have seen it is not without its faults and therefore its critics. A major criticism of the regulatory framework in the UK is this division between the Bank of England and the FSA, a topic we touched on in the chapter on Central Banks. There are those who say that, whilst the FSA strives to follow the banks since it is not

---

[3] Bank of England.

actually involved in the markets, it is not so sensitive to events until they reach a critical point. They are not close enough to the cash flow to see where the banks themselves see risk which they translate into a change in their lending patterns, as we saw with the interbank market in 2007/8, with the banks becoming extremely reluctant to lend to one another and so exacerbating the liquidity problems that were already there. We have also seen another example of this in 2010 with the markets' reaction to the European sovereign concerns, when again there was pressure on interbank lending with the banks once more being less willing to lend out funds in this uncertain period. The FSA would obviously refute this, putting forward the case for objective supervision, which is why both models of single and multiple regulators do exist globally. Interestingly, we will see in the chapter on Germany a similar two-agency structure but one that seems to draw a lot less criticism.

Another key factor in any form of regulation is the international aspect of banks and financial markets. It is important that regulators pay attention to international accords, such as implementing the Basel II Directive that we mentioned earlier, but they also have to pay attention to their own country's competitive position. This has been a particularly sensitive issue for the FSA, following the Financial Crisis. The UK, particularly London, for a variety of reasons including history, location and language, holds an important and influential place in the markets as a whole. We spoke at the beginning of this chapter of the importance of banking to the overall economy, and the FSA, along with the UK government, has been faced with the challenge of protecting this business but whilst still sticking to the core mandates of creating a stable financial market environment and, of course, protecting the users of these markets. At times it has seemed that these two facets, protecting the UK's competitive position and protecting the market environment and its users, are in conflict. Whenever reforms are suggested that may to some seem too radical the threat is always made that the industry will move to another location. So the UK government and the FSA find themselves having to carefully balance the need to reform with respect for these concerns.

COMMERCIAL BANKS AND LICENSED DEPOSIT-TAKERS

In December 2009 there were 329 institutions authorized as licensed to take deposits in the UK. They were divided as shown in Table 8.1:

Table 8.1 Licensed Deposit Takers

Incorporated in the UK	152
Incorporated in another EEA country	96
Incorporated outside the EEA	81
Total	**329**

Deposits in UK banks are covered by the Financial Services Compensation Scheme (FSCS), and in 2010 are covered to a level of £50,000.

Earlier in this chapter we spoke about the five largest banks in the UK, Barclays, HSBC, Lloyds, RBS and Standard Chartered, and of these the first four are amongst the names most commonly seen on the high street. In the chapter on Commercial Banking we spoke of the nationalist nature of this business, and this is clearly reflected in the UK, with the exception of the Spanish bank, Santander, that has a highly visible presence owing to a series of takeovers. We should say a word about HSBC because this may seem an anomaly. Although HSBC stands for Hong Kong and Shanghai Banking Corporation, the name of the founding firm that was established in 1865 to promote trade between Europe and China and India, its headquarters are in London. In 1987 it bought a 14.9% share in Midland Bank, which it then converted to full ownership in 1992 so to all intents and purposes it is a UK bank. Standard Chartered is however different from the other top five banks, as, in the UK, its focus is not on retail banking but instead on wholesale and private banking, making them more akin to the merchant banks that we will discuss a little later. For the others, they are, to a greater or lesser extent, full-service banks, with Lloyds being the lightest in investment banking. In the field of retail and corporate banking their services are much the same, offering the range of deposit accounts, financing and FX that we discussed in the chapter on Commercial and Retail Banking. So we will see these names regularly in the FX and money markets, particularly in the sterling market. RBS is unusual in that it operates under two names in this banking market, RBS and NatWest, whilst Lloyds Group is even more unusual with four names, Lloyds TSB, Halifax, Bank of Scotland and C&G, all operating in the same markets. This is a product of the legacies of the bank but strangely it also means that there can be competing branches of the same firm on a high street. Even though the banks have operated strategies to minimize this, with the growth of internet banking this strategy may only mask the internal competition.

Corporate business is also crucial to the cash flow of these banks. They all have long-lasting historic relationships with the major UK borrowers, often with a geographic bias, such as RBS' relationships with Scottish firms. They benefit from the UK's position as a major economic centre, particularly in the service sector. Corporate banking services will cover the full range of products that the firm is likely to need, tailored to represent the size and scope of the firm. Corporate banking is a very relationship-based business and many of the corporate customers of the bank will be examples of long-standing relationships. The banks though should not rest on their laurels as we know that in the 21st century this area, like so many other parts of the industry, is becoming increasingly competitive so history is not necessarily an assurance of future business. However given that the product offering is not likely to differ substantially between rivals the decision on counterparty is likely to be driven by a perception of efficiency forcing the banks to focus attention on many areas of their whole operation.

All of these banks also operate investment banking operations, with Barclays Capital being probably the most well-known amongst them, although interestingly in 2009 not the most profitable. We have come across Barclays Capital several times in our league tables as they have built up a strong base of clients and market expertise beyond the UK market. HSBC is also a very international bank probably with a natural bias towards its Asian roots, whereas RBS and Lloyds have tended to appear more geographically restricted, concentrating more on domestic business and clients than the other two seem to have done. However when we looked at the largest banks by asset size we saw RBS at number one, so we should not dismiss these banks as less significant; it is really more to do with the focus of their business. To take RBS as an example, their international presence is restricted to key areas in Europe, Asia and North America, and their primary business model is offering commercial and retail banking to these customers through their acquisitions of such banks as Citizens in the US and ABN Amro in the Netherlands. Barclays, on the other hand is well-known for its successful investment banking arm. Interestingly, though, in 2009 the year of the great bankers' bonus debate,[4] the profits made in investment banking at RBS far outstripped those of Barclays Capital.

---

[4] 2009 saw a lot of attention paid to the bonuses given to bankers, particularly those of banks that were either partially nationalized or had taken advantage of government funding facilities. Many felt it was unacceptable for these banks to be paying bonuses to their employees before they had repaid taxpayer funds. Much as these payments were disparaged they were still made, causing the government to become firmly embroiled in the whole debate with the subject of limiting bank

Since these departments are often called the 'Markets' divisions of the banks this also tends to be where we see them trading a range of financial products often including FX and money markets just to keep most of the trading activity of the firm under one umbrella. When we looked at the GEMMs[5] we saw three of the Big Three banks in the list, so we know that they are involved in the UK government bond market and as a follow-on from this they are also likely to be involved in UK corporate bonds. However not only are they present as traders but also as originators and issuers themselves. It was Lloyds Group that actually reopened the sterling RMBS[6] market in 2009. As well as sterling markets these banks will also be players in other currencies, notably the US dollar and euro, but also other currencies that often fit in with their natural strengths and business flows. For example, HSBC will show its strength in Asia in its trading and origination of Asian currency securities, and Barclays' strength in Africa, an area where they have made a series of acquisitions, can be seen in its vigour in this area of emerging markets. They are also all active in the equities markets, if nothing else in order to have a full range of investment products to offer their customers. This being the case it is worth their while to become members of the relevant exchanges, so all will be members of the UK exchange and some, such as Barclays Capital, will be members of numerous major exchanges globally.

Private banking is also a key area for all of these banks. RBS owns the prestigious brand of Coutts, one of the oldest UK private banking firms, with roots tracing back to the 17th century. In the 21st century private banking and wealth management have been identified as key areas for UK banking to cope with an increasingly wealthy population in their home markets, even bearing in mind what we said about changes in HNWIs in the chapter on Private Banking. Probably the biggest growth area is in the mass affluent, which is the group below the high net worth, and it is this group that already comprises a key customer of the UK banks and their model has been to offer premium product packages to these customers, including tailored loans and savings accounts and access to securities services, whilst on a lower level and without the personal contact afforded to the true private banking customers. By doing this the banks aim to retain this core business in-house, and as

bonuses and forcing a restructure of the whole compensation culture of the industry being firmly placed on the agenda.

[5] Gilt-Edged Market Makers.

[6] Residential Mortgage Backed Securities.

we said in the chapter on Private Banking, maximize potential business opportunities.

Building Societies

The first UK building society was founded in 1775 in Birmingham. Their purpose was home financing, and in their original structure they were called *terminating* societies, as when all the members of the society had been housed the society itself would be wound up. This concept actually existed until 1980 when the last of the terminating societies, First Salisbury, was dissolved, but 1845 saw the creation of the first permanent society, The Metropolitan Equitable, which is the structure with which we are more commonly familiar. By 1860 there were over 750 societies in London and more than 2000 in the provinces, illustrating the breadth of coverage of these organizations. Their intention was to embed themselves in local communities so that savers and borrowers could feel closer to the institution that was managing their money. The names of the building societies today still reflect these geographical roots. Building societies are primarily savings and home loan institutions, functions that are also carried out by the commercial and retail banks that we have already looked at, but their core difference from a bank comes in their structure, the ownership of the society being in the hands of the members. In 2009, there were 52 societies, although in 2010 a merger had already been announced between two of them; between them they hold total assets of £375 billion. Table 8.2 shows the 10 largest societies:[7]

In 2008 the top five societies held 74% of the total assets in the sector, and we can already see the size of the gulf between Nationwide at number 1 and Norwich & Peterborough at number 10. As of December 2008 the smallest was Century Building Society of Edinburgh, with assets of just £24 million. Equal first in the league table is Britannia which in 2009 merged with Cooperative Financial Services, part of the Cooperative Group, which is the country's largest consumer cooperative association, and it is this cooperative status that allows Britannia to still be classed as a building society, as this is the core distinction. By definition building societies do need to be mutually owned, owned by the members of the society. They are regulated by the FSA, falling under different legislation, notably the Building Societies Act 1997,

---

[7] Building Societies Association.

Table 8.2   10 Largest Building Societies

Rank	Name of Society	Asset size
1	Nationwide	201,101
–	Britannia*	33,153
2	Yorkshire	28,157
3	Coventry	20,163
4	Chelsea**	15,209
5	Skipton	14,101
6	Leeds	10,156
7	West Bromwich	8,781
8	Principality	6,396
9	Newcastle	4,974
10	Norwich & Peterborough	4,988

* Merged with Cooperative Financial Services in August 2009.
** Merged with Yorkshire BS in April 2010.

which laid out the framework for the constitution of the societies along with restrictions on mergers and, crucially, funding. One of the major differences between banks and building societies in the UK is that the latter are subject to a strict restriction on how they are able to meet their funding needs. At present they are not allowed to raise more than 50% of their funding from sources other than their members. This is intended, partly, to protect them from the vagaries of the financial markets, but was also a key factor in the fall of Northern Rock, that we discuss in Appendix B. However in 2007 an enabling Act was passed, the Building Societies (Funding) and Mutual Societies (Transfers) Act, that could change this. An enabling Act is one which needs secondary legislation to actually bring the proposals into law, but if this happens then the funding ratio could change significantly, rising to as much as 75% non member funding, which will potentially completely alter the balance sheets of these societies. It will also make it easier for the societies to merge, and it is thought that these reforms would prevent more demutualization. Demutualization is when the society elects to go public, and become a publicly listed entity, with shareholders rather than members, and so moves to the bank side of the spectrum. The first building society to do this was Abbey National in July 1989, followed by nine others (see Table 8.3).

Most of these are now owned by major banking groups so no longer exist in an independent form.

Since building societies are so restricted in their funding this impacts on how we see them in the financial markets. Obviously since they are

Table 8.3   Demutualized Building Societies

Alliance & Leicester
Birmingham & Midshires
Bradford & Bingley
Bristol & West
Cheltenham & Gloucester
Halifax
National & Provincial
Northern Rock
Woolwich

mutual societies they will not be seen in the equity market raising funds but they will borrow in the money markets and in the long-term debt markets, although we will not expect to see them with anything like the visibility of the commercial and retail banks. One area in which we do see the building societies is in the creation of residential mortgage-backed securities (RMBS),[8] an important source of funding for them as it ties together the cash flows of the funding with the primary source of assets to be funded. Despite all the problems of 2007 and 2008 this is not a dead market and in 2009 Nationwide issued £3.25 billion of RMBS.

Building society is an expression most commonly heard in relation to the UK but it also exists in Commonwealth countries, such as Australia, Canada, New Zealand where there are relatively large markets of building societies. However this mutual structure is one that we will see in many of the markets that we are going to look at later in this book.

MERCHANT BANKING

In the chapter on Investment Banking we looked at the history of this type of banking and we used Baring Brothers as an early example of one of these banks. In actual fact Baring Brothers was considered a merchant bank rather than an investment bank. Partly this is geographical – the UK equivalents to the US investment banks were the merchant banks – but if we look a little more closely we see that traditionally their models

---

[8] These are a form of asset-backed securities in which the collateral behind the deal will be residential mortgages. We give more of an explanation of this structure in the section on Quasi-Sovereigns when we look at agencies such as the US FNMA which is a major issuer of asset-backed securities.

of business were slightly different. In the chapter on Banking in the US we will look at the US investment banks and we will see that their core business is decidedly raising funds and trading securities. With the merchant banks this is slightly different. Whilst they were also in the business of *disintermediated financing* we tended to see that, as well as raising money, they were also committed to lending money. So if we look at the types of business carried out by the likes of Barings, Cazenove, Schroders, some of the famous names of merchant banking, we will see a long tradition of project finance and direct lending. Today the names we have mentioned are no longer independent merchant banks. Barings as we have already said, was acquired by ING, Cazenove by JPMorgan Chase and Schroders sold its investment banking business to Salomon Smith Barney, now part of Citigroup, so we can see that a lot of the distinction is now irrelevant. In the 21st century the business that we would have described as merchant banking will be carried out by the investment bank divisions of the full-service banks such as HSBC Global Banking and Markets. As we said earlier all of the major banks in the UK will have some form of investment banking divisions and these departments now carry out the traditional merchant banking activities.

The UK, London in particular, is a major location for the financial markets but many of the firms we see active in London are not British by origin, although many of them are incorporated in the UK. This internationality is particularly clear in the area of investment banking which is appropriate given the nature of these markets themselves. So if we are talking about banking in the UK we have to mention these international firms as well as the traditional British names as these firms are major contributors to the business and its impact on the economy. If a UK-based corporation is thinking about raising funds in the capital market, in sterling, they are unlikely to limit themselves to the UK banks so the mandate bid process that we discussed before is likely to involve an international list of firms.

SOCIAL BANKING

Not all banking is driven by purely commercial motives. There are a number of structures that combine the core business of banking, as we described in the Introduction to Banking, with altruistic elements. These sorts of structures will be found in many countries, including the UK. The following are examples of these institutions.

Friendly Societies and Credit Unions

Friendly societies and credit unions carry on the theme of mutuality that we saw with the building societies. These institutions combine not just a vehicle for placing and taking funds, but also a social welfare aspect to them, through providing insurance services of varying types from life cover, to health insurance, to cover for funeral expenses. They are therefore somewhat of a hybrid institution, being a mixture of savings and insurance. If you look at the offerings of Liverpool Victoria, the largest of the friendly societies, there certainly appears to be more of an insurance bias than anything else, as they offer insurance that goes beyond the historic roots to include car and pet insurance! Historically friendly societies were set up as a means of self-help for the less affluent parts of the community. The intention was to encourage savings and offer welfare in the times before the welfare state. By 1945 there were 18,000 societies with 14 million members. In 2009, since we do have a welfare state, the number of these societies has dwindled, with the Association of Friendly Societies showing only some 45 member firms, but still with five million individual members. These firms between them held assets of £15 billion, and the top 10 were as shown in Table 8.4.

As with the building societies we can see a massive difference between the largest, Liverpool Victoria, and the tenth on the list, Dentists' Provident Society. These two names are also very indicative of how the societies were formed, either through a geographical connection, or maybe a professional (or trade) one. In the first instance of the society being created the members would have contributed a small sum of money each week from which they could draw if need be to cover sickness, death expenses etc. From this many have grown into more sophisticated

Table 8.4   10 Largest Friendly Societies

	Assets
LV= (Liverpool Victoria)	6,280,800,000
Royal Liver Assurance	3,526,601,000
Family Investments	1,075,133,000
Police Mutual Assurance Society	931,479,000
Scottish Friendly Assurance Society Limited	701,651,000
The Children's Mutual	599,215,000
Engage Mutual Assurance	508,121,000
Ancient Order of Foresters Friendly Society Limited	167,945,000
National Friendly Society Limited	150,107,042
Dentists' Provident Society	132,012,539

financial institutions whilst still staying true to their principles of mutuality and welfare. As with all of our other financial institutions they are
regulated by the FSA.

Credit unions are at present still a very small part of the UK financial landscape. In 2009 there were 509 unions regulated by the FSA
representing 605,000 members, but this is a structure that appears to
be growing. As with the friendly societies and building societies they
work on the idea of pooled money, with the funds being placed in
savings accounts being used to finance loans, and even a structure called
a Credit Union Current Account, reminiscent of a bank account, that
allows the holder to set up direct debits and use ATM machines. Whilst
credit unions are very common in other countries, such as Ireland where
some 50% of the population are said to be members of a union, they are
still really in their infancy in the UK. We will talk some more about the
concept of credit unions in the chapter on Banking in the US.

Charity Bank

Charity Bank is a licensed deposit-taker regulated by the FSA and
covered by the FSCS[9] but unlike other banks 100% of the deposits it
receives are used to finance charity and community initiatives. Charity
Bank was launched in 2002 with a balance sheet of £6,000,000, which by
2009 had grown to £60,000,000. In competition with other commercially
motivated banks Charity offers a range of savings accounts open to all
but its loans are only available to approved organizations.

Social Investment Wholesale Bank

In July 2009 the UK government issued a consultation document on
its intention to create a wholesale social bank. Social investment is
investing in society, so the bank would have to carry out the dual aims
of creating social and financial value. The bank would provide financing
to established intermediaries, such as Charity Bank and other ethical and
charitable trusts, to help to improve the liquidity and structure of the
market. It is envisaged that the bank would undertake many of the classic
investment bank functions, advisory, trading, raising capital, investment,
but exclusively in the social sector. It is not intended that the bank should
be government-owned; rather it would look for independent financing,

---

[9] Financial Services Compensation Scheme.

possibly listing on an exchange, so that it could run as an independent enterprise. This would be an innovative structure in the markets and could provide great benefits for raising the profile of social investment, particularly at a time when this appears to be picking up investor interest following the Financial Crisis and when interest rates stand at such a low level that people are looking at alternative ways to invest their money.

9

France

HISTORY

Banking in France has often been referred to as a slower starter than, for example, the development of banks in the UK. We should remember though that when we look at the 16th and 17th centuries we are looking at times when trade, particularly international trade, was in its infancy but already fast developing and a lot of that development was, of necessity, centred on ports. So we do tend to see the dominance of places such as England and the Netherlands with their trade routes, and cities sitting on the major waterways like London and Rotterdam, although this was surpassed by Amsterdam. However if we look at Paris in these early days we can still see that the patterns of trade also dominated banking there, but maybe without such formalized structures. At the beginning of the 18th century, though, events started to change this, notably the institution in 1716 of John Law's Banque Générale that we will talk of a little later.

As we have already seen and will continue to see when looking at other countries, the 19th century saw a real period of growth in the banking industry and in France we focus on the development of the *hautes banques*. These are generally defined as a combination between merchant banks and private banks, but in reality this reflects very much the trade of most banks in those days. As we saw in the UK, banks were very closely linked to trade and merchants, with banks often being established by these merchants involved in the trade of wheat, tobacco, and, of course, railway construction. An interesting thing with hautes banques, though, was the nationality of many of the bankers, since they came not just from France but also from the Netherlands, Switzerland and England, so showing a very international perspective. One such was James de Rothschild who was sent by his father Mayer Amschel Rothschild to set up a branch of the UK bank in Paris, as he did with his other four sons to other European cities. James de Rothschild became extremely successful and influential in the French banking industry, even becoming a director of the Banque de France. All of this means that from the outset the French banking system was being established with good international ties, and this was reflected in the number of investment associations that were established, particularly with London, all with the aim of improving trade relations and associated funding.

Whilst the hautes banques were dominating Paris there was also a network of provincial banks being established. By 1870 there were some 2000 of these banks. They operated an interesting relationship with the Paris banks, one of correspondent banking. This is where banks have mutual accounts with one another, and is still seen today in bank relationships, particularly with regard to FX deals. These correspondent relationships meant that funding from the Banque de France could be passed through to the provincial banks to support the network. A downside to the system, though, was that these banks did not have limited liability and the economic and political crises of 1848 showed the weaknesses of this system. This led to bank failures and a lack of trade financing that culminated in the government having to step in and make funds available through the creation of discount banks like the Comptoir Nationale d'Escompte de Paris. Jacques Lafitte, who had been a governor of the Banque de France from 1814–18 before allying himself to Louis-Philippe, leading to him becoming Prime Minister in 1830 (a post from which he resigned in 1831 as a financially and politically ruined man), was to prove very influential in the history of French banking. He had already tried to make a limited partnership of banking and trade in 1827, but in 1837, after his fall from favour, he founded the Caisse Générale du Commerce et de l'Industrie which was a joint stock company, focused on providing credit to trade, to try and develop the sector on a firmer footing than before, a significant development for French banking.

The second half of the 19th century saw the creation of many of the names that are either still in existence or have only disappeared in the past couple of decades. In 1852 Louis Wolowski, originally from Poland but naturalized in 1834, started Crédit Foncier, the first mortgage bank. It was modelled on the German model of mortgage financing and originally was intended to service the agricultural community but due to a lack of demand they changed the focus of their business to mortgage financing in the cities, originally in Paris, but moving on to other areas. In the same year Crédit Mobilier was born. This was a bank specifically created to finance industry. It was supported by the government and given the right to issue debt in its own name, all, this time, on the principle of limited liability. They often swapped this debt, and their equity, for similar of firms in which they invested creating a network of interdependence. However, Crédit Mobilier lost its government support in 1886, leading to its decline, but the name lived on elsewhere notoriously in the US with Credit Mobilier of America.[1]

1859 saw the founding of Crédit Industriel et Commercial (CIC), 1863 and 1864 we saw the birth of Crédit Lyonnais and Société Générale, long-standing names within the French banking system. These banks modelled themselves on the evolving English model, with strong branch networks, but were also notable for the pains they took to attract business, such as by advertising and even employing door-to-door salesmen. Whilst witnessing the creation of these commercial banks we also saw the growth of the investment banking part of the business, with the creation of banks such as Banque de Paris et des Pays-Bas (Paribas) and Banque de l'Union Parisienne, which were noticeably different from the commercial banks in their targeted markets and their structure. These banks did not have branch networks and focused primarily on bonds and long-term deposits.

So, into the 20th century we saw a firmly established privately owned banking industry, but in 1878 the Banque Populaire à Angers was founded, the first cooperative bank, set up with the intention of promoting enterprise and investment in small and medium-sized businesses. In 1917 the state adjusted the balance in favour of these banks which was a precursor to how the banking sector was going to change as the century progressed. Through the 1920s there was growth of these cooperative banks, and also agricultural banks, such as Crédit Agricole, another long-lasting name in the industry. However, the period between the two world wars saw a decline in the private banking sector, although by the time of the Second World War there were still 550 banks in France. The next key event was to fundamentally change the structure of French banking. This was the government's nationalization of the Banque de France, and four leading banks, Banque Nationale pour le Commerce et de l'Industrie (BNCI), Comptoir Nationale d'Escompte de Paris (CNEP), Crédit Lyonnais and Société Générale. This was the beginning of a trend of nationalization and merger that was to continue during the following decades, including the merger in the 1960s of BNCI and CNEP to form Banque Nationale de Paris (BNP).

---

[1] Credit Mobilier of America was actually a construction company involved in a massive fraud in the US. It was created by the Vice President of Union Pacific Railroad, and the fraud involved the company making contracts with Credit Mobilier to build the railroad. These contracts were paid for by cheque and these cheques were then used to buy stocks and bonds in the railroad at low prices which were then sold on the open market for huge profits.

More nationalization occurred in 1982 when investment banks and all banks with deposits greater than 1 billion French francs were nationalized. This meant that pretty much all the banks in France were either state-owned or mutual. It was also a period of great strength for the French banks internationally, and probably not coincidentally. Crédit Agricole, Crédit Lyonnais, BNP and Société Générale were amongst the largest banks in the world by deposit size, however over the next few years pressure was increased to privatize these banks to make them truly competitive with the increasingly internationalized market. The first of these privatizations took place in 1987 and over the next 15 years we saw further privatizations of the banks including the notable deals listed in Table 9.1:

Table 9.1   Bank Privatizations

Privatization date	
1987	Société Générale, CCF, Paribas
1988	Credit Agricole
1993	BNP
1999	Credit Lyonnais*
2001	Banque Hervet

* The government maintained a 10% stake which they finally sold in 2002.

The period following privatization saw a number of mergers: BNP launched a takeover for both Société Générale and Banque Paribas, successfully merging with Banque Paribas in 2000; Crédit Lyonnais was acquired by Crédit Agricole in 2003; and most recently the merger of Caisse d'Eparne and Groupe Banque Populaire to form BPCE in 2009. However the only international inroad into the French banking sector has been by HSBC with their acquisition of CCF in 2000 and Banque Hervet in 2003. This is in contrast to the French banks' foreign acquisitions, most notably BNP Paribas' acquisition of Fortis Bank of the Netherlands in 2009.

REGULATION AND THE BANQUE DE FRANCE

As of 2008 there were some 450 banking businesses in France, with the Banque de France at the industry's heart as its central bank. We spoke earlier of John Law and the Banque Générale that was established in 1716 and this is seen as the precursor to the Banque de France, but not a particularly successful one. John Law was appointed by Philippe d'Orléans to set up the Banque Générale, which whilst privately owned was 75% financed by government debt. It started the issuance of paper money, and two years later in 1718 was renamed Banque Royale as its notes were guaranteed by the king. So far everything sounds fine and pretty much in line with how we saw the Bank of England coming into being, but unfortunately a great scandal was brewing. John Law had bought a company in America, the Mississippi Company, apparently to help the French residents of Louisiana. He floated this as a joint stock trading company that then built up a monopoly on trading with North America and the West Indies. From there he carried on to expand into trade routes with Asia, again building up monopolies. The more successful the company became the more people wanted to get involved and so Law started to trade shares in the company for government debt, effectively tying the value of the company to the value of the government securities. In 1720 the bank and the company were united, and Law was given a government post to attract more capital. He succeeded, for a while, in trading the shares against the debt but underlying all this was a fundamental lack of value leading to price inflation and ultimately a loss of confidence. Later in 1720 both the bank and the trading company collapsed, with Law being dismissed and fleeing France. So, this first attempt was not successful and was actually damaging to France's reputation and ability to raise funds.

In 1800 the Banque de France was set up, again charged with issuing banknotes. Once again this was a private company, set up as a joint stock bank, although in 1806 the government passed a statute giving it the right to appoint a governor and two deputies within the bank, thereby taking on some influence. The bank was based in Paris and initially had little exposure outside, but soon established a strong branch network, which grew through the second half of the 19th century to reach 160 by 1900 before growing to 259 in 1928. Today there are still 129 branches of the bank around France.

The bank stayed in private hands until the process of bringing it under state ownership began in 1936, culminating in nationalization on 1 January 1946. As with the Bank of England, though, the trend today is for independent central banks, and the Banque de France received its independence in 1993. In 1998, with the introduction of the euro, France joined the ESCB.[2]

[2] European System of Central Banks.

The functions taken on by the bank will be very much the same as we see for all central banks:

- issuing notes and coins;
- implementing monetary policy through open market operations;
- contributing to foreign exchange policy and international relations;
- managing the country's reserves;
- bringing government debt to the market via the primary dealer network of SVTs;[3]
- regulation.

The first three of these are matters where the bank cannot act unilaterally. Whilst they definitely have a major consultative role to play in determining policy this must be to the benefit of the eurozone as a whole, not just France, so the actions taken have to be in line with a central policy. Nonetheless it is the individual central banks that we will see actually in the markets, carrying out the day-to-day money market and FX trades, which again we discussed in the chapter on the UK, and also building the links with the banking community in order to maintain a close watch on these institutions and the markets in which they are acting.

In terms of regulation, the actual process is divided into committees focusing on different elements of banking and the financial markets. Bank authorization is carried out by the Comité des Etablissments de Crédit et des Entreprises d'Investissement (CECEI) whilst supervision falls under the umbrella of the Commission Bancaire. The two committees must work in concert, along with the Association des Marchés Financières (AMF) an independent public body focusing more on the investment market, authorizing and regulating investment products and those that create and sell them, along with the market infrastructure itself. This structure is intended to split responsibilities to allow concentration on a particular part of the landscape, whilst obviously understanding the links with one another and so a process of information-sharing and co-operation is essential to make the system work. However, it is important to realize that bank authorization and supervision is maintained under the umbrella of the central bank, and so the Governor of the central bank sits as chair of both these committees, and is also represented on the AMF. So contrary to what we have seen in recent times in the UK, the key functions of monetary stability and regulation are carried out by the same body. This idea of uniformity is also seen in the French

---

[3] Specialistes en valeur de trésor.

banking laws, particularly the lack of distinction between commercial and investment banks, to create an industry fundamentally based on the idea of universal banking.

Along with other countries the French government had to take measures to cope with failing banks during the Financial Crisis. In its strategy the French government created two agencies, one, Société de Prise des Participations de l'Etat (SPPE) is wholly state-owned and takes on the role of recapitalization, whilst the other, Société de Financement de l'Economie Française (SFEF), is a public-private enterprise, 34% owned by the state and 66% by the top seven banks, that concentrates on refinancing. SPPE was established with €40 billion available to the banks, whilst SFEF was authorized to issue up to €265 billion of government guaranteed debt, with a maximum maturity of five years, for the purpose of refinancing the banks. These securities were very well received by the market so proved an efficient funding tool. We speak a little more about SFEF in the chapter on Government Agencies.

COMMERCIAL AND RETAIL BANKING AND THE COOPERATIVE BANKS

As we have already seen there are two types of credit banks in France, the privately owned and the cooperative. These cooperative banks carry a lot of importance in the French banking system and have been supported by the government, not least through the Banking Law of 1984 which established a level playing field for banks of all types, putting what have previously been savings banks on a par with their commercial counterparts and therefore opening up the range of activities they could undertake. These cooperative banks are typically local or regional banks, which despite having increased their product range over the past 25 years are nonetheless still firmly affiliated to their original customer base, often focusing on retail and the smaller to medium-sized end of the corporate market. The cooperative structure works on the idea of independent banks forming into groups to benefit from economies of scale by sharing various things such as IT, risk control, etc. If we take a look at Crédit Agricole we can see how this translates into a business model.

Crédit Agricole

The bank was founded in 1894 by the government to facilitate agricultural borrowing, hence its name. The bank was created as a decentralized institution and so at the same it was authorized to create Crédit Agricole's local banks which were owned by farm unions. These local banks were pretty much by definition small, and so ran into liquidity problems that required the government to allow for the creation of Crédit Agricole regional banks in 1899. These banks were formed to be the structure through which government advances could be distributed. This is still the format of the bank today. In 1920 the Office Nationale de Crédit Agricole was formed, renamed Caisse Nationale de Crédit Agricole in 1926, and this became the central clearing organization for these regional and local banks, and then in 1966 it began the process of becoming independent from the government, leading to its privatization in 1988. When this happened 90% of the shares were sold to the regional banks and 10% to staff. Following this in 2001 it listed on the stock market, taking the name of Crédit Agricole SA, but the purpose of this was to give its major shareholders, the regional banks, the ability to more easily make major acquisitions, which it has continued to do during this century, including, notably, the acquisition of Crédit Lyonnais. Today the bank is still majority-owned by these 39 regional banks, representing 2549 local banks, but 45.2% of its equity is free floating within the market and so has been bought by a range of investors both institutional and individual. This means it is basically a hybrid, part cooperative, part private, but since the majority shareholding is in the cooperative sector this is still its dominant feature.

Crédit Agricole is one of the largest banks in France, taking 28% of the French household market, putting them at number one in terms of activity and market share, and ranking third in France by asset size. The two larger banks are both privately owned, BNP Paribas being the largest by asset size, followed by Société Générale. All of these banks offer very much the same range of commercial banking products for both retail and institutional customers that we saw in the UK market, and as we will see below they are also very active in investment banking.

INVESTMENT BANKING

We have already spoken about the idea of universal banks in France, and a lot of this came about after the Debré-Haberer reforms of 1966–69 that loosened the restrictions separating commercial and investment banking activities, encouraged competition and focused more attention on risk management within the bank for this new era. As of 2009 the four banks with the greatest involvement in investment banking were BNP Paribas,

Calyon, Natixis and Société Générale. These names also show us the two ways in which the banks approach the market. BNP Paribas and Société Générale trade under the same name in all sides of the markets, whilst Calyon is the investment banking arm of the Crédit Agricole group, and Natixis, the investment banking arm of the merged BPCE. Investment banking is seen as an important part of the whole banking industry, recognized by the state with various initiatives such as Finance Innovation,[4] promoting Paris as a centre for banking, and particularly advocating several key activities, with investment banking being one of the industry's core future developments. The French banks have a very international presence, and if we think back to the lists of government bond primary dealers we saw in the chapter on Investment Banking, BNP Paribas was present in the list not only for France, but also UK and USA, which is a reflection on its international presence and ambitions.

The types of activity that the banks will undertake will once again include advisory, origination, trading, just as we have seen before, and whilst naturally their greatest strength will be in French names, the single currency has made it easier for the large banks to migrate across geographic borders by showing their expertise in the currency. So we are very likely to see these banks very actively involved in equity and debt deals in euro, but also the other major currencies, and of course derivatives, although in recent times a lot of coverage has been given not to the banks' skill in this area but more to their failings. In January 2008 the market found out about a trading scandal at Société Générale when a rogue trader managed to lose the bank around €5 billion. Then later in the same year Caisse d'Epargne reported a loss of €600 million as a result of another unauthorized trading scandal. Derivatives was actually an area in which the French banks had been seen to be very dominant and well respected, but as a result of these incidents, particularly that of Société Générale, they experienced a big fall in market confidence, resulting in a fall in revenues. However, we should say that BNP Paribas still managed to be named Equity Derivatives House of the Year 2009 by Risk magazine, so things were clearly not all bad for the French banks. Indeed the French banks can still be seen very actively in the derivative markets, despite this fall in confidence, both as traders of the instruments and also through incorporating them within their offerings to their customer base, as part of financing or risk management strategies.

---

[4] A government initiative set up in 2007 to bring together industry and research partners to further research in and development of the financial services industry in France.

10
Germany

HISTORY

When we looked at the UK we saw how the UK banking industry had grown around trade and established its roots early on, with that very firm link with the merchants, but actually relatively little government involvement – until now. In France we saw the same trade links but then in the 20th century a very different pattern evolving, with the nationalization and then subsequent privatization of the French banks, which created a different feel to this industry. In Germany we are going to see another different development, an industry that by comparison seems to have grown relatively late, but owing to events in history it has had to take a very different turn in the 20th century. This is important to us because these three locations represent the three major European banking centres in the 21st century, yet their development has been so different that it is bound to have impacted the industry that we see today. It also shows that whilst we talk about European banking we should be very aware of the differences that exist and that always have existed within Europe.

As we have been looking at the history of banking we have focused much of our attention on the 16th and 17th centuries as showing us the earliest examples of banks. However if we were to look at, say, Italy we would see that the roots go further back than this. In Italy we have the same old story of banks established by traders, but we can see very early on these banks, such as those of the Bardi and Peruzzi families, in the 14th century, and then the famous Medici Bank that was established in 1397. The business of these banks was dominated by the use of bills of exchange, where loans and deposits were made and bills issued for redemption at a later date, not necessarily at the same value. This was to avoid being accused of usury – charging interest on loans, a practice that was banned by the church. We will talk more of this later in this book when we look at Islamic Finance Institutions. So, to bring this back to banking in Germany, the first financial institution we tend to see are the *Fuggers* money lenders and early bankers of the 15th and 16th centuries, with their business based on the Italian model.

In fact they derive from Hans Fugger a wealthy 14th century weaver, and over time his family increased this side of their business, such that ultimately they really bankrolled the Hapsburg Empire, dominated metal trading and managed to amass a great fortune, building up the model of merchant banking that we have already seen in the UK. They set up branches initially from their Bavarian roots in Augsburg and then extending outwards and were very successful until the 17th century when they were brought down by their own expansion, since during this expansion they managed to amass very large loans.

In the 17th century we start to see a few important developments, not least the founding of Germany's oldest bank still in operation, Berenberg Bank. Of course back in the 17th century Germany was not one unified country, but rather a series of states and so much of the development in banking finds links to the Hanseatic League, an influential alliance of trading cities that held the monopoly on trade from the Baltic to the North Sea. Given everything we have said already about the links between trade and banking it is not surprising that we find many of our bank structures setting up in towns within this league. The downside to this is that we struggle to identify any single centre to the market such as we saw with London, Paris or Amsterdam, and so this in turn impacts on the creation of a central bank and the unity that this brings. We can see a couple of precursors, though, such as the Hamburg Giro Bank that was created in 1619 along the lines of the Bank of Amsterdam, which we spoke of in the chapter on Banking in France. This, though, was not the first bank to issue money. The first to do this was the Königliche Giro- und Lehnbanco, established by Frederick the Great, and which ultimately evolved into the Prussian Bank, which was established some 150 years after the Hamburg Giro Bank. The amounts issued were very small, as was the capital of the bank, but the bank did start to set up an important framework for the business of banking. However even then this was not going to happen quickly because, over time, we saw as many as 31 banks being designated as notenbanken and so authorized to issue money on behalf of the various states. Clearly, therefore, it was a very regionally fragmented market.

It was not until the 19th century that we started to see a cohesive banking industry beginning to build up, and it was at this time that the business really entered its boom period. For example in 1816 M. A. Rothchild & Söhne was established by another son of Mayer Rothschild, this son being sent to Frankfurt, like his brothers elsewhere, to open this branch of the family business. Just two years later they brought the first foreign government loan to the market in London on behalf of the State of Prussia. M. A. Rothschild continued in Frankfurt until 1901 when it transferred its business to Diskonto-Gesellschaft, although Rothschilds did re-establish an office in Frankfurt in 1989. However going back to the 19th century we saw the market continue to develop at a moderate pace until we reached the middle of the century, the period of the Crimean War, which saw the market making a bit of a jump. This was a period of great speculation which was then followed by the creation of yet more banks, nine in Prussia and 15 in various other states, so by then we could say that there was a thriving banking business.

1870 was an important point in the history of Germany, with the beginning of the Second Reich, and the founding of two important bank names, Deutsche Bank and Commerzbank. Deutsche Bank was founded in Berlin, although the next couple of years showed their expansion not just in Germany but beyond with the bank opening offices in Bremen and Hamburg but also London, Yokohama and Shanghai. Commerzbank, originally called Commerz- und Disconto- Bank in Hamburg, was formed as a coalition of trading companies and merchant banks, with their initial purpose being to finance trade in the Hamburg area. Here were two ways in which the banking system was developing, one outward looking and one inward. Both banks were established as joint-stock banks, but two years later came the creation of Dresdner Bank, again established through a consortium of banks which started trading in December 1872 and was then listed on the Berlin stock exchange in January 1873 – becoming a public company. The consolidation within these banks became a major theme throughout the 19th century and on into the 20th century. Another important thing that happened in 1870 was the passing of a law that stopped the creation of any more central banks, and then in 1875 the first unified central bank, the Reichsbank, was formed. Since we then had a new currency introduced, the Goldmark, which proved to be a pretty stable currency for the next few decades, we can definitely see that a solid banking structure had emerged from rather patchwork beginnings.

However this period of strength and consolidation came to an end in 1931 when a lack of liquidity brought about a major banking crisis in July of that year. This led to a limit on payments, with the banks only paying 20% of the requested amounts and the Reichsbank having to buy shares of Dresdner Bank to shore up its capital base, and also negotiating a merger with Darmstädter und Nationalbank – does this sound similar to actions we have seen recently in the markets? Dresdner was not the only bank to need this sort of support so the Reichsbank was very involved in the market at this time.

Naturally the period of the Second World War was a particularly difficult one in the history of the German banks as they carried out government policy, much of which led to decades of controversy in the period following the war, particularly in regard to the assets of their Jewish customers. However on a more corporate level this strategy also included the banks being required to make acquisitions in strategic locations, followed by the need for branch closures as the war progressed. Deutsche Bank probably had the most problems resulting from the Second World War; both the bank and the market had to come to terms with some of the actions taken during this time. Its role as a key banker to the government meant that activities they undertook during the war have had a very far-reaching impact on the bank, and this is a part of its history, and of German banking in general, that has taken a lot of resolution. After the end of the war we saw head office closures of the main banks, and a serious disintegration of their asset positions, notably due to their large holdings of government debt whose value was dubious. After the war significant structural changes happened to these banks, dividing them into numerous units. In 1947 Deutsche was divided into 10 units, Dresdner into 11. Gradually over the following years the situation started to normalize, especially after the introduction of the Deutschemark, and from 1952 we start to see some re-consolidation in the sector, very much on regional lines. From this point the banks continued to establish themselves as major institutions not just in the German market, but internationally as well over the decades, as they continued to merge, predominantly with other domestic institutions, although Deutsche Bank made some famous overseas acquisitions of its own such as with the purchase of the UK merchant bank, Morgan Grenfell in 1989. A similar acquisition was Dresdner's purchase of Kleinwort Benson in 1995, and then 10 years later, in 1999, Deutsche made their famous and landmark acquisition of Bankers Trust of the US, one of the largest US commercial banks. So the pattern we see is very much of German banks buying overseas rather than overseas banks buying into Germany. In May 2009 we saw another significant domestic merger with Dresdner being acquired by Commerzbank, who were looking to further consolidate their competitive position relative to Deutsche and through which we now have a banking picture which is dominated by two large banks, Deutsche and Commerzbank, although still nowhere near equal in size.

This said, though, as of 2009 there are approximately 2300 credit institutions in Germany,[1] of different types and nationalities, including the regional banks that we will discuss below.

THE BUNDESBANK

The Bundesbank is the central bank of Germany, and being part of the euro we are going to see that it will operate under the same restrictions as we encountered with the Banque de France. Unlike both the Bank of England and the Banque de France the Bundesbank has not been in operation for centuries but instead only came into being in the 20th century. Germany has had its fair share of challenges to cope with in the banking industry, such as the effects of the Second World War, which also brought with it another challenge relating to the division of the country into East and West Germany. This had a major impact on banking as it brought with it issues to be dealt with in relation to the role of a central bank. So we see that until 1990 German effectively had two central banks, both issuing currencies, and with two different economies to support. In 1957 the Bundesbank became the central bank of the Federal Republic of Germany and after unification the central bank of Germany as a whole. Its head office is in Frankfurt but it also has nine regional offices and 47 branches. Before entering the ECSB the Bundesbank had a reputation as being a strong central bank that kept close contact and control over the banks in Germany and over monetary policy. It was not afraid to take decisions on interest rates, for example, that sometimes surprised the markets and may have appeared aggressive, but if the move was considered warranted in Germany's best interests then this is the route they would take. Since the introduction of the single currency its role has had to change in that, like the Banque de France, many of its actions must be dictated by the ECB, but the Bundesbank will contribute fully to its policy-making role and takes its duty of researching and understanding the markets very seriously.

The Deutsche Mark and the Ostmark

In order to understand the significance of two central banks it is important to remember a little about the situation in Germany during the 40 or so years between the Second World War and unification.

---

[1] Bundesbank, 2009.

The Reichsbank was dissolved after the Second World War when the allies took charge of immediate post-war monetary policy in Germany. It was replaced in 1947 by the Bank Deutsche Länder, later to become the Bundesbank, in West Germany and the Deutsche Notenbank, later the Staatsbank der DDR, in East Germany. The primary purpose was to stabilize the currency and in 1948 the Deutsche mark was introduced as the currency of the western occupied zone. However this caused unforeseen difficulties since the currency of the Soviet-occupied zone was still the Reichsmark, so this currency came flooding from West Germany into East causing massive inflation. In July 1948 East Germany also received a new issue of currency, Deutsche Mark von der Deutschen Notenbank, also known as the *Ostmark* and so we had two German currencies. This division was to continue until the Berlin Wall fell in 1989 and the subsequent adoption of the Deutsche mark in East Germany in July 1990. Officially there was always parity between the currencies, but the Ostmark was never a convertible currency;[2] the East German authorities actually imposed a compulsory amount that foreigners entering East Germany had to exchange rather than allowing freedom of exchange, and therefore a black market developed, valuing the Deutsche mark far higher than the Ostmark. This is why different conversion levels had to be used on unification, with wages, prices and first-level savings converted at parity, whilst home and business loans and larger savings were converted at a rate of two Ostmarks for one Deutsche mark. This is the legacy adopted by the Bundesbank after unification. Whilst they should have been looking, in theory, at a straightforward integration, in practice it was much trickier. They also had to cope with a great deal of debt issuance to finance this unification, the cost of which exceeded expectations and had financial ramifications for the country for many years.

Government Debt Issuance

As with other central banks the Bundesbank acts as fiscal agent to the government and so brings its debt securities to the market. Once again, the auction method is the most commonly used mechanism and again we find a list of primary dealers that will bid at the auction and then trade the securities. The Bundesbank issues an annual ranking of these dealers, according to how much paper (securities) they underwrote

---

[2] A convertible currency is one that can be freely traded and exchanged in the markets without controls and restrictions.

Table 10.1   Bund Issues Auction Group (Primary Dealers)

Members of the Bund Issues Auction Group

Citigroup Global Markets Limited
Deutsche Bank AG
Merrill Lynch International
UBS Deutschland AG
The Royal Bank of Scotland Frankfurt Branch
Barclays Bank PLC
HSBC Trinkaus & Burkhardt AG
Morgan Stanley & Co. International plc
Société Générale S.A. Zweigniederlassung Frankfurt am Main
Goldman Sachs International
J.P. Morgan Securities Ltd.
Commerzbank AG
BNP Paribas S.A.
Calyon
DZ BANK AG Deutsche Zentral-Genossenschaftsbank
Nomura Bank (Deutschland) GmbH
Landesbank Hessen-Thüringen Girozentrale
Credit Suisse Securities (Europe) Limited
Bayerische Hypo- und Vereinsbank AG
ING Bank N.V.
Bayerische Landesbank
Natixis
WestLB AG
Landesbank Baden-Württemberg
Norddeutsche Landesbank Girozentrale
DekaBank Deutsche Girozentrale
BHF-Bank AG
Jefferies International Limited

during the issuance process so making everything very transparent and encouraging competition. In 2009 the government brought 60 issues to the market, not all successfully as the first five-year issue of the year, back in January, failed to raise its required €6 billion, but this is a very rare occurrence and this particular auction was a victim of the market conditions and uncertainty at the time. There are 28 firms in this group, and as of end 2009 their rankings were as shown in Table 10.1.[3]

When we look at this group we see the same international names as we have seen previously, but also a good diversity of German financial institutions, with, not surprisingly, Deutsche Bank and Commerzbank, being the two largest German banks, topping the list of domestic names. It is important that this is an efficient group as the German government

[3] Bundesbank, 2009.

is a large borrower in the markets, with, for example, debt issuance for 2010 forecast by the German Finance Minister, Wolfgang Schaeuble, in December 2010 to be €357 billion, in various maturities and structures, higher than the €323 billion it had forecast for 2009. Of course this was before the sovereign debt crisis of Greece that resulted in Germany committing to its loan of €22.4 billion, over three years, to support Greece that may well have a significant impact on this number.

Monetary Policy and the Financial System

As we have already said, with Germany being part of the single currency, the status for the Bundesbank is much the same as for the Banque de France, in that the Bundesbank's primary function on monetary policy will be to gather information that will be used to formulate policy. They will then act on behalf of the ECB, where required, and, of course keep a close eye on money supply in Germany. This is such an important area for the currency that more than half of the short-term central bank lending in euro comes from the Bundesbank. In the chapter on the UK we spoke about the need for the central bank to ensure that the infrastructure was in place to allow payments to be made within the banking system, and again, euro-wide there is also this requirement. So alongside any national payment systems there is also a pan-euro one. This is the TARGET2[4] system, a wholesale real-time payment system, for transfers such as the banks and other limited large institutions will make with one another, which was developed and operated by the Bundesbank, along with the Banque de France and the Banca d'Italia. In January 2008 another payment system, SEPA, was introduced, which allowed for easier payments and transfers between the banks and their customers, and again the Bundesbank was instrumental in the adoption of this system for easier flow of funds. So we can see that the Bundesbank plays a very active role in ensuring the efficiency of payments across the euro system as it believes this to be a crucial element to the successful functioning of the single currency.

Regulation and Supervision

These tasks are carried out by the Bundesbank and the Bundesanstalt für Finanzdienstleistungsaufsicht (BaFin). BaFin looks after not only banks

---

[4] Trans-European Automated Real-time Gross Settlement Express Transfer System.

but also insurance companies, pension funds, investment companies and other financial service providers, whilst the Bundesbank concerns itself with banks, and principally their operation. It is BaFin that authorizes these banks and sets out the standards required to maintain their licences, but it is the Bundesbank that really analyses the reports to ensure that the banks are meeting their requirements. So we see here a system of cooperation between the two authorities to try and ensure financial integrity, such as we said was an essential component of a principles-based system of regulation. Of course, this will not always prevent all problems as we have seen in 2008 and 2009. In common with many other countries Germany had to set up a fund to support financial stability in 2008 – Soffin[5] – established under the auspices of BaFin. The fund was created to offer recapitalization, guarantees and assumption of risk positions, and by 2010 its biggest position was its takeover of Munich's Hypo Real Estate Bank, a mortgage and public finance bank.

THREE PILLARS OF BANKING

We mentioned earlier that the German banking system was based on three types of bank, the private commercial banks, such as Deutsche and Commerzbank, the state-owned Landesbanks, and their affiliated savings banks, and the cooperative banks. We will take a look at each of these, but one thing we will see is the overriding principal of universality in German banking. There is no distinction between the functions of commercial banking and those of investment banking. For the most part the banks do not even use internal subsidiaries to differentiate the business flows (such as Barclays and Barclays Capital). So we are therefore likely to see these various institutions in the markets in proportion to their business flows from their customers and their international presence, rather than being able to say that one part of the bank does this and another part something else. Part of the universal model should be that the bank responds as a whole to areas of activity, assuming, of course, that it is sufficiently well managed to take advantage of this structure. A criticism often made of Deutsche Bank is that it is now too big to efficiently operate this model. Its very size will make it slower to react to changes in the flows going through the firm, and if we add to this labour market restrictions that have been introduced in Germany over the past decades these too do not help in creating a flexible organization.

---

[5] Finanzmarktstabilisierungsanstalt.

Private Commercial Banks

These are the banks such as Deutsche Bank and Commerzbank that we discussed earlier. These two names are the dominant ones, not only in terms of market presence, but also asset size, with Deutsche Bank in 2009 still dwarfing the combined assets of Commerzbank and Dresdner since the merger, and ranking as the second largest bank in the world. The third largest bank in Germany is a Landesbank, Bayern LB, and then the cooperative bank DZ Bank. When we looked at the history of banking we saw how some banks, particularly Deutsche Bank, really looked towards development of their international business, along with their domestic business. If we take Deutsche Bank as an example we will see them active in pretty much all the major financial centres, as well as many of the lesser ones, giving them a global presence. In fact, in 2008 Deutsche Bank had 1981 branches, of which less than half were located in Germany. Since the 1970s the bank has adopted an aggressive policy of acquisition to build up their international presence; aside from buying the banks we have already mentioned in the UK and the US the bank has also made acquisitions in Italy, Spain, Belgium, Turkey, Switzerland and Russia, as well as the domestic acquisitions of Norisbank and Berliner Bank, and the large stake taken in Postbank. We can see the international ambitions of the bank, but also how it has consolidated itself within its domestic market. The portfolio of products and services they offer covers both retail and institutional customers and both traditional commercial and investment banking products. However as well as the obvious financial markets such as equity and debt they also look at other markets where their customers could have interests. An example of this is their presence in the commodities markets, not an obvious core market for them but one in which they have built up expertise as they appreciated this market as a potential asset class for their customers. From their very beginning they took cash deposits which, strange as it may now sound, was at the time revolutionary business. Then in the 1950s they started to build up their retail banking side, which explains some of the acquisitions they have made subsequently as they increased their presence. On the investment banking side, again from the 1950s onwards they have achieved landmarks in this marketplace. An example of this was their bringing to the market a bond for Anglo-American Corporation of South Africa, in 1958, which was the first foreign bond in Germany since 1914, so reopening the international debt market in Germany. And of course we should mention their presence as primary dealer in so many international government bond markets.

Commerzbank's offerings will be similar in product to those of Deutsche Bank, but it is hard not to think of them as a younger sibling. Their customer base will be similar but smaller, but with the same mix of corporate and individual customer. They will offer the same range of commercial and investment banking and will therefore have the same financial market exposure, although of lesser size and less globally diverse.

Cooperative Banks

This is a large and important sector in the German banking industry, with some 60 million customers for these institutions, of which there are around 1200 in 2010. There are also two banks that operate a central bank service, uniting these individual units – DZ Bank and WGZ Bank – and the sector as a whole holds assets of more than €1 trillion. DZ Bank actually holds 35% of these assets, with a value of €410 billion, highlighting its dominance and accounting for its ranking as the fourth largest bank in Germany. So we can see that whilst acting as a central bank for business flows, particularly the international business flows of the cooperative banks, these two banks also operate large banking operations on their own account. Since the banks are cooperative in structure a large proportion of their customers are members of the bank, although not all of them, and they operate the concept of pooled money, which stood them in good stead during the Financial Crisis. Having said this, though, Germany operates a two-tier deposit protection scheme, with an additional scheme applying to cooperative banks, guaranteeing 100% of deposits, underlining the safety and attractiveness of these institutions for the retail customer. The products offered by the cooperative banks focus primarily on retail savings and loans, including mortgages, but in line with the universality idea they will also offer insurance, asset management and investment products, along with corporate and investment banking products to the institutional market, albeit typically at the smaller end of the spectrum.

Thinking about how these cash flows will translate into financial market exposures, we can expect to see them most actively in the money markets, as they manage the flows of their customer base, with some long-term funding and structured product presence as they look at the long end of their loan book. As we have said they quite often channel their exposures through the two central banks so it is from these names that we can expect to see a broad range of market exposures, encompassing capital markets, foreign exchange and derivatives as well as the core exposures.

Savings and Landesbanks

By business volume this is the largest sector of the German banking industry. Savings banks are retail-oriented banks, offering the typical range of savings and loan products. Whilst their primary focus is retail they also cover the smaller corporate market, and offer a lot of services to the self-employed. The Landesbanks are regional banks falling under state law that until July 2005 carried government guarantees. Since then they are limited liability companies, but with a large proportion of state ownership as shareholder. These banks form part of the network of savings banks across Germany, with the Landesbanks being the regional central banks for these firms. Since they lost their government guarantees they have faced problems in the markets, including the need for public bailout funds, such as were given to Landesbank Sachsen AG; more recently EU approval has been given for bailout funds to be given to LBBW, the largest of these banks. This approval was granted on condition that the bank cut its balance sheet by 40% and reorganized its internal management. This was necessary for the bank to prove itself viable and therefore eligible for bailout funds and this is at the heart of what many see as being the problem facing the Landesbanks: whether they are still financially viable in today's markets.

When some Landesbanks first started to experience liquidity problems it was assumed that the savings banks that are their members would be the ones to recapitalize them, but this proved not to be necessarily true. Savings banks in Bavaria and Schleswig-Holstein decided not to raise funds for their Landesbanks, whilst those in Baden-Württermburg took the opposite view. Since this region is covered by LBBW this may prove to be a very costly decision for them, with the state agreeing to inject €5 billion into the bank in April 2009. We should remember though that despite the bad headlines that have come out since 2008, not all Landesbanks are in difficulty – some even managed to record profits in 2008, and the savings bank sector as a whole is a very healthy one. In 2008 the 438 German savings banks managed to record billion euro profits and increase their balance sheets to €1.071 trillion whilst many other banks were posting losses.[6] However some Landesbanks have adopted a far more international profile over the past few years, and it is thought that this is a key factor to their problems. There have also been some scandals, including an ongoing investigation into executives at LBBW for involvement in improperly investing in US mortgage bonds, so the bank is under attack from many directions. Some of these banks are also being mentioned in relation to involvement in derivative deals, taking the risk of Greece in the credit derivative market, which has proven to be a highly speculative and unprofitable trade for them as Greece faces its own significant financial crises. So for these various reasons the future for these Landesbanks is looking very uncertain, particularly as there have been many calls for mergers between them to improve their efficiency. Some people have even questioned whether they are necessary at all in the markets or are fulfilling a function that could be taken over by one single entity as opposed to seven regional ones. Since an agreement has now been approved to facilitate these mergers we are likely to see considerable change, which is probably going to be good news for the commercial banks like Deutsche and Commerzbank who can see business opportunities arising here.

It is unusual for a country to have a banking system that is so dominated internationally by such a small number of firms. This is probably because the German banking industry as a whole is predominantly a very domestic one, and many of the institutions we have looked at, particularly the savings and cooperative banks, will not be well-known outside of Germany. Recent events within the Landesbanks may well serve to strengthen this domestic focus. Having said that, the banks that we do see on the international stage are very successful. There have been many periods when Deutsche Bank in particular has been not only one of the largest banks but also one of the most active in all areas of financial markets.

---

[6] Deutsche Sparkassen-und Giroverbund.

11
USA

Banking in the US is, by dint of its relatively shorter history, going to be a newer industry than some of the other countries that we have considered, but what it lacks in depth of history it more than compensates for in its contribution to the internationalization of the industry and its influence.

Before 1780 there was not really a banking industry in America. For a start the Currency Act of 1764 forbade colonies such as America to print or circulate their own money; it was an Act passed in response to the British parliament seeing more and more bills of trade circulating, becoming a de facto currency, but with fluctuating values as changes in the economic conditions affected the names attached to these bills. So to regularize things this Act was passed to prevent the logical development from trade bill to banks issuing currency. Of course there is also the matter that these notes were not producing any income for any UK lenders or taxes for the government which may have had an influence on the government's actions. This Act coupled with the Sugar Act, a law passed increasing duty on non British goods imported to the colonies, were spurs to the unrest that led to the Revolutionary War but inhibited the development of a banking system. A currency was issued at this time, known as the Continental, that was meant to be used to raise money for the war, but it was produced in such quantities that its value became negligible. However in 1780 we can see the very first forerunner of a central bank, the Bank of Pennsylvania, that was established primarily to fulfil this function of raising funds for the war. This bank was then superseded the following year by the Bank of North America, modelled on the Bank of England, and designed to carry out the functions of issuing currency and regulating the market that were beginning to emerge in the UK. Then in 1791 came the creation of the First Bank of the United States, which was initiated by Congress but set up not as an agency but rather being established as the largest corporation in the America, and therefore dominated by the influences of industry and banking. This is why the bank found itself with a lot of opposition and finally led to its charter not being renewed in 1811.

Around this time we can really begin to see how the industry was building up. Banks were being created in various states, amongst them the Bank of New York in 1784, a name still in today's market, the Bank of Massachusetts in 1783, which formed one of the earliest parts of what is now Bank of America, and in 1799 The Manhattan Company, one half of the union that became Chase Manhattan, ultimately becoming part of JPMorgan Chase. So we can start to trace the roots of present-day banking back more than 200 years. At this time there were also many savings institutions in states beyond the obvious northeast coastal ones with their trade links, such as Kentucky and Maryland. These savings banks did not have the business reach of the state banks but instead focused on more local cash flows and encouraging individual savings. We can equate this to the idea of city and regional banks that we have seen in other countries, but we do also need to remember the size of this country which, even more than somewhere like England, would naturally have caused geographical segmentation.

In 1816 another attempt at creating a central bank was made with the Second Bank of the United States. Unfortunately this was only marginally more successful than the first – its charter lasted 20 years but was then not renewed in 1836, which left the US without a central bank for the next 73 years. During the period in which the central bank did exist the banking industry moved on by leaps and bounds. By 1820 there were 266 banks in 23 states.[1] Unfortunately we also saw our first real bank failure, the Merrimack Bank of Massachusetts, and as we will see this was not to be the last. During the next decade there was a period of retrenchment but this was temporary as by 1840 there were 702 banks. This may sound like a good development of the market until we remember that from 1836 there was no central bank. With no central bank, government of the banks was on a state-by-state basis, so of course standards varied, and there were severe problems with the issue of currency. In order to make loans the banks individually issued currency so that by 1860 there were more than 10,000 different banknotes in circulation. Along with this there was plenty of bank fraud, with banks being set up and issuing as many notes as they could before they then went out of business, so we have a pretty chaotic situation and, of course, between 1861 and 1865 a country in the midst of a civil war.

---

[1] Federal Reserve Bank Minneapolis, 2006.

In 1863 the National Banking Act was passed to try and bring some order to this market. This act introduced the idea of nationally chartered banks that would be authorized to issue currency. Banks that received the charter would be regulated by the newly established Comptroller of the Currency. These national banks would issue uniform banknotes and had to hold substantial reserves against the currency issued. These reserves would be government securities as in the event of a bank failure the reserves would be sold to cover the demands against the notes, and so these government securities would have the liquidity necessary to allow this. The first bank to apply for a charter was the Pittsburgh Trust and Savings Company which after the granting of the charter became First National Bank of Pittsburgh, today PNC Bank. To remove the banknotes of state banks from circulation the government passed a law in 1866 imposing a 10% tax on these notes, which resulted in a surge of applications for national bank status and the effective removal of the notes. It did not, however, mean that the state banks ceased to exist because despite being called national banks these banks could not create branch networks, unless allowed to do so by their home states, and they could not cross state lines. So there was still plenty of opportunity for other types of bank in the marketplace even if they did not issue currency. Therefore by 1920 there were more than 30,000 banks in the US – more than the rest of the world put together.

As we have already seen with the banks in Europe the end of the 19th and the beginning of the 20th centuries was a period of great unease in the banking industry, with many bank failures and runs on money, when depositors would swarm on a bank demanding return of their deposits for fear that the bank would fail – often causing just that to happen. In 1893 a banking panic threw the US into depression, followed by an even worse one in 1907 that led to the passing of the Aldrich-Vreeland Act. This established the National Monetary Commission to look into the state of banking and ultimately led to the establishment of the Federal Reserve System, the central bank that we know today. After the First World War there was a lot of speculation in the markets, with many observers fearing that this stock market speculation would prove dangerous to the banks; notable amongst these was Carter Glass, former Chairman of the House Committee on Banking and Currency, and subsequently Secretary of the Treasury. In 1929 they were proved right with the stock market crash of that year followed by the Great Depression and the ensuing banking crisis that lasted from 1929 to 1932. From this came the passing of the Glass-Steagall Act.

Box 11.1 The Glass-Steagall Act

This is the Act that, amongst other things, separated activities in US banking. It is still important for us today to understand why Glass-Steagall was passed, particularly since we hear so much talk of the concepts being reintroduced. Its intention was to shore up the banking industry and protect investor funds from market vagaries. The period of speculation of the 1920s showed up serious flaws in the universal banking model, not least that funds placed with a bank were being used by the banks to fund their speculative business, and so therefore the customers' funds were being exposed to greater risk than they believed to be the case through looking at the credit of the receiving bank. Under Glass-Steagall the Federal Deposit Insurance Corporation (FDIC) was established, offering depositor protection of up to $2500 – now this is $250,000 – and since this was a federal agency the risk came back to the government. This being the case the need to quantify this risk became more apparent and it was felt that by dividing the business model the government could have the clearest view of the exposure to depositors' funds. So we ended up with the divisions stating that commercial banks, investment banks and insurance companies should be separate from one another. The downside to this is as that as the 20th century evolved it was felt that this legislation was hindering the competitiveness of American banks, especially since the universal banking model seemed to be working so well in other countries, so the end of the century saw a lot of lobbying to repeal the law.

It also has to be said that by the 1980s many of the banks who wanted to be involved in this business were doing so through over-seas subsidiaries, finding ways to exploit loopholes, such as booking trades offshore, irrespective of where they were actually dealt. This became particularly clear as the decade saw a real move towards globalization of the markets, with many institutions such as stock exchanges opening themselves up to foreign membership, and the American banks did not want to be left behind and even hoped to take a leading role in this. So in the late 1980s there was some loosening of the Act with the commercial banks being allowed to create securities corporations within the banks that could carry out investment banking activities, and then eventually in 1999 the Gramm-Leach-Bliley Act was passed effectively repealing the Glass-Steagall Act. Just 10 years later the situation looks to be changing again. Following the Financial Crisis there have been widespread calls to reinstate the Act, and not just in the US. Many European countries have been considering instituting Glass-Steagall-like legislation to protect commercial and retail banking and restrict the activities of the 'too big to fail' banks. At the end of 2009 legislation was introduced into the House of Representatives to re-enact part of the Act, and in January 2010 President Obama proposed limiting the size and scope of banks to prevent a recurrence of the events of 2008, again reminiscent of Glass-Steagall. So it seems as though this Act will be still be discussed for some time to come and is not confined to the history books.

Interstate Banking

Another restriction in the US system, and one we have already touched on, was the restriction on interstate banking. This was a law passed in 1956[2] that prohibited a bank holding company registered in one state from acquiring a bank in another. This meant that banks were unable to spread themselves too thinly across the whole US, but the downside was that we inevitably saw that a tiered system of banking evolves reflecting the different pockets of wealth and liquidity around the US. The biggest winners were the banks on the northeast coast, the *money center* banks we will look at below. This restriction on interstate banks was lifted with an Act in 1994[3] which allowed mergers between adequately capitalized banks, and subject to restrictions on concentration of banking within the state. One of the first mergers to take place after this was Bank of America's acquisition of Illinois-based Continental Bank. This was the renamed Continental Illinois National Bank and Trust Company, which, in 1984 had been bailed out by the Fed and the FDIC since it was then considered 'too big to fail'. Up until Washington Mutual's failure in 2008 this was still the biggest bank failure in US history.

Bank Failures

Bank failure has unfortunately been a consistent theme in the US for the past 25 years. The period from 1986–95 was one of the blackest as this covered the Savings & Loan crisis, when we saw a staggering

---

[2] Bank Holding Company Act, 1956.
[3] Riegle-Neal Interstate Banking and Branch Efficiency Act (IBBEA), 1994.

1043 banks fail.[4] A Savings & Loan bank is a form of thrift institution whose primary business was financing home loans. These banks had been working in a difficult climate for quite some time, with a volatile and high interest rate environment in the 1970s and 1980s, along with a weaker economic situation and crash in real estate values, which all contributed to these banks running into problems. Many of them were also under-capitalized and under-regulated. These banks were covered by the Federal Savings and Loan Insurance Corporation (FSLIC) but this itself became insolvent in December 1986. A new agency, Financing Corporation (FICO), was then created to fund the FSLIC in 1987, and in 1989 another agency, Resolution Trust Corporation, was created to handle the failed banks in this area. Another financing arm, Resolution Funding Corporation (REFCORP), was created to raise money in the debt market to finance the activities of Resolution Trust. Both FICO and REFCORP were government-backed agencies but they had to pay a premium above the government's cost of funding to raise money, sometimes quite a significant one, with that premium representing the market's fear at the scale of the problem. The final cost of this crisis turned out to be $153 billion, with the taxpayer bearing the lion's share ($129 billion), although at the height of the crisis in the early 1990s it was feared that this could be as high as $500 billion. However this seems relatively small in relation to the $700 billion pledged to insure or purchase bank assets under the recent TARP[5] scheme.

The first decade of the 21st century started calmly but by the end of the decade we were in another banking crisis. The Table 11.1 shows the number of bank failures between 2000 and 2009.[6]

Embedded in the comparatively modest figure for 2008, modest that is by comparison with what happened in 2009, is the failure of Washington Mutual, the largest US Savings & Loan bank, which failed in September 2008. The FDIC promptly sold the banking subsidiaries of the holding company to JPMorgan Chase who immediately reopened them under their own branding. As of today, there is a legal case going through whereby the holding company is suing the FDIC for inappropriately seizing assets and selling them to JPMorgan Chase at too low a price, which, of course, is a claim that is being countersued by the bank.

---

[4] FDIC.
[5] Troubled Asset Relief Programme.
[6] FDIC.

Table 11.1   Failed US Banks 2000–2009

	Failed US Banks
2000	2
2001	4
2002	11
2003	3
2004	4
2005	0
2006	0
2007	3
2008	25
2009	140

Then in 2009 with the Financial Crisis we see a massive jump in bank failures, as we can see in Figure 11.1.

What may be even more worrying is that in January 2010 there were 15 failures with the number reaching 78 by the end of May, so we cannot even say that the worst is necessarily over, especially since, worryingly, in April 2010 we saw 23 bank failures, only one less than the peak of July 2009 when 24 banks went down. Obviously the economic situation has had a major part to play in this, with an increase in nonperforming assets on the banks' portfolios, but we also need to look at how the banking crisis has affected the liquidity of these banks and also consumer confidence. We spoke earlier of runs on banks and how they can push the firm over the edge, and this sort of activity happens when the public

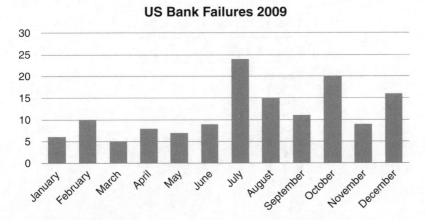

Figure 11.1   Bank Failures 2009

loses confidence not just in an individual bank but in the system as a whole, which could well describe the feelings we have at the end of the first decade of the 21st century.

THE FEDERAL RESERVE SYSTEM AND BANK REGULATION

We have spoken above about the FDIC and some other regulatory agencies of the 1980s and 90s, so we should take a look at the role of the central bank and the other regulators that are involved in the financial markets in the US.

The central bank, the Federal Reserve System, is established on a national and regional basis. At the national level is the Board of Governors, consisting of seven governors, including the Chairman, who is typically the public face of the bank. The governors are appointed by Congress, on a 14-year term, with the Chairman being appointed from amongst them on a renewable four-year term. The governors all sit on the Federal Open Market Committee (FOMC) which is the committee that determines monetary policy and its implementation as well as setting reserve requirements for the banks. Along with the governors there will be representatives from the Federal Reserve banks, the regional representation. The structure consists of 12 Federal Reserve banks, named for the cities in which they sit, and these are shown in Table 11.2.

There are also 25 branches of these regional banks and their purpose is to be even closer to their member banks. The local Federal Reserve banks

Table 11.2   Federal Reserve Banks

Federal Reserve Banks
Boston
New York
Philadelphia
Cleveland
Richmond
Atlanta
Chicago
St. Louis
Minneapolis
Kansas
Dallas
San Francisco

will interact with the members to carry out research or transactions, as required, to implement the policy of the FOMC, in other words the open market operations. As of 2009 there were 8039 banks in the US with about 30% of these being members of the Federal Reserve System. All national banks must be members of the system; state chartered banks can be members. The 5000 or so banks that are not members would include credit unions, and savings and loans, which we will discuss below.

This central bank structure is very different from the others that we have looked at so far, but their duties are not. Monetary policy and financial stability are again the two core pillars of the bank's responsibilities, and clearly regulation and supervision will form a part of this, along with other agencies such as the Comptroller of the Currency that still regulates the nationally chartered banks. One interesting thing about this central bank is that it does not create the currency. When we look at a five pound note in the UK we see the Bank of England printed on it, on a five euro note we see the ECB, but on a five dollar note we see Federal Reserve Note, because the note is not issued by the Federal Reserve Note but by the Department of the Treasury.

Regulation of a bank can be the responsibility of one of a number of agencies depending on the type of bank. As we saw in the US banks will have either a federal or a state charter and this, along with the type of business, will define how and by which agency they will be supervised. These different agencies include:

The Federal Reserve – overseeing members of the Federal Reserve System, e. g. national banks and some state-chartered banks.
Comptroller of the Currency – specifically overseeing national banks.
FDIC – overseeing non member deposit-takers as they fall under the deposit guarantee scheme and so are a direct exposure to the agency.
Office of Thrift Supervision – looks at savings and loans, credit unions, etc.

It is unlikely that this will remain the same. As we have already said the end of 2009/beginning of 2010 has seen a couple of bills going through Senate and the House of Representatives proposing reform of this system. In the Senate the Dodd Bill has proposed amalgamating all of these offices into a single regulator, whilst the House Bill merges the Comptroller of the Currency and the Office of Thrift Supervision, so we are almost certain to see some reduction in the number of bank regulators.

Another agency involved in regulating financial markets is the Securities and Exchange Commission (SEC) that has regulated the securities industry since 1934. Their focus is on the firms involved in the securities industry, so, for example, the traditional definition of investment bank would have fitted perfectly into the model of the type of firm that comes under the SEC.

US BANKING IN THE PRESENT DAY

As we have seen the last few decades have brought in some major changes to the US banking industry – and more than a few crises that have had to be weathered. Finally we are going to take a look at some of the key structures that we will come across.

Money Center Banks and the larger banks

These are the largest commercial banks. Traditionally they have been primarily based in New York, and this is not by accident. One of the impacts of the restriction of interstate banking was the clustering of banks and therefore the uneven distribution of funds. If you look at the geography of wealth in the US you see that it is very heavily biased on the northeast coast. That is not to say that there is not wealth elsewhere in the country, nor high net worth individuals, what we are talking about here is the historic accumulation of wealth. This is why we see the dominance of the New York Stock Exchange over the other regional exchanges, why we see more of the New York Federal Reserve Bank than the others, why New York is the pre-eminent financial centre in the US. The industry has grown up around the wealth, in the same way that it has in London, Tokyo or any of our other major financial centres. Along with a strong domestic presence these banks also have a strong international presence, so it's not surprising that these will be the largest banks in the US. In the 1980s the *money center* banks were considered to be:

- Manufacturers Hanover Trust
- Chemical Bank
- Chase Manhattan
- JPMorgan

- Citicorp
- Bankers Trust
- Bank of America.

In the 21st century the first four of these are all part of one bank, JPMorgan Chase. Bankers Trust has been acquired by Deutsche, and only Citicorp and Bank of America remain close to how they were in the 1980s, although far expanded in terms of reach by dint of mergers and acquisitions, including an investment bank each, Salomon Smith Barney for Citigroup and Merrill Lynch for Bank of America. Today we also need to include Wells Fargo in this list since they are now one of the largest banks in the US.

Another feature of the *money center* banks is their commitment to nationwide banking, as opposed to the second-tier group of banks, the regionals, which tend to focus their attention in the region in which they are incorporated.

Traditionally the *money center* banks were commercial banks, but since the repeal of Glass-Steagall we would now definitely say that they are universal banks offering the full range of commercial and retail banking products, as well as providing investment banking to global institutions. So we are likely to see them active in most markets, trading, bringing deals to the markets for their clients, but also actively using the markets to fund their own requirements.

Regional Banks

These are banks that operate only in one state or region. They will offer loans, deposit facilities, credit cards, and all the normal range of products one would expect to see but remaining in a confined geographic location. This can be very successful for them as they do not have the international exposure of the *money center* banks. In fact, at one time Wachovia was the last remaining US bank to hold a top-quality triple A rating, for precisely this reason. The downside, of course, is that they are so tied in with their local economies that they are susceptible to systemic effects within that region. This is something we have definitely seen in 2009 and was probably a major contributor to Wachovia's downward change in fortunes and its acquisition by Wells Fargo. When we look at *Community Banks*, below, you might struggle to see the difference between these and regional banks, but this difference really lies in scope. The community banks are even more geographically limited. The regions covered by the regional banks can be far broader, incorporating whole states, and there is even a group of super-regionals that cross state lines, such as those operating in the region of New England, for example. The other thing that differentiates these banks is their size. Whilst not comparable to the *money center* banks these super-regionals will typically be top 100 companies, so carry large balance sheets.

Investment Banks

As we said in the earlier section on Investment Banking there are very few pure investment banks left in the market. However what we often see is the legacy of how investment banks were integrated into the universal banks. For example, it is JPMorgan that carries out the investment banking business of JPMorgan Chase, and Bank of America uses the brand Bank of America Merrill Lynch (which whilst not a snappy title nonetheless points to the acquisition of expertise), and so on. Goldman Sachs is the exception in that whilst it has a banking licence it appears to have chosen not to build a significant depositor base so far, but instead to stay true to its investment banking roots. The significance of the licence was to allow Goldman Sachs easy access to Fed bailout funding if required. This all comes down to the different relationships between central banks and commercial and investment banks. In the past when the division was clear cut we would always say that central banks would not bail out investment banks, but they would do their best to support commercial banks. Now since the distinction is blurred we cannot make this statement. By providing liquidity to Citigroup the Fed has supported its investment banking business along with the commercial and retail banking side, which brings us right back to the discussion on Glass-Steagall. One of the reasons that the bonuses paid by the banks in 2009/10 have caused so much fury is because these bonuses are based on profits that probably could not have been made if the banks had not been supported by the Fed. Irrespective of which side of the business made the most profit, the core question is would the bank have even existed if the Fed, and the other central banks working on behalf of their governments, had not done all they could to shore up the financial system? If the answer to this is no, as it certainly was for at least some of the major banks, then this raises a very difficult issue for the regulators, hence the calls for segregation of the business. It will be interesting to see how this pans out.

Community Banks

Community banks are defined by the FDIC as banks with less than $1 billion in assets and operate in restricted geographical areas, thereby embedding them in their local communities. This definition is not quite accurate as there are a number of community banks that hold assets of more than $1 billion, but their business model is still that of the classic community bank. Although these banks represent collectively only about 23% of the total assets of US banks, by number they represent more than 90%. In structure they can be thrift associations (savings and loans), independent banks, cooperatives, a variety of different forms, but what links them is their size and their business model. They have also shown themselves to be very vulnerable in this latest Financial Crisis by dint of these two factors: their relatively small size and geographical concentration. If we look at the number of bank failures in the southeast this will tell a story of how hard hit these communities have been in the recent recession. Community banks focus on retail and small business customers, offering products that really revolve around savings and loans, often home and farm loans. Since the deregulation of interstate banking and the growth of branches of the large banks this sector has faced increased competition and they have lost business to the large banks. Interestingly, though, a survey of community bank executives undertaken by Grant Thornton in 2003 and referenced by the FDIC shows that the banks themselves see their greatest competition as being other community banks, followed by credit unions and only then the large banks.[7] Community banks can be found all across the US and the chart in Figure 11.2 shows their distribution.[8]

When we spoke of the *money center* banks, representative of these large banks, we said that they were often seen in the financial markets to fund themselves; this is not the case with the community banks. Their funding tends to come predominantly from their depositors and funding from the Federal Home Loan Banks (FHLB) agency set up to facilitate the flow of mortgage funds.

Credit Unions

As we have seen in previous sections these financial institutions are not-for-profit cooperatives. In 2009 there were 7881 credit unions in the

---

[7] The Future of Banking in America, FDIC Banking Review, January 2005.

[8] Independent Community Bankers Association.

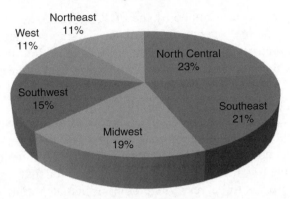

Figure 11.2   Geographic Location of Community Banks

US, of which 4847 were federally chartered and 3034 state-chartered. As with all the other banking institutions we have looked at we see again this choice of state or federal charter, with the choice of which to go for being determined by the union's individual objectives. These unions are created by groups of connected members. The connections can come through living or working within a specified geographical area, being employees of a certain trade or employer or maybe through religious affiliation. The scope of the membership criteria is set out in the charter of the union, often in very specific detail. In Table 11.3 shows a league table of the 10 largest credit unions.

Table 11.3   10 Largest Credit Unions

Credit Union	Asset size
Navy Federal Credit Union	$36.4 billion
State Employees Credit Union	$16.7 billion
Pentagon Federal Credit Union	$13 billion
Boeing Employees	$8.6 billion
Schoolsfirst Federal	$7.8 billion
The Golden 1*	$6 billion
Alliant*	$5.9 billion
Suncoast Schools Federal	$5.3 billion
American Airlines Federal	$5.1 billion
Security Service Federal	$5.1 billion

*These two credit unions are geographically based.

All of these are federal credit unions apart from Boeing Employees (BECU), The Golden 1 and Alliant. The Navy Federal CU is a very large union, the largest in the world, but there are also some very small ones, such as Destiny Credit Union, Wisconsin, that had assets of just $8508 in 2009.[9] Deposits in credit unions are predominantly insured by the National Credit Union Share Insurance Fund (NCUSIF) up to $100,000, although this was temporarily raised to $250,000 in 2008 through to December 2009. A small minority of credit unions are insured by American Share Insurance, a nonfederal insurer of credit unions. The products provided by the credit unions will again be typical retail products such as home and car loans, but there is also a strong emphasis on savings and, as we have seen before with credit unions, the idea of encouraging self-help.

One of the most noticeable things about banking in the US is not the variety of structure, which is very similar to what we have seen elsewhere, but the sheer number of banks, even today. On the one hand this will be a reflection of the size of the country and of the customer base, but in the 21st century you have to wonder whether all of these institutions are still necessary. The US has had by far the greatest number of bank failures, and, excluding the exceptional such as Washington Mutual, the bulk of the failures are of small, localized banks. Maybe this is where the problem lies. Often these banks fail very easily and so you have to question their capitalization, and since they are so regionally focused they are very susceptible to local economic change. The problem lies in how to restructure the market. The 'easy' solution is to merge the small, more vulnerable banks into the larger ones, but this may be like feeding the lions. If the natural buyers are banks such as Citigroup and Wells Fargo, we have already spoken a lot about the dangers of allowing these banks to become too big, so is it wise to make them even bigger or even to create new mega-banks? So maybe the solution is to keep them regionalized but just insist on better capitalization – a regulatory issue. Unfortunately this was said after the 1980s Savings & Loan crisis, and yet here we are just 20 years later facing another banking crisis. So perhaps the answer is something we have not yet thought of, but whatever it is let's hope we can find it before we have another banking crisis – possibly in another 20 years' time or, worryingly, considerably sooner.

---

[9] National Association of State Credit Union Supervisors.

12
Japan

Over recent decades the Japanese banking system has seen some great highs and lows. As we will see the glory days were in the 1980s followed by the series of crises of the 1990s. Going into the 21st century we can see the major position that Japan holds in financial markets. The Japanese yen is a major trading currency and the fourth largest central bank reserve currency, albeit well below the US dollar and the euro, but only marginally less than the British pound. Some of its banks are amongst the largest in the world, active in many international financial markets and we have even seen a Japanese bank taking a large stake in a US bank, so we can appreciate that we have an established banking community, but unfortunately one that has encountered some difficult times over the past decade, as we will see below. Once again we will be looking at the types of bank in the market to see if we can find similar institutions to the ones we have identified elsewhere, but we will also find some purely domestic Japanese structures that reflect the heart of the economy of Japan.

HISTORY

The Japanese banking industry really came into being at the end of the 19th century. Prior to then the firms that performed the banking functions were not really set up as banks at all and it was not until the Meiji period (1868–1912) that a more formal banking industry began to grow under the encouragement of the government through the Ministry of Finance. This was spurred on by the increase of international trade and the call for trading rights, but it was the administration at this time that looked to other countries – the UK, Germany, France – and copied much of their infrastructure in many ways, including the encouragement of trade and investment. By 1900 there were more than 2000 banks in Japan, primarily set up to finance trade. Two notable institutions to be created at this time were the Bank of Japan and Dai-Ichi Bank. The latter was originally named Dai-Ichi Kokuritsu Bank, meaning First National Bank, which is what it was – the first official bank to be established in Japan in 1873. At the time it was given the right to issue banknotes, although when the Bank of Japan was created in 1882 this function was moved to them, leaving Dai-Ichi Bank to operate as a commercial bank. However this set a precedent of banking that other investors were quick to follow in establishing new banks. There was an interesting relationship between the banks and the government in that at this time the government were large issuers of debt and it was the banks that became the biggest buyers of this debt. By 1900 the government had some ¥500 billion of government bonds outstanding, with another ¥200 billlion of military bonds. In the late 19th century securities exchanges were established in Tokyo and Osaka, and the debt became traded on these exchanges, so we can see the beginning of a well-formed capital market in place.

In 1897 the government created Nippon Kangyo Bank to finance agriculture and light industry, and then in 1902 they created Industrial Bank of Japan (IBJ) to finance heavy industry. Both banks were to provide medium and long-term funding, and to do this they were authorized to issue securities. In 1911 Nippon Kangyo had its charter reformed allowing it to take on the functions of a commercial bank, accepting deposits etc., whilst over time IBJ focused its attention more on investment banking-type activities, not just in Japan but overseas as well, lifting the international profile of the Japanese banks as well as financing Japanese industry and infrastructure such as the railways. Both of these banks were privatized after the Second World War. Also in this period just after the war we started to see the industry become more organized, with the city commercial banks building up their business with the larger corporations, whilst the smaller regional banks built their strength with the small to medium-sized customers.

In the 1980s the Japanese financial institutions went through what seemed to be their strongest period, building up a strong international presence and building their business not only with Japanese clients but many international ones, including some of the most blue-chip names such as the World Bank, and achieving primary dealer status for the various major government bonds. However it was also at this time that cracks began to show in how the banks did business. For a start, in 1985 restrictions on paying interest on deposits were removed, leaving the banks in the position of having to compete with one another for funds, which ended up costing them more and more. However instead of charging more for their loans the banks absorbed this reduction in profit and instead boosted this figure by selling stock that they had held for a long time and realizing profits. Unfortunately in Japan there is a cross-ownership mechanism, *keiretsu*, an alliance of corporations around a bank, that required the banks to buy back the shares to maintain these relationships, but at the new higher prices. To deal with any deficits in cash flow they borrowed heavily in the capital markets. At the end of the 1980s when new capital requirements were introduced by the Bank for International Settlements (BIS) the banks were hit heavily by not having enough capital and as an accommodation to them the BIS agreed that tier two capital should include so-called 'hidden assets' such as 45% of unrealized capital gains on the equity holdings of the banks. Whilst this enabled them to meet their capital requirements it also made them very vulnerable to stock market moves as a fall in value would reduce their capital holdings and leave them needing to urgently increase capital. If we think about what happened to the equity markets in 1987, the global stock market crash that many believe was partially triggered by inflated values in Japanese equity, and again just a few years later, the second Japanese crash in 1990, we can start to appreciate how vulnerable the banks were. This is one of the reasons that the 1990s proved so difficult for them. If we also take into account the collapse of the real estate market in Japan that had been heavily financed by these firms, either directly or indirectly through the banks' lending to non bank mortgage companies,[1] we can appreciate what a traumatic period this was. We must also mention again the cross-ownership idea, *kereitsu*, because this also had an impact. The typical shareholders of the banks were insurance companies, the corporations to whom the banks lent money on their corporate banking side, the employees of the bank and very likely the firms that were the customers of the banks and then other banks. This repetition of exposure proved to contribute to the systemic failures we were to see in the 1990s.

It seems that the trigger for these failures was the collapse of a securities house called Sanyo Securities in 1997. A securities house is a firm whose primary business is trading in securities, although through time some of them became increasingly involved in origination. Despite the fact that this was not a licensed deposit-taker such was the exposure of other firms to Sanyo Securities that this failure was followed, in the same year, by the fall of another securities house, Yamaichi, which had been one of the biggest and most internationally accepted of the Japanese

---

[1] These mortgage companies were often set up by the financial institutions and financed by the cooperative banks, and are known as *Jusen*.

securities houses, and two banks, Hokkaido Takushoku and Tokuyu City Bank. This was not the end of the story because the following year saw problems arising in two more high-profile banks, Long Term Credit Bank (LTCB) and Nippon Credit Bank that led to them being nationalized. LTCB was then sold to a consortium of foreign banks in 2000. A landmark deal in terms of increasing the involvement of foreign firms in the Japanese banking industry, it was renamed Shinsei Bank and went public in 2004. Nippon Credit Bank was bought by a consortium of Japanese firms and renamed Aozora Bank. Interestingly these two banks announced their intention to form a cooperation agreement in 2010 with a view to merging. By 2000 the central bank had dissolved 110 deposit-taking institutions and spent ¥86 trillion in dealing with problem loans, equivalent to 17% of Japan's GDP.[2] To cope with the current Financial Crisis the Bank of Japan has had to join with the other central banks in setting up liquidity arrangements to support the Japanese banking system, including a stock purchase scheme under which they agreed to buy some of these infamous shares held by the banks. To their credit no banks failed during the recent Financial Crisis, with the last bank to fail in Japan being Chubu Bank in 2002, although in December 2003 Ashikaga Bank was placed under special measures to prevent its collapse. However, interestingly, if you were to compare a list of Japanese bank names in 1985 with a list of the same in 2010, you would struggle to find many of the same names. Not only have the banks collapsed, but they have also merged, as we will see, and quite often have taken completely new names for the new merged identities.

MARKET STRUCTURE

In Japan there are various types of financial institutions, as we have already seen. These include city and regional banks and cooperatives such as Shinkin banks and agricultural banks. Then there are the securities houses that undertake investment banking business. We spoke a little earlier of the division between banks based on size and this structure still exists, along with a regional division, meaning that many of these firms offer a similar service but will differ in terms of the size of deals and also their international presence.

---

[2] The Financial Crisis in Japan in the 1990s: how the Bank of Japan responded and the lessons learnt, BIS, 2001.

City and Trust Banks

Following many mergers over recent decades there are now five city banks left which are registered with the Japanese Banking Association:

- Mizuho
- Mizuho Corporate Bank
- Sumitomo Mitsui
- Bank of Tokyo-Mitsubishi UFJ
- Resona Bank.

These are the full service commercial banks, although as we can see from the list above Mizuho separates its retail business from its corporate business by using two separate companies owned by the holding company. Resona Bank is also somewhat different from the others since this Osaka-based city bank focuses its attention more heavily on the retail and small to medium corporate business, leaving the other three to be the most high profile names in international Japanese banking, the mega-banks, equivalent to Deutsche Bank, JPMorgan Chase or Barclays. There are also another 19 banks which are authorized to carry out trust business. These are banks that, along with lending activities, also carry out asset management and pension-related businesses, including the servicing of these activities, which will include such things as custody and asset administration. These banks are listed in Table 12.1.[3]

At the end of 2009 two of these banks, Sumitomo Trust & Banking and Chuo Mitsui Trust Holdings, agreed a merger deal to be completed in 2011 which, if it completes, will create the fifth largest Japanese bank by assets. Amongst these 19 banks we will find three foreign banks, State Street, Bank of New York Mellon and Société Générale, who all have licences to carry out this type of business. Bank of New York Mellon and State Street offer asset management and servicing in Japan, which is their core business. Société Générale offers asset management, corporate and investment banking and private banking, but none of these banks are offering the full-service model. Only Citigroup, through Citibank Japan Limited, does this. They were the first foreign bank to change status to be authorized alongside the domestic Japanese names, as a Japanese entity, offering full-service products to both retail and corporate customers. This is a different status from the 59 foreign banks that are authorized to offer their international products in the Japanese

---

[3] Japanese Banking Association, 1 January 2010.

Table 12.1   Trust Banks

Japanese Trust Banks
Aozora Trust Bank
Orix Trust & Banking
Trust & Custody Services Bank
Shinkin Trust Bank
Shinsei Trust & Banking
State Street Trust & Banking
Sumitomo Trust & Banking
Société Générale Private Banking
Chuo Mitsui Trust & Banking
Chuo Mitsui Asset Trust & Banking
Nikko Citi Trust & Banking
JSF Trust & Banking
Japan Trustee Services Bank
The Master Trust Bank of Japan
Bank of New York Mellon Trust Bank Japan
Norinchukin Trust & Banking
Mitsui Trust & Banking
Nomura Trust & Banking
Mitsubishi UFJ Trust & Banking

market, but not to compete for the domestic business, such as the retail banking products, as they are not listed as Japanese entities. This is why there has been such a call for the Japanese market to deregulate further and allow more foreign involvement, either through allowing foreign ownership of Japanese banks or broadening the spectrum of products that can be offered by the foreign banks. Of course, if we think back to when we looked at banking in the UK we had to comment on the nationalist nature of this type of banking, with Santander's slow movement to rebranding as an example, so simply allowing foreign ownership will not necessarily change the face of banking in Japan.

These city and trust banks have been the ones primarily, but not exclusively, to benefit from the cash injections following the Financial Crisis, and in the case of Resona Bank prior to this, since they received government funding back in 2003. This has probably been a motivating factor in the merger discussions between Sumitomo and Chuo Mitsui, to create a more solid base, and we are likely to see more mergers in the coming years.

Regional Banks

The regional bank market is divided into two, with first and second-tier banks. As of 2010 there were 64 first-tier banks and 45 second-tier banks.

They work firmly in their local areas, helping to serve the economic needs of the region. Nationally there are 7500 branches of the 64 first-tier regionals so as a group they are highly visible in the banking system. Their focus is on individual and smaller corporate business, but some of them have built up an international presence as well. An unfortunate example of this is Aozora Bank which is listed as the largest creditor to Lehman Brothers, and also had an exposure of ¥12.4 billion to Bernie Madoff's ponzi scheme. A problem for the regional banks is that they have seen a fall in their traditional customer base over recent years, a situation that has affected their performance and stability, meaning that some have had to approach the central bank for liquidity funding and the market has had fears for some of their less well-performing loans.

Cooperative Banks

The biggest category of cooperative banks is the Shinkin banks, which operate as commercial banks, but in theory restrict their lending to their members. As of 2010 there were 281 Shinkin banks and their customer base, like that of the regional banks, is individuals and smaller corporate customers. As a way of supporting the network the Shinkin Central Bank (SCB) was established in 1950 to provide central banking services to its members. By consolidating in this way the SCB is able to more efficiently raise funds and is one of Japan's largest institutional investors. Through managing the individual Shinkin banks' supply and demand the SCB aims to stabilize the sector and achieve the best funding and investment rates. To this end in 1990 it established a subsidiary in London, Shinkin International, to raise the profile of the bank and carry out its international business, both in investment and fundraising. Since then this subsidiary has expanded its business model to carry out this function for other Japanese institutional clients as well as the core base.

Another cooperative institution is Norinchukin Bank, which was established in 1923 as the central bank for the agricultural coopera-tives. It is set up as a cooperative entity itself and has 4093 members comprising agricultural, fishery and forestry cooperatives, along with associated organizations. These are core elements of Japan's economy which is why they receive particular attention for their importance to the infrastructure of the economy. The bank is funded primarily through de-posits of its members but it also issues debt in the capital markets. They also invest in the securities markets to enhance returns and make loans to the cooperative members as part of the support network that is the over-riding principle behind the organization. The cooperative structure is set up with the members forming part of regional associations who offer, amongst other things, banking services through the bank system, and these associations are in turn connected to Norinchukin which operates at a national level as their central bank. These banking associations are JA, covering the agricultural cooperatives and JF Marine Bank, which covers fisheries. They have developed systems for deposit insurance and bankruptcy protection to help support and promote the cooperatives within their system, and JA bank has set up initiatives working with Mitsubishi UFJ Group to offer cash cards and ATM access. This is a model that is likely to develop further. All the services offered by these banks are rooted in protecting and developing the economy for those working within these core activities and so are having to respond to changes within the activities themselves that have impacted on the patterns of savings and loans coming through the cooperative bank systems.

Securities Houses

A securities house is like an investment bank although its original focus was more on trading and sales than origination. Over the years, though, the Japanese securities houses broadened the model to include more origination to raise their profile in the market. In the 1980s there were four major Japanese securities houses that made a great name for themselves internationally. These four were Nomura, Nikko, Daiwa and Yamaichi. Today, only one remains as an independent firm. We heard how Yamaichi failed in 1998, and then Daiwa and Nikko were also both bought up and integrated within other banks, following the pattern that we have seen elsewhere of integrating commercial and investment banking business. Nomura, though, is the name we still see today. Nomura Securities Co. was founded in 1925 as a spin-off from a bank, Osaka Nomura Bank. Since then it has established itself as a global player, building up strength through various acquisitions, including in recent times the acquisition of Lehman's Asia-Pacific franchise, along with some European and Middle Eastern business, although not the prime London business that was purchased by Barclays at the end of a bidding war with Nomura. Again, if we think back to the lists of primary dealers in the US, UK, Germany and France, we saw Nomura's name on these lists as pretty much the sole representative of the Japanese market. They offer a range of services to their customers from retail securities trade execution through to wholesale origination and full corporate finance services, with – as their roots would suggest – a strong base in trading and sales, and so they fit perfectly into the profile of investment bank that we discussed earlier. In 1993 they established Nomura Trust & Banking, offering a full range of banking services to its Japanese customer base, transforming it into the universal bank model, although if we look at the bias of Nomura's business, we will see that it is heavily weighted on the investment banking side.

Of the types of bank that we have discussed here it will be Nomura and the Big Three city banks that will be the most prominent in international financial markets, but that does not mean that the others will be invisible. They will certainly use the financial markets to raise funds and invest their considerable assets, but their focus will be far more on the side of servicing their domestic client base needs. So we will see them in the FX markets, given the strong import-export business in Japan, and we will see them looking to raise and invest funds efficiently, hence their use of the central bank structures to improve this. For Nomura and the Big Three there is also the strong history of trading that means we will see them in equity and debt markets, and whilst their native strength will be in Japanese names their work over the past decades has meant that they are often involved in international markets.

REGULATION

In Japan there are a number of organizations that have been involved in regulating banking and financial markets. As with all the other central banks that we have looked at so far the Bank of Japan concerns itself primarily with monetary policy and financial stability, meaning that they have to interact, and again intervene if necessary, to support their banks. Since the Financial Crisis we have seen them initiating special measures to aid the liquidity situation in Japanese banking, such as the stock purchase scheme that we spoke of earlier. It was only in 1998 with the passing of the Banking Act of that year that the Bank of Japan moved towards independence. In the past it had often been claimed that both the Bank of Japan and the Ministry of Finance were very heavily politically influenced, but under this Act it was made clear that the central bank was expected to act independently and transparently and without undue political influence. Until the 1990s the Ministry of Finance took primary responsibility for supervision of financial markets and the institutions that were active in these markets, but in the interests of independence 1998 saw the establishment of the Financial Services Agency. This agency was gradually given responsibility for standard setting and supervision, along with financial crime prevention (such as anti-money laundering and insider trading). Securities and futures were put under a separate regulator, the Securities and Exchange Surveillance Commission. The Commission describes itself as a watchdog maintaining daily surveillance over the market, looking for unusual movements and following up on reports from the industry and the public.

The Bank of Japan follows a pattern rather similar to that of the Bundesbank in that it makes regular inspections of the institutions holding accounts with them, but also dedicates a lot of time to analysing reports to look for signs of weakness in the banking system. It is not only banks that hold accounts with the central bank but also other financial institutions, so they are able to have a broad overview of the marketplace. Their role as lender of last resort has come under a lot of scrutiny over the past decades, as they were criticized for not offering this facility to Sanyo Securities back in 1998, a criticism that is eerily reminiscent of that made against the US Federal Reserve Bank in connection with Lehman Brothers. Up until 2005 Japan offered 100% deposit insurance, but since then this has been reduced to ¥10 million, which is offered through the Deposit Insurance Corporation of Japan. As we mentioned earlier, there have been no bank failures in Japan since 2003, but 2008 did see ¥1.7 billion of asset purchases, and a grant of ¥260 billion, again to Ashikaga Bank, to shore up the Japanese banking system.

The banking sector in Japan is very similar to those we have seen elsewhere with the mixture of banks and the dominance of an elite group of universal banks, at least in the international perspective. The market away from these, though, falls into a model that is much compartmentalized, with banks being licensed for very specific roles. It is also a particularly domestically dominated market, with, as we have seen, relatively little foreign exposure in the very heart of the industry. Foreign involvement is focused more on the corporate side than the retail side, but then this is the picture that we have seen in the other countries that we have looked at, showing that the industry still has far to go to become truly an international marketplace at all levels.

13

China

In 2009 combined assets of banks in China stood at RMB 78 trillion (approx $11.6 trillion), an increase of 26% on the previous year.[1] This is an indication of the size and importance of banking in this area. However the nature of the industry is very different in China from the other countries that we have looked at. This lies primarily in the level of government ownership of the industry. RMB 40.1 trillion of these assets are held by the majority state-owned commercial banks, illustrating their dominance in the market. This, though, is a moving landscape, and the past two decades have seen great changes in banking in this country, with more likely to follow. Given the strength and increasing importance of the economy, and the speed with which it appears to have recovered from the effects of the global recession of the end of the first decade of the 21st century, the continuing development of this economy will be carefully monitored. This is likely to increase the international significance of the banking industry in China.

HISTORY

China has a long history of banking, with paper currency first being seen in China in 1024, in Sichuan. This is not something that we have seen in the other countries that we have looked at, so the logical conclusion is that if there was evidence of paper money, so there must have been some form of banking industry. However, we cannot really find a recognizable structure of currency available beyond this until quite a few centuries later, bringing it in line with what we have seen elsewhere. If we go forward to the 18th and 19th centuries and look at the province of Shanxi we will find the Piaohao (Shanxi banks). Once again we will see links with trade driving the business of banking and in this region we can pick up on the influence of one particular company, Xiyuecheng Dye Company of Pingyao, which by 1823 was so well-established in the world of financing that the owners effectively changed their business

---
[1] China Banking Regulatory Commission.

plan to focus on banking, and set up a network across China – effectively a branch network. This is very reminiscent of the stories of the merchant bankers we came across in the UK, apart from the establishing of branches which had never really been part of the British model. At the same time we also find the Chinese equivalent of the provincial banks, the qianzhuang. These banks were set up to cover small regional areas and worked in close contact with the merchants, and by the 1890s there were some 10,000 of these around China.

So the latter half of the 19th century in China, as elsewhere, was a time of great strides forward for the creation of the business of banking. As international trade increased we have spoken of banks moving to set up branches in other countries, and China was a prime location. The first foreign bank to open in China was the Bombay-based British Oriental Banking Corporation in 1847. This was followed by others but in 1865 we saw probably the most significant, the opening of the Hong Kong & Shanghai Banking Corporation (HSBC), which was the largest foreign bank in China. Whilst British banks dominated the Chinese market there were also banks from other countries and by the end of the century the international banking community comprised banks from Britain, France, Germany, Japan and Russia. These banks were not regulated by the Chinese government and so they were free to issue banknotes, accept deposits, set up banking relationships with the qianzhuang as they chose, which all in all led to a very fragmented marketplace.

At the end of the century we also saw more development of the domestic banks, with the first national Chinese bank opening in 1897 – Imperial Bank of China, later to become the Commercial Bank of China after the Xinhai revolution. We also saw the establishment of the first Chinese Central bank in 1905, the Bank of the Board of Revenue (changed to Great Qing Government Bank in 1908, and then Bank of China after the revolution), and this bank was then given exclusive rights to issue banknotes to try and bring some order into the currency in circulation. In 1928 the Central Bank of China was created and the business model of the Bank of China was changed: this was now to focus on foreign exchange, working with a government charter to stabilize the currency and manage foreign exchange flows.

So at this point we can actually see a somewhat similar environment to that in other countries, with a central bank and numerous independent banks, albeit probably not as advanced in form as we might have seen in some other countries, but the framework was similar. However we then saw a massive change when in 1935 the government seized control of 70 banks – known as the Chinese Banking Coup. Putting these banks into state hands completely changed the market environment as, under the direction of the state, the banks became very inward-looking and invested heavily in domestic industry, so tying their fortunes to those of the domestic economy. Following the Second World War the banking system was set up on the lines of the Soviet model. A new central bank was established in 1948, the People's Bank of China (PBOC) which was made through a combination of three commercial banks, and whilst we call this a central bank in actual fact many of its functions in these early decades were those of a commercial bank rather than the roles of central banks that we have looked at elsewhere. The commercial banks, which had either been taken over or integrated within the structure of the PBOC, worked under direction and so had no incentive to be competitive with another. Instead they were assigned functions according to location, requirements, etc., so the core of the industry was stunted in how it could develop through most of the 20th century, until after the Cultural Revolution 1966–76, when we started to see the introduction of some banking reforms. One of the first of these was the separation of the Big Four commercial banks from the PBOC. These banks are the four cornerstones of the Chinese Banking industry:

- Bank of China
- China Construction Bank (CCB)
- Agricultural Bank of China, and
- Industrial and Commercial Bank of China (ICBC).

Originally these banks were restricted to offering their services in the areas suggested by their names, but over time the restrictions were lifted allowing them to compete with one another for loans and deposits, creating more of a natural market. An important part of this was the change in the law that came about with the passing of the 1995 Commercial Bank Law of China. This officially defined the Big Four as commercial banks and promoted the idea that they should be run as commercial enterprises rather than instruments for policy lending, and so opened the door to this new competitive industry. The mid-1990s also saw the establishment of a number of new banks, owned primarily by institutional investors, again adding to the competitive landscape, with another change being the establishment of the local city cooperative banks. In 2010 the Chinese banking industry consisted of the mix of institutions shown in Table 13.1.

Table 13.1   Chinese Banking Industry

Majority state-owned banks*	5
Privately owned commercial banks**	12
City Cooperative banks	90

*this includes the Big Four we have already discussed and Bank of Communications Co. Ltd.
**this can include banks where the government also has a majority holding, although the original idea was for institutional ownership.

Banks in China are also restricted in the types of business they can operate, so there is a sort of Glass-Steagall law in play. In 1995 we saw the opening of the first real investment bank, China International Capital Corporation Limited, which was formed as a joint venture between Chinese and foreign financial institutions, notably China Construction Bank and Morgan Stanley. This bank carries out the typical investment banking functions of advisory, origination and trading and building up business and reputation for bringing equity and debt deals to the markets domestically and internationally.

Foreign Ownership of Chinese Banks

The 1990s saw the government first starting to allow foreign banks entry into this market, albeit on a very limited basis. Firstly by allowing a limited amount of deposit and loan business in local currency in a specially defined economic zone, then by granting licences to carry out more local business, and to allow a very limited amount of foreign ownership of domestic banks. This began in 1996 when Asian Development Bank (ADB), the supranational agency, bought a 1.9% stake in China Everbright Bank Co. Ltd. This was followed by more small purchases but really they were rather insignificant owing to the government restrictions. However this was to change when China joined the World Trade Organization in December 2001 and made undertakings agreeing to open up the banking industry to foreign involvement. This is why in the first half of the 21st century we saw this business beginning to pick up. In 2003 the state issued guidelines to encourage international share purchases, saying that foreigners could buy up to 25% of a domestic bank, with any single investor being allowed to hold up to 20%. If a bank goes public, which is another pattern that we have seen in recent years, then this restriction no longer applies, so we have witnessed

Chinese banks bringing IPOs[2] in various markets, often to allow ease of investment into the banks. This does, though, affect how the banks are defined. If we think about CICC as an example we said that Morgan Stanley was a major investor, actually owning 34.3% of the company. In this instance because the bank has such a high foreign ownership stake the bank can no longer be defined as domestic but is now classified as a joint venture. One of the most significant purchases was HSBC taking a 19.9% stake in Bank of Communications, and along with this it also secured the rights to double its holding when regulations permitted. This started the partial privatization of the Big Four, with Bank of America, RBS and Goldman Sachs, amongst others, taking stakes in these banks.

We do have an interesting side note to this story, though, which is an unexpected trend that seemed to be developing in 2009. This was a lessening of foreign investment and an increase in state-entity investment. China has a very large sovereign wealth fund that we will discuss later in this book and we saw the domestic arm of this fund increasing its share holdings in the banks. For example, both UBS and RBS sold their entire stakes in Bank of China, whilst others such as Goldman Sachs, Allianz – the German insurance company – and American Express sold part of their holdings in the Hong Kong listed shares of ICBC. Maybe the most significant of these was Bank of America's reduction in its holding of China Construction Bank from 19.1%, which had been near the threshold and therefore signalling the bank's desire to take on a greater stake as deregulation advanced, to a new level of less than 17%. The reasons for these sales could well be commercially motivated, but it raises an interesting question about how the internationalization of banking in China will continue in the 21st century.

BANKING SERVICES

When we look at the commercial banking services offered by these Chinese banks we tend to see a smaller range of products on offer than we have seen in other countries. They will offer a range of deposits and loans, for various purposes, including home loans, but without the variety of structure that can be seen in the financial products offered by institutions of other countries. The market, at the moment, does not have this variety of savings structures and loan repayment and interest patterns that may be demanded in more competitive markets, but the

---

[2] Initial Public Offerings.

banks are developing their product range, particularly in light of the changing population. An example of this can be seen in wealth management and private banking. The country does have an increasing number of HNWIs[3] and the banks are beginning to offer wealth management products to this growing marketplace. You can also see a number of FX and precious metal products for retail customers, including trading products, again to reflect a changing culture. For the corporate customers they will offer the larger value loans and deposits, but also a large range of products to facilitate international trade, such as import-export financing, leasing, etc. In other words, again the banks tailor and publicize their products to match the business needs of their customers in this very export-biased marketplace.

We are starting to see the larger banks increasingly in the overseas markets on a global basis, not just in Asia, through branches and subsidiaries. We said earlier that the commercial banks were limited in the way in which they could be involved on the investment banking side, but ICBC is the first of these commercial banks to try and build up this business. Their focus is on M&A and the advisory side of the business rather than origination and trading, leaving these activities traditionally to the investment banks. These investment banks are predominantly joint ventures with foreign firms but their existence is subject to approval from the authorities which tends to be only sporadically granted. We are likely to see an increase in the number of these joint ventures, such as Deutsche's venture with Shanxi Securities, to form Zhong De Securities Company Limited, which was announced in July 2009, as these joint ventures can carry benefits that would not be available to foreign banks in their own right. These benefits would include things like receiving licences to carry out more activities than would be granted to a foreign firm. The investment banking industry has already increased substantially, with more Chinese companies opting to raise money onshore than offshore in 2009, a situation very different from just a few years previously, but potentially the industry can go far further. The regulators, though, have kept strict control on the granting of licences, with still more uncertainty as to how long their willingness to further open the market would continue. So, the large international banks are actively looking for partners in 2010 whilst the opportunity is there.

---

[3] High Net Worth Individuals.

14
Islamic Finance Institutions

We spoke earlier about usury and how this was banned by the church leading to the Italian banks in the 14th century focusing their banking models on the trading of bills of exchange to avoid being accused of usury. This is defined as the charging of excessive interest, and comes up again when we look at Islamic banking, which also prohibits usury, known as *riba*, and from this has grown a model of banking that differs fundamentally from those we have looked at in how the products are structured.

Islamic banking is more than just prohibiting excessive interest. Its principles come from the Shari'ah, the law of Islam, and so this form of banking has been around for centuries. However it was in the 1970s that we started to see the development of the market as we know it today. The market is centred on the Middle East but there are many pockets of activity elsewhere, and the UK has the 8th largest centre for Islamic banking in 2009, according to the DTI.[1] The largest Islamic bank is Al-Rajhi bank in Saudi Arabia, but then six of the rest of the top ten banks are based in Iran. Table 14.1 shows the top 10 Islamic banks, by asset size, in 2009.[2]

If we think back to when we spoke about the largest bank in the world by asset size, Royal Bank of Scotland, with assets of $3.5 trillion, Al-Rajhi looks very small by comparison, but this is a growing sector, with an estimated size in the industry of over $750 billion, and a relatively small geographical concentration, so really a like-for-like comparison is not possible.

The principles of Islamic banking are based on an understanding of the scriptures and to ensure this understanding the financial institutions will use Shari'ah boards to ensure their compliance. These are boards comprising three or more Muslim scholars who determine whether the activities of the bank adhere to the principles. These boards will typically include member(s) from one of the organizations that sets standards for

---

[1] Department for Trade and Industry.
[2] The Asian Banker, 2009.

Table 14.1   10 Largest Islamic Banks

	Country	Assets $million
Al-Rajhi Bank	Saudi Arabia	43,981
Bank Mellat	Iran	39,781
Bank Saderat	Iran	39,319
Kuwait Finance House	Kuwait	38,209
Bank Tejerat	Iran	29,885
Bank Sepah	Iran	23,625
Dubai Islamic Bank	UAE	23,153
Bank Maskan	Iran	17,632
Agricultural Bank of Iran	Iran	16,675
Abu Dhabi Islamic Bank	UAE	13,944

this industry, a sort of trade association such as we discussed earlier when talking of the ACI and ICMA, a notable one of these being the Islamic Financial Services Board (IFSB) in Malaysia. The core ideas behind this form of banking include the following:

- prohibition of excessive interest
- sharing of risk
- no speculation
- ethical investment: no investment in anything related to unacceptable activities such as pornography, gambling, pork products, weapons, alcohol and conventional banking.

In order to respect these restrictions and yet still offer financial services to their customers the Islamic banking institutions have developed a range of Shari'ah compliant products and services that form the basis of their offering to their clients. At the heart of this is the need to have a flow of funds between banks and customers, so there are a number of ways in which the bank can accommodate this whilst staying within the accepted principles.

If we look first of all at the core business of savings and borrowings we will find Shari'ah compliant savings accounts. Sometimes when you look at these you will see an interest rate quoted, but this is not what it appears to be. Money, as a commodity, is deemed to have no intrinsic value of its own and so it cannot earn interest, and yet the banks need to attract funds and also to be competitive with one another in today's marketplace. Therefore funds that are placed with the bank will receive a return, based on the profit made by the institution and so not directly related to the funds placed on deposit with the bank. The interest rate that is quoted will just be a guide to how much the funds could earn, but is not saying that this is the rate your actual deposit will achieve. In some cases, such as for Islamic banking operations in the UK, the quoting of this rate is a legal requirement, but the distinction remains that the rate and the deposit are not intrinsically linked.

If a client wants to borrow money there are several ways in which this can be done. The two most common are *murabahah* (cost plus sale) and *Ijara* (leasing). If a customer wants to buy a car, using the murabahah model, the bank will buy the car on the customer's behalf and then sell it to the customer at a pre-agreed premium. The payment can then be managed by instalments and once the final payment has been made the car is owned by the customer. Under an ijara agreement the car is leased to the customer at fluctuating rates according to the changing values of the car. Typically there will be an element of the leasing payment that goes towards a final purchase of the car, and once it has been fully paid ownership will transfer to the customer. These arrangements can be used for the financing of any tangible assets. Trying to find an acceptable equivalent of an overdraft facility is more difficult, but if a customer does have need of this kind of financing it is possible using the principle of *tawarruq*, a sort of reverse murabahah. An example of this would be a bank buying something such as a precious metal on behalf of the customer that they would sell to them at a pre-agreed price, and agreeing a payment schedule, just as we have seen before. The customer, though, wanted cash not a commodity and so the bank will immediately sell the commodity on the customer's behalf, and credit the funds to their account, giving them the liquidity they required. This does not exactly mimic the cash flow of a typical overdraft but it does allow non asset-based borrowing.

There is also an insurance product, *takaful,* that is based on the idea of pooled resources and shared responsibility with contributions being pooled and the liabilities shared amongst the members. Contributions, therefore, have to be sufficient to meet the expected exposures of the group so this eliminates uncertainty and allows for the idea of mutual support, as well as including a certain portion that must be perceived as a gift in order to fulfil the requirement of helping one another in times of need. The rest is the contribution to this joint pool, which represents the total extent to which liabilities can be covered so there is no uncertainty.

CAPITAL MARKETS AND DERIVATIVES

If we look at wholesale institutional borrowing, we can see some asset-based financing that is very much the same as we have in the examples above, just on a larger scale, such as arranging loans for property. However there are some issues when it comes to creating capital market products and managing risk. In terms of equity, as long as the companies are not involved in the unacceptable activities the concept of buying shares is fundamentally fine, since this represents a shared risk proposition. However debt financing is trickier, because of the issue of interest, but today there is an active sukuk market, being the nearest thing to the bond market. A sukuk is not defined in the same way as a bond, as a debt of the issuer, instead it is a certificate based on assets with revenue flows linked to the flows on the assets. This is a growing market – in 2009 we saw the issue of a sukuk for Saudi Electric Company of SAR 7 billion ($1.7 billion equivalent), the largest deal to date, and we have had a number of major international borrowers coming to this market.

So we can see that here we have the basics of a capital market but derivatives are more problematic. Under Islamic law gambling – *gharar* – is forbidden, and this translates to the purchase or sale of something that may not exist. Similarly, speculation – *maysir* – is also forbidden. So if we think about futures contracts where commonly people buy or sell a contract on a notional underlying with the intention of trading out before the expiration of the contract, this is clearly not acceptable. Similarly if we look at an option contract, where the buyer of the option pays the premium for the right to buy or sell, and if the option expires unexercised will lose all their 'investment' in the premium, which again would not be acceptable. This is because by paying the premium the buyer was only buying the right to do something, not the underlying commodity, and so this was speculating on a future movement, maysir. Even FX forwards can be difficult to justify because of the way they are calculated, looking at the interest rate differentials in the two currencies, although forward FX is carried out by some Islamic banks. This is because there is a need for risk management tools, as prudence is advocated in Islamic law, particularly given the amount of international trade and exposures likely to be taken, and so again we need to find Shari'ah compliant alternatives. One such alternative is *salam*, where a deal is struck today to deliver a commodity at a point in the future. The full payment must be made at the time the trade is struck and the commodity cannot be specific but must be fungible, for example US dollars as a currency rather than specific dollar bills. This is very different from conventional forwards where payment is made at the conclusion of the deal rather than the beginning. Another example is an *arbun* contract, where a buyer commits to a deal on a future date and makes a payment, like a deposit. If they then pull out the deposit is lost, but if the deal goes through the deposit is deducted from the final purchase price. This is like an option but the crucial difference is that the premium element is inherently linked with the cost of the asset and not just with the right to do something and so this deal is not speculating on future movements.

Islamic banking has grown in popularity not just in the Muslim world but also elsewhere and part of that may be a reaction against what some see as the excessive profitability and influence of conventional banking, so at the beginning of the 21st century it has received a lot of exposure. The effect of this has been to focus more attention on what is allowed as opposed to what is not allowed, in other words we are seeing further developments in the industry as it tries to find ways to manage cash flows without compromising the integrity of Shari'ah.

15

Microfinance Institutions

Microfinance is the business of providing financial services to the poorest people, and the Microfinance institutions (MFIs) are the institutions that do this on a global basis. Microfinance began after the Second World War, with the support of government and supranational agencies, but developed by the initiation of non government organizations (NGOs). There is a key difference between microcredit and Microfinance. Microcredit is about providing finance to the poor, either by loan or by grant to the poorest. Microfinance aims to go beyond the limits of pure lending to the poor. It aims to provide more financial services as required to help to create a financial infrastructure. Microfinance institutions can typically offer lending of course, but also other products including home loans, savings, insurance and money transfer. All in all these will be the sort of services that their customers might require and very similar to those we find in mainstream banking but just on a completely different scale. The key difference comes from the customer base, which, as we keep seeing, will affect the cash flows through the firm. The customers of the MFI are those living below or near the poverty line, in some of the poorest areas in the world. The loans they make will not be for large sums, but often for extremely small amounts. They will not make house loans based on a multiple of earnings as their customers will often not have regular incomes, so their whole business model has to be adjusted. Traditionally, lending through the MFIs will be to finance entrepreneurial activities, to allow their customers to take up business activities that may require a little seed money. However, in 2010 the pattern is changing somewhat, and the firms are also seeing some borrowers of funds for consumer goods, but the underlying ethos is still to fund these customers to help themselves.

Grameen Bank of Bangladesh is generally considered to be the first example of an institution set up specifically to provide these services. It was established in 1976, becoming a bank in 1983 using the cooperative structure, 95% owned by its customers and 5% by the government. Grameen Bank operates in rural areas, dealing with the typical Microfinance customer, with 97% of their customer base being women. They also operate a campaign called the Struggling Members Programme, aimed at the very poorest who have no other option than to take to the streets to beg for survival, and even here the bank tries to offer financing, by helping these customers to buy things to sell in order to build up a livelihood of some sort. This illustrates a firm doctrine of Microfinance: it is not simply charitable giving, it is financing to build a future. The customers are given loans that they are expected to repay, but without the penalties that are often attached in conventional banking if they are unable to do this. Deals may regularly have to be rescheduled and refinanced, but overall the industry actually sees a repayment rate of more than 95%.

Whilst it is easy to see how lending fits into the world of the MFI, savings products may seem a bit less obvious. Again we are talking about small-scale deals that are sold on the basis of financial responsibility. The customers need to plan for their futures, even their funerals, and so the MFIs try to encourage them to put away any extra funds they may have. Along similar lines is the sale of insurance. Obviously this will be a far smaller business than the loan side of the book, but it carries a financial importance in that it is part and parcel of how a cooperative institution funds itself. Clearly the ratio of deposits to loans will be very different from that we might see in a conventional bank, but this is also instilling a cultural change, and the business model for this sector is very much a forward-looking one. We should remember that this is also not that dissimilar to the friendly societies in the UK or some of the credit unions in the US and elsewhere, both of which emphasize saving for major events and encouraging self-help in a financial sense.

MEANS OF FUNDING

MFIs can finance themselves through issuing equity, depending on their structure. Not all are established in the cooperative model, but whatever structural model is used they will borrow money and will issue debt, but as we will see at the moment this is not yet normally on the public markets. They can use their shareholder capital as leverage for raising debt, with the most conservative of these MFIs doing so to a small extent, whereas the larger MFIs have adopted a greater leveraged model, again similarly to a mainstream bank. We tend to find that the MFIs with the higher leverage are those which are based where there are established financial markets, and therefore the possibility of varied sources of funding. The MFIs will also look for other sources of funding, including investment from the investment management side of the market. The MFI promotes itself as the conduit for lending to the poor and so looks for the investment funds that take an active stance in Socially Responsible Investment (SRI) to provide them with funds. There are two distinct types of these investment funds, not-for-profit and commercially motivated.

Not-for-profit

These are funding sources often from government and government agencies, as part of their commitment to alleviate poverty, but also through non government funds set up specifically for altruistic lending. One example would be the Deutsche Bank Microcredit Development Bank. This is set up as a not-for-profit fund, financed through endowments of the bank and through its wealth management division, that makes loans to MFIs. These loans are low interest-bearing and given out on a leveraged basis, meaning that the MFI has to use the money to generate more funds, that can then be lent on to the end customers.

Apart from grants and donations, these not-for-profit donors, particularly the government-owned ones such as USAid can also help financing through mechanisms like credit guarantees. Anything that can increase the perceived safety of funds can reduce the overall funding cost, so to have a triple A rated guarantee to a loan can make a big difference to the rate paid by the institution to borrow money.

Commercially Motivated Funds

These are funds where the donors expect to receive a return. An example of this is the Dexia Micro-Credit Fund, which was the first commercial fund established in 1998 for socially responsible investing. It is managed on behalf of the bank by specialist Microfinance fund managers, and in 2009 the fund held assets of just over $541 million, of which loans to MFIs accounted for nearly $385 million, having invested in 101 MFIs in 35 countries. They buy debt from these MFIs with a maximum maturity of 3 years, and set a return target for the fund of 6 month Libor $+ \frac{1}{2}\%$, and so they have a commercial target that they look to achieve whilst investing in this area. Clearly, though, they have to keep a proportion of the fund in liquid instruments, which will not be the MFI loans, which means that on average somewhere around 25–30% of the cash within the fund cannot actually be invested in this marketplace.

There are also some funds that tend to work in a middle ground here, particularly just after a fund has been set up. Whilst the long-term aims will be for the fund to become profitable this may not happen in the short term and so their investment strategy has to be to look for long-term potential.

These sources of funds are often structured as investment vehicles that can be sold to both institutional and retail investors, thereby tapping the largest possible investor base, and have successfully sold themselves on the basis of the growth of the Microfinance market.

FUNDING STRUCTURES

One of the most important elements to the funding given through the investment funds is this idea of increasing the potential investor base so it is important that we understand how the investment funds invest in the MFIs. Because of the nature of their business we have already said that the MFIs can attract only limited funds from their own core customers, and when it comes to attracting retail investment elsewhere their attraction is limited by their small, concentrated business models. This is why disintermediation is vital to them. Most of the Microfinance funds want to build up balanced portfolios so that investors can spread the risk of their investment whilst staying within the sector. So the MFIs need to provide a range of investment products that they can buy.

Debt

This is the most common means by which the MFIs will raise money. The MFIs issue debt that tends to have a maximum maturity of five years, although probably more often out to three years. This debt will be privately issued to a bank or consortium of lenders, and so will not be liquidly traded. This is why we saw the high percentage of the Dexia fund not being invested in Microfinance which is a problem of wasted opportunity. So the public capital markets are likely to play a larger role in funding in the future. In 2009 we saw SKS Microfinance of India come to the public market for a small deal, $16 million equivalent, but on the back of this they announced their intention to raise a further $104 million equivalent. There are obstacles to using this route, not least being the lack of investor familiarity, but Standard & Poor's, the rating agency, embarked on a project in 2008 to set up a methodology for rating MFIs, and as of 2009 there were 14 such rated entities. A rating is a means for an investor to benchmark the credit risk of one borrower over another, but evaluating this credit risk for the MFI sector is not the same as the process for a standard corporation. However, having these ratings and the commitment of the agencies to provide them in the future is a pretty significant step forward.

Another debt-related means of raising money is through securitization. This is where the MFI packages together assets on their books and then sells the cash flows from these assets to banks in return for capital. Obviously this is going to make everybody think of the sub-prime mortgage crisis in the US, which is the same concept, and there are those who fear a similar situation could arise in this sector of the market, but as of 2010 this would seem unlikely. This is because the market is still so relatively small and, as we said, the repayment rates are high. However we will still see the effect of the Financial Crisis on this part of the market. As it stands the securitization model is an important funding mechanism for the larger MFIs, and we are seeing growth in the sector.

Equity

As well as their public debt issue, 2009 was an important year for SKS Microfinance for another reason. This was also the year in which they listed on the Mumbai Stock Exchange, the first MFI to have a listing. This structure opens the door to significant potential public investment, but its primary purpose was for the listing of their debt securities. Up until now the equity investment has come principally through the private equity funds, but again if we see increased exposure through the ratings agencies and potential debt issuance we may see more of the MFIs going for a public listing.

Microfinance is all about socially responsible financing, as we said at the beginning of the chapter, helping the poorest to have access to financial services. At the beginning of the 21st century we are seeing this market mature and develop on the back of greater international investment interest, not least because of financial market conditions and low interest rates in the traditional markets, but at the moment we are only at the tip of the iceberg in terms of the potential size and visibility of this industry.

Part III
Quasi-Sovereigns and Supranational Agencies

16

Introduction

In this section we are going to look at a group of institutions that have a particular legal status, institutions that are not banks or corporations in the normal way, such as we have already looked at, but instead have very close links to governments – without being governments. This is the group that we collectively call quasi-sovereigns, and in this section we will look at three different types, municipalities, government agencies and supranational agencies. We will see these institutions in the markets as borrowers and as investors, and they form an important group, although more visibly active in some markets than others. Another expression you may hear used to describe this group is sub-sovereigns, which quite aptly describes how they would fit in a risk profile, not as good as the sovereign issuer of the country, but above the more mainstream corporate names.

When we see these quasi-sovereigns in the markets we see them as borrowers raising funds for their primary purpose and leveraging off their status. Some of the issuers will carry explicit government guarantees behind their debt issuance, while others, whilst not explicitly guaranteed, will carry an implicit guarantee in that the market would not expect their governments to allow these agencies to fail – a faith that may be misplaced, but we cannot help but think about the US Federal National Mortgage Association.[1] At other times they carry neither explicit nor implicit guarantees and yet still they maintain an unusual status in that because of who they are the normal rules of default and bankruptcy do not apply. If we take, for example, a municipality such as Vallejo, California, that declared itself bankrupt in May 2008, this left its holders of $200 million of debt in a tricky situation. The city could not be forced to liquidate assets to pay off this debt and avoid default, nor could it be sold to another city, as might happen with a corporate borrower. We will look a little more at this situation in the following chapter, but for now it goes to illustrate that the risk is different here, both the risk of default and the consequences when this does happen.

---

[1] See the chapter on National Agencies for more about what happened to FNMA.

As a rule of thumb these institutions should be net borrowers rather than net investors, but some of them will operate sophisticated models whereby they are able to take advantage of their good credit ratings to borrow cheaply and then invest at a higher rate and use the margin to help finance their core activities. This is particularly true of some of the supranational agencies that carry particularly good credit ratings. These supranational agencies are agencies owned by more than one country so giving a diversified credit exposure. Many of them are development banks, set up to provide economic support to specific regions, but others are industry-specific, such as EUROFIMA, set up to support the development of railways. They typically attract top-quality triple A ratings from the international ratings agencies so when they issue debt it is actively bought by the sorts of investors we will look at in the next section, particularly the more conservative investors such as the pension funds.

We should not underestimate the importance of this group of institutions in the financial markets. We are likely to see them as active borrowers and investors, often in very large size on both sides of the equation. As we have already suggested, quasi-sovereign debt can be very attractive to investors, both institutional and sometimes retail, as we will see when we look at municipalities, and so these institutions can sometimes be innovators in the market, using untested structures because they offer the safety of credit to compensate for the potential risks that can accompany lack of familiarity. An example of this is the German federal state of Saxony-Anhalt's issue of the first European sukuk bond, a bond issued under the rules of Islamic finance also known as Islamic bonds, in 2004. This was a five-year borrowing, raising €100 million. At the time this issue was launched this was a very young market, with relatively little international exposure. Prior to this quasi-sovereign there had been three sovereign deals, but this issue was seen as moving the market forward towards more comprehensive market issuance. This met with some success as, since then, we have seen more borrowers in the market, and names that we would not necessarily expect to see, such as General Electric with their issue of a $500 million sukuk bond in November 2009, the first for a US corporate borrower. But it should be said that the development of this market has not been as fast or as extensive as many hoped. However Saxony-Anhalt's deal illustrates well that these institutions are not necessarily over-conservative but will be willing to look at innovative structures if the costs and returns can be favourable to them. In 2009 41% of the international debt issuance was by sovereigns and quasi-sovereigns, and this excludes the debt issued on domestic markets which are often the markets of choice for this group of institutions. As investors they contribute significant amounts to the market. As an example the World Bank manages asset portfolios of financial securities amounting to more than \$70 billion, some in liquid trading portfolios, others in more dormant long-term portfolio, and that is just one of these institutions. In the following sections we will take a closer look at each of these types of quasi-sovereign and get a feel for why they use the financial markets and how they impact them.

17
Municipalities

The first group of quasi-sovereign institutions we are going to look at are the municipalities, or local governments. By the far the most visible of these are the US local governments who are very active issuers of debt and have their own market sector, the municipal (or muni) market. However, as we will see, these institutions appear in other markets such as in Europe and Asia, although not on such a large scale. These municipalities will also be investors to some extent, with normal excess cash flows to place in the markets sporadically during the year, which will push them towards money markets, and also their long-term asset holdings that give them a level of financial stability. As an example, in Germany in 2008 this group held securities worth some €9 billion and currencies and deposits of about €36.5 billion,[1] a relatively small holding by comparison with some of the amounts we have seen elsewhere and small by comparison to their credit market debt which stood at about €560 billion. So it is not surprising that it is as borrowers that they will be most visible in the market.

There are three core ways in which a municipality can fund itself, by borrowing through the central government, by borrowing from banks or by using the financial markets to issue debt, either public or privately traded. In the UK the local authorities tend to conduct their public borrowing through the government, although that may change in the future. In 2004 the UK's Transport for London issued the first of a series of bonds, and this was effectively the first municipal debt that had been seen in the UK market for decades. However between 2004 and 2009 no other city or area had followed suit, although in 2009 the city of Birmingham raised the possibility of issuing a bond itself so we will wait to see what happens there. In Germany the regions have historically used the Landesbanks[2] to finance themselves, with the Landesbanks issuing debt to on-lend to the regions. However in the last few years we have also seen a change here, with the regions issuing

---

[1] Federal Statistical Office.
[2] See Part Two, Chapter 5.

directly and in differing structures, such as the sukuk bond for Saxony-Anhalt that we discussed in the introduction to this section. Over the past decade the international bond market has seen issues from a number of European cities and regions such as France's Marseille and nearly every region of Italy. However this has not been without problems as we will see later.

If a city or region does decide to issue bonds there are two main structures that they can use: the first is to issue debt that is a general obligation, and the second to issue a revenue bond. A general obligation is a debt that is backed by full faith and credit of the issuer. They will pay the interest and the redemption on this from their general revenue flows such as taxes. This is the type of debt they will issue to cover general shortfalls on overall financing requirements. A revenue bond is one that is issued to finance a specific project that will ultimately bring in its own revenue stream and therefore pay for itself. Examples of this have been bonds issued for toll roads or buildings that will be leased and so create an income flow. Not all countries will use both structures, although if we look at all the international municipal debt issuance we see a strong bias towards raising money for infrastructure projects as opposed to general financing, although whether the cash flows would cover the cost of the debt is not always so clear cut.

MUNICIPAL BOND MARKETS

We are now going to take a look at a few of the major markets, so we can see how these institutions appear in different areas.

US Municipals

In the US we find a very deep, well-established municipal bond market. In 2009 the total US municipal bond issuance was $409.6 billion, with more than half of this issued as revenue bonds (see Figure 17.1).[3]

This is a very mature marketplace, with issuance dating back to the 19th century. In 2009 there were about 50,000 active issuers with some $2.7 trillion of debt outstanding, with about half of these bonds being insured by one of the 11 established primary bond insurers, five of which are rated triple A. We do have to say that one of them, ACA, is in serious financial difficulty following the Financial Crisis, and at the

---

[3] SIFMA US Key Statistics 2009.

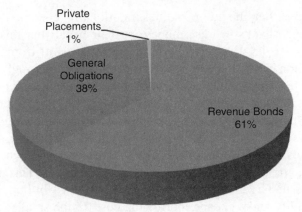

US Municipal Bond Issuance 2009

Private Placements 1%

General Obligations 38%

Revenue Bonds 61%

Figure 17.1 Municipal Bond Issuance

beginning of 2010 was itself rated below investment grade. Often known as the muni markets on the whole they create an attractive destination for investment and a good source of financing for these borrowers. To further enhance its attractiveness these bonds can also be tax-efficient for domestic investors, which is why they have increasingly been bought by retail investors over the past couple of decades. Whilst this all sounds very good the picture has not been completely rosy for these institutions. Between 1986 and 2007 there were 1100 municipal bond defaults,[4] a small percentage of issues overall but not a totally insignificant number. This is enough to make the markets fear default in hard times as we saw recently. In 2008 the market suffered, along with all the others, from a big drop off in liquidity, which affected not only existing deals but also the issuers' ability to raise money. Overall issuance only fell by about 10%, but the way in which some deals were brought to the market had to change. There was a swing away from general obligations to revenue bonds, and where these borrowers in the past had been able to issue debt on a competitive basis, asking the market to bid for the paper, instead they had to turn more to a negotiated model where they allocate the deals to underwriters to price and bring to the market the paper, which generally carries a higher overall cost. This said, though, municipals are still considered solid borrowers, with a very low default rate across the sector, and so the market is still a willing buyer of their debt.

---

[4] Standard & Poor's.

German Municipal Bonds

As we said earlier, the municipalities traditionally relied predominantly on the Landesbanks to raise money on their behalf but this has been changing over the past decade with a significant shift from 2007. The largest region is North Rhine Westphalia, and not surprisingly this is the most visible issuer in the market, borrowing not just in euro but in other currencies as well. At the end of 2008 they had €136.9 billion debt in the credit markets. The smallest borrower was Saarland, with just €10.2 billion.[5] Some of the smaller regions have joined together to issue Jumbo deals, bonds issued by groups of typically five to seven regions, although the largest group was one of 10 for one of these bonds. This means that they can issue larger deals, typically greater than €1 billion, leading to more liquidity and a cheaper borrowing cost for the smaller areas than by going it alone. Whilst these regions are considered very safe, their safety was called into question when in 2003 the state of Berlin made a petition to the Federal Constitutional Court for an increase in federal grants. They said these were needed to improve their financial situation that was still suffering from the financial implications of the unification of East and West Germany. In 2006, though, their request was refused. This was very significant for the markets because it made people realize there was no automatic bailout heading to these municipalities if they ran into financial problems, and so they could not be considered to be as safe as the German government as a borrower. This had some impact on market prices, but thankfully not as negatively as it could have been. At the end of the day if these regions are coming to the markets without explicit guarantees then there is always the risk that they could default so it is the responsibility of the investor to decide if they are happy to accept this risk and at what cost.

Japanese Municipal Bonds

In 1992 bond issuance by the Japanese municipalities stood at ¥61.1313 trillion. In 2005 that had risen to ¥139.9292 trillion.[6] This coincided with a move towards making fundamental changes to how these municipalities could issue in the markets. Before 2001 the terms for all regions were uniformly set in line with government issuance, then in 2002 Tokyo decided to set its own terms, followed by Yokohama in 2004 and then

---

[5] Federal Statistics Office.

[6] White Paper on Local Public Finance, 2007, Ministry of Internal Affairs and Communications.

Kanagawa and Nagoya, and thereafter it was felt that each region and city should set their own terms if they came to the markets to reflect the diverse risks. This was particularly important following the financial collapse of the city of Yubari in 2006 when it had to be classified as a city under 'rehabilitation', effectively becoming bankrupt. There has also been a policy of merging the municipalities to make them run more cost-effectively and efficiently and in the period from 1999 to 2007 the number dropped from 3229 to 1804, with this consolidation also serving to ensure good credit ratings for their debt. The average rating for a Japanese municipal bond in 2010 was AA, a very solid rating.

BANKRUPTCY

Unfortunately we do have to think about what happens when things go wrong. As we said earlier, when a municipality declares itself bankrupt it is not the same as a corporate bankruptcy. We mentioned in the introduction to this section of the book the current situation in Vallejo, California. In May 2008 they filed for bankruptcy and in December 2009 they produced a five-year bankruptcy workout plan in which they proposed, broadly, to suspend interest accrual on their bonds for four years and defer payment of interest and principal for three years, so bondholders are left with what we class as nonperforming assets. Another difficult situation in the markets at the moment is that facing Jefferson County, Alabama, who have $3 billion of debt and in July 2009 defaulted on a $46 million principal repayment and then a week later missed an interest payment. To make matters worse, the principal was insured on a quota basis by two insurance companies,[7] one of which, Syncora, was itself suspended from making payments in April 2009 and so defaulted on its insurance obligation to Jefferson County – a double whammy. As of the beginning of 2010 Jefferson County had not declared itself bankrupt, but as with Vallejo it is working on a plan to reschedule payments. This, then, is the crux of the risk: with luck and patience the municipality should be able to repay its financial obligations – the difficulty lies in where these stand relative to their other obligations such as pensions, healthcare, etc. So the bondholders can find themselves in for a long wait. Revenue bonds are considered riskier than general obligations as

---

[7] Quota split insurance is where the exposure is insured on a proportional basis by two or more insurers. So in this case whilst Syncora may not pay out the other insurance company will meet their claim on the proportion of the risk that they were underwriting.

the projects may never produce the revenue predicted. This was certainly the case with the Washington Public Power Supply System's (WPPSS) default in the 1970s, when it defaulted on $2.25 billion of debt after it only built one of five projected nuclear power plants. If one of these municipalities does default the lenders will receive some of their money, although in the case of WPPSS the amount recovered was very low, around 25%. This is known as the recovery rate. On the whole, though, municipals do tend to pay out high recovery levels from 100% down to 40% for the riskiest sectors.[8]

Whilst financial markets can provide this group with a good source of funding, often at very competitive levels, they can also cause them expensive problems. In November 2009 the SEC ordered JPMorgan Chase to pay $50 million and forfeit $647 million in claims against Jefferson County after accusing two directors of the bank of making undisclosed payments to certain commissioners of the county to solicit business and then covering these costs in the rates charged on derivative contracts they undertook against the county's bond offerings. This is not the only scandal involving derivative transactions and local government authorities. One of the most famous was the Hammersmith and Fulham scandal in 1989 when this UK local authority had taken loss-making derivative positions that it could not afford to cover. When the banks made their legitimate claims the authority failed to pay which led to the trades being declared *ultra vires*, meaning Hammersmith & Fulham had no legal right to enter the deals and so they were ruled invalid. This resulted in a subsequent legal turmoil that ultimately involved 75 banks and 130 local authorities, costing the banks an estimated £750 million. In 2010 we are seeing another situation unfold in Italy where Bank of America Merrill Lynch and Dexia are being investigated for derivative deals with Italian municipalities linked to their bond issuance in 2003 and 2004. So whilst on the one hand the markets have served them well, on the other hand they have not. Whether they are ill-advised or ill-informed the risk remains but the fact is that the financial markets are necessary for these borrowers to raise the size of funds they need and to manage risks in raising these funds.

To finish, in Text Box 17.1 there is a brief summary of how we might see these municipalities in the market to a greater or lesser extent, dependent on any internal restrictions that may be imposed by their national governments.

---

[8] Default Risk and Recovery Rates for US Municipal Bonds, Fitch Ratings, 2007.

Box 17.1 Summary of Municipalities Activity in the Financial Markets

Their role in the markets:

- These municipalities are most likely to use the markets as issuers raising funds for general purpose (general securities) or to finance a specific project (revenue securities).
- They are seen as investors but mainly in the money markets to invest any excess liquidity they may have.
- They will not normally take on the role of financial intermediaries.

The markets in which they are most active:

- They can be active in the money markets, and would probably do a lot of their cash management in this market, but would usually not have a great deal of FX exposure. An exception to this is to manage any exposures they have from financing in foreign currency debt markets.
- They will typically use both the long- and short-term debt markets depending on their needs and the acceptability of their names.
- Equity is not a market that would be of much interest to them.
- They are users of derivatives for risk management, particularly the long-term interest rate derivatives, such as swaps.

18
Government Agencies

Now we are going to look at some of the agencies that we see in the markets. These agencies will all have been set up under government sponsorship to carry out a particular purpose, most commonly it will be for some sort of infrastructure financing, and as such we are going to see them again predominantly as borrowers as they raise the funds for their main purpose. As with the municipalities we are going to see a difference between the US and the rest of the world when it comes to this group. In the US there are a group of agencies which are very active in the financial markets, both domestically and increasingly over the last few years internationally, whilst in Europe and Asia they are seen less. However in pretty much most countries we will find examples of these types of institution, even if they do not represent a large part of the market. The alternatives to using the markets directly are again borrowing from banks or the central government raising funds on behalf of the agency. This is the case in the UK, which as we saw with the municipalities is not a market where local governments nor this type of agency typically borrow directly at the moment. In the section on Municipalities we spoke about Transport for London being issuers of a series of bonds that we defined as municipal bonds. This was because of their geographic focus. You might have thought that this would have been classified as an agency bond since Transport for London is an agency, but it is an agency set up by the Greater London Authority, not by central government. This is a crucial difference. An agency can be set up to provide for a certain region but it must be set up by the central, not regional, authority. So, even though the UK has a large, well-established presence in financial markets, there is not a large market presence of UK agencies. Size of market is not necessarily important, though. For example, if we take a look at the bond market in Korea, which is small by international standards, we will see that in this market corporate bonds outnumber government issues, and of these corporate bonds the bulk are actually state agencies raising funds for infrastructure. So this shows us a very different development of the market in Korea from the UK.

In this section we will take a look at some examples of the agencies that we see in the financial markets, looking at some representative examples from the US, Europe and Asia so we can get a feel for their presence. We will also take a look at the way in which they raise money and the structures they will use, as this will impact on how they are perceived and their ability to use the market successfully.

These agencies are all set up with a particular purpose. This could be to build some infrastructure project, such as motorways, and as an example of this the first Eurobond[1] was issued by an Italian agency, Autostrade Concessioni e Construzioni in 1963. The company was privatized in 2000 which also illustrates how the status of agencies can change and often has changed. Other agencies will be set up to promote development in a specific area or to make investment in a particular part of an economy, such as EUROFIMA, the railway agency that we mentioned elsewhere. There are also agencies for specific financial purposes such as the US mortgage agencies, which we will look at below, and the agencies that have been set up to raise funds to support the markets since the Financial Crisis. So all in all we have a diversity of purpose, but one thing they all share in common is the need to raise wholesale amounts of money.

In the introduction to this section we spoke about quasi-sovereigns carrying explicit or implicit guarantees, and this market is a mixture of both. Having an explicit guarantee would always be preferable as it removes any uncertainty. If we think about Autostrade there could be a big difference between a government-owned road builder and a private company operating in the same industry so when the markets commit to lending long-term this will obviously influence their decision. If the debt issued carries an explicit government guarantee then this clearly reduces risk and should also lower the borrowing cost. It is interesting, though, that even with government guarantees these borrowers typically have to pay more than the government to raise their funds, because they are still one step away and there is a timing risk here. If you buy a government guaranteed bond you will get your money back in the event of a default (we hope!) but there could be a delay before this happens as the legal issues are sorted out. This is why in times of uncertainty the investors tend to demand a higher risk premium than would logically be expected. This risk premium shows itself in the yield of the debt, the

---

[1] Eurobonds are a form of international bonds and now make up the largest corporate bond market in the world as they cross international borders.

Figure 18.1   Asset-Backed Agency Debt Structure

cost to the borrowers. There are two main debt forms that the agencies use when borrowing in the financial markets. On the one hand they issue standard debt, which is issued with the full faith and credit of the issuer, or sometimes they will use an asset-backed structure. In general the structure looks like the diagram in Figure 18.1.

This is the basic structure but it can quickly become far more complex as we involve Special Purpose Vehicles (SPVs) which are created to buy the assets, repackage them and then issue the securities into the market. This diagram, though, shows in a nutshell the flow of funds which is the all-important point to an asset-backed security. This is the structure used by FNMA, one of the US mortgage agencies that we will look at below. One of the most common asset-backed securities we will find in the markets is the mortgage-backed security (MBS) and it is this security that has caused so many of the problems we have encountered in the market. In theory the asset-backed structure should be safer than just relying on the general credit of the issuer as the cash flows to service the debt should come from the specific pool of assets, and should anything go wrong they could be sold on in the markets and so generate the cash to meet the principal payments. Typically there will be more assets underlying one of these bonds than there is money raised through the issue, in other words the bond will be over-collateralized, to allow a safety net in case any of the assets fail to perform, such as any of the assets defaulting. Unfortunately again we have seen things behaving differently in the past couple of years as both the safety and the value of the assets underlying these securities have come into question and so doubts have been cast about how safe these structures actually are. An example of this is the sub-prime mortgage-backed securities. Here the securities are loans to higher risk borrowers, and so the collateral itself is far from perfect. As default rates within the loans rise so it increases the probability that the securities will default, thereby removing the safety nets of over-collateralization as we begin to reach levels where the buyers of the securities are at risk of not receiving income and even capital loss. These products can also become even more complex as they incorporate not just pure loans but also derivative contracts, making ever more complex products. In theory, though, asset-backed securities should offer a double level of protection and we have seen instances in the markets when borrowers with this sort of asset-backed debt have gone into bankruptcy and the structure has worked perfectly returning 100% of lenders' funds in a very short space of time. The keys must lie in the assets but also in the house that originates the securities. So as long as the assets are secure, stable in value and can be easily sold in the market then there should be no problems in the market – it is just a shame that this may be asking too much of many of the asset pools.

US MORTGAGE AGENCIES

Probably the most famous agencies in the financial markets are the US agencies, particularly Federal National Mortgage Association (FNMA – often referred to as Fannie Mae) and Government National Mortgage Association (GNMA – Ginnie Mae). Both of these agencies are involved in mortgage financing but are very different from one another in the scope of their business and their presence in the markets. To look first at Ginnie Mae, this agency is a perfect example of a government agency as its aim is to enable mortgages for affordable housing. It was established in 1968, and carries with it a full US government guarantee making it one of the safest borrowers in the market. It is also famous for being an innovator of the mortgage-backed security market, asset-backed securities in which as we said the asset pool is a collection of mortgages. These individual mortgages have to meet certain criteria such as being insured by approved insurers to increase the security of the deals. Any banks and mortgage companies from which Ginnie Mae accepts loans for their backing also have to be approved. The securities themselves are created when the banks and mortgage companies (the issuers) pool a group of mortgages and securitize them leading to the issue of MBS, with Ginnie Mae guaranteeing timely payment of the interest rates on the bonds and its principal repayment. The issuer name will not be GNMA as it does not directly issue the securities; instead it will be one of the SPVs we spoke of earlier, but when an investor buys into one of these deals it is the agency risk that they are buying. This is what gives uniformity to the market and allows the securities to be traded as liquid instruments. Since 1970 they have guaranteed $3.3 trillion of MBS, with $418.9 billion being issued in 2009, a significant rise from $220.6 billion in 2008.[2] So when we see this agency in the market it is not as a borrower in the traditional sense in which we have come across borrowers before. In fact, GNMA makes much of its limited exposure to financial markets. It does not carry large positions in financial assets, in fact on its balance sheets out of total assets of $15.674 billion this will include funds with the US treasury of $5.2 billion funds and $9.2 billion US government securities of which 31% are for maturities of less than a year and then a further 64% for maturities out to five years.[3] All of this illustrates how very conservative they are as investors. So whilst GNMA is a name we often see in the markets it is clearly not as an active broad-based investor nor as a traditional borrower.

The other major US mortgage agency is FNMA, although this is not the only other mortgage agency. FNMA (Fannie Mae) as an agency predates GNMA, having been established back in the 1930s, and indeed it was from FNMA that GNMA was created. Originally established by government in 1938, in 1968 it was divided into two. One part, GNMA, was established as a government guaranteed agency, the second, still retaining the name of FNMA was to be a privately owned government sponsored agency. So unlike Ginnie Mae, Fannie Mae did not carry an explicit government guarantee, but as a US agency it ranks, in terms of risk, below US treasury risk but above a non agency triple A (AAA) corporate. As we have said before we have often had the idea of an implicit guarantee for these government sponsored agencies and this theory was tested in 2008 when in September of that year Fannie Mae had to be bailed out by the US government and placed into a government conservatorship run by the Federal Housing Finance Agency. The treasury committed to providing $200 billion in capital, as and

[2] GNMA Financial Reports 2009.
[3] GNMA Annual report, 2009.

US Market Outstanding Debt

Figure 18.2   Agency Debt Market

when needed, to the agency, but in January 2010 this cap was removed, suggesting the government would do whatever was necessary. The business model of Fannie Mae is very different from that of Ginnie Mae. Fannie Mae actually buys mortgages from the mortgage lenders. It funds its purchases with borrowings from the financial markets, including issuing MBS that it creates itself in its own name. This is one of the largest borrowers in the financial markets with, at the end of 2009, $200 billion short-term debt and $585 billion long-term debt outstanding in the market,[4] issued in a broad spectrum of structures and markets, both domestic and international. It therefore plays a very significant role in the financial markets, with US agency debt, of which Fannie Mae is the biggest issuer, accounting for 8% of a total market of $34.6 trillion (see Figure 18.2).[5]

Some other names that you may come across in relation to US agencies include:

- Federal Home Loan Housing Corporation (FHLMC – Freddie Mac) – this is the other agency that was taken under conservatorship along with Fannie Mae. It operates the same business model, buying mortgages from mortgage providers and issuing debt to fund this operation.
- SLM Corporation (Sallie Mae) – Sallie Mae is actually not an agency. It was when it was originally created in 1972, but as with Fannie Mae, it became privatized, although in this case it lost its federal charter in

---

[4] FNMA Funding Summary.
[5] SIFMA.

2004. There is still a link with the government, though, in that Sallie Mae is the largest provider of federal student loans.

ZAITO INSTITUTIONS

These are the Japanese agencies, government-owned corporations. There are currently about 47 of these institutions of which 22 have debt outstanding in the financial markets. Whilst not as well known as the US institutions we have just been discussing they are an increasingly visible group in the financial markets. If we look at this group we can see a broad range of different types of agency that all take part in the government's Fiscal Investment and Loan Programme (FILP) to finance infrastructure projects, such as expressway building, airport expansion, hospitals, education, and providing economic support to trades and industry including fishing and agriculture and others. There has been some reorganization of these zaito in recent years to create more efficient business models, such as the formation of Japan Finance Corporation (JFC), created in 2008 from a merger of four corporations (with a fifth to be incorporated after 2012):

- National Life Finance Corporation
- Agriculture, Forestry and Fisheries Finance Corporation
- Japan Finance Corporation for Small and Medium Enterprise, and
- Japan Bank for International Cooperation.

Bringing together these different elements JFC becomes a cross-border agency providing financing to not only the small and medium-sized (SME) sector, but even on the smallest level it is there to help individuals in their business projects. This type of project represents the largest destination of the financial support given by these agencies. A large part of the business of JFC is to provide safety-net loans and to do this it will need to raise funding. At the end of 2008 this group in total had debt issued amounting to ¥131.1 trillion bonds, all of which was government guaranteed.[6] JFC itself had nearly ¥6 trillion outstanding, including 15 international bonds in the market, 14 denominated in US dollars, and one in Thai Baht.[7] On the other side of their balance sheet JFC also holds ¥49.6 billion in securities, not a particularly large amount but enough to show that they are an investor in the financial

---

[6] Ministry of Finance, Summary of Fiscal Loan Fund Management Report.
[7] This includes legacy debt from the agencies before the merger.

markets as well as a borrower. What this group of agencies really shows us is how the financial markets can be used to provide financing all through an economy. In order to achieve this, though, these agencies carry the government guarantee, and there have been failures of zaito institutions in the past, so we know that these are not infallible, hence the reorganizations. This is particularly important for the agencies such as JFC which borrow actively and have a very international presence in order to try and attract the maximum international funds. Between June 2009 and January 2010 JFC issued three US dollar bonds, totalling $6.75 billion, so we can gauge the importance of their profile against raising this sort of size of financing.

SPECIAL PURPOSE AGENCIES

The last type of agency that we are going to look at is exemplified by France's Société de Financement de l'Economie Française (SFEF). This agency was created in October 2008 and announced its closure one year later, in October 2009. Its sole purpose was to raise money in the financial markets to support the French banking system. We have come across an agency of this sort before when we looked at US banks and we spoke of Resolution Financing Corp (REFCORP), which raised financing in the US for bank bailouts in the 1980s, so the idea is not a new one, although the structure of this agency differs. This agency was set up as a part-ownership project, formed as a limited company, with ownership divided between the state, holding 34%, and the major banks, holding 66%. Whilst the ownership is shared, control is firmly in the hands of the state. During its one year of active life the agency issued debt in euro, US dollars, British pounds and Swiss francs, totalling €77 billion, all of which was guaranteed by the French Republic, under an overall guarantee scheme of €360 billion. This is one of only two agencies carrying a government guarantee in France so all of its issues were well received as investors appreciated the rarity and quality and so were happy to buy the issues. These investors were not just domestic but international as well, which is why the agency chose to use different currencies to maximize the potential investor base. The funds that were raised were then used to support the French banks by making loans to them against receiving collateral. The banks that were eligible to borrow from SFEF had to be solvent and there were limits set on how much banks could borrow, although some of these had to be adjusted to higher levels. This was all part of the refinancing plan for the French banking system. There was also another agency developed to recapitalize banks, effectively to bail them out, and this was the Société de Prise de Participation de l'Etat (SPPE).

These agencies differ from the ones we looked at previously because they were always intended to be limited life, specific purpose institutions. The Finance Act of 2010 does give the government the right to reactivate if necessary, but the SFEF announced that it had finished raising funding as soon as it felt the market was able to fund the banks itself and so no longer needed state involvement. That being the case there was no longer any need to borrow more money.

This French agency is an example of an unusual form of government agency, one with a limited purpose and life in the markets. It had a specific project for which it was raising funds and when this was achieved the agency was no longer needed and so is no longer visible in the markets, beyond servicing long-term debt. For most of the other agencies that we see in the market their business remit is ongoing and so they are likely to continue using the financial markets as long as the markets provide them with the liquidity they need. We have seen, by some of the size of issuance that we have looked at, that the financial markets are crucial to these agencies – where else could they find funds of the magnitude that we have been considering? And we have only looked at a small, representative subset. Most countries will have agencies, both in developed and developing markets, and for these agencies being able to use the financial markets is a great benefit.

As with the municipals in the previous chapter, in Text Box 18.1 is a summary box of how we might expect to see these agencies in the financial markets, and again we have to add the caveat that there may be domestic restrictions on the activities of these agencies.

Box 18.1 Summary of Government Agency Activity in the Financial Markets

Their role in the markets:

- Government agencies will most commonly be issuers in the market using both debt and money markets, often quite prolifically.
- They are seen as investors but mainly in the money markets to invest any excess liquidity they may have.
- Some, such as the US mortgage agencies are intermediaries, taking risk from the banks and using this to raise money to be lent to them,

but this is not the same as the intermediary model that we saw in trading and sales.

The markets in which they are most active:

- They are very active in the money markets but would not normally have a lot of FX exposure.
- They will sometimes use both the long- and short-term debt markets, particularly in recent times but the bias will probably be to issuing long-term debt as they often use the markets to finance large infrastructure investment.
- Equity is a market in which they are rarely involved, only in very unusual circumstances such as when an agency moves from public to private ownership. Having said this, FNMA has tapped the equity market in various locations in recent times as another funding mechanism.
- They are likely to use derivatives for risk management but unlikely to trade them.

19

Supranational Agencies

In the last chapter in this section we are going to look at supranational agencies, agencies owned by more than one country. These agencies are very often seen in the market, yet again as net borrowers, but this time we will see that they are also significant investors. We will see that their borrowings far outweigh their investments in the financial markets and yet such is the size of both that whilst the picture is not very balanced we can nonetheless see the importance of this group on both sides of the market.

Supranational agencies are created to promote development in either a specific region or on a global basis. They are amongst the best names that we see in the markets as their ownership by more than one country makes them very safe credits. The typical structure is that the shareholders have both a subscribed and unsubscribed commitment to the agency, and so if liquidity problems arise for the agency they can call on the unsubscribed portion of its capital, which has been committed by the shareholders. Obviously if these shareholders were themselves in financial difficulties they may not be able to meet their commitments, but the probability of this happening to every shareholder country is far lower than it happening to any single one of them. This is why these supranational agencies typically carry top-quality triple A ratings. Clearly the better the shareholders the less the risk which is why it is important to know who owns these agencies and which are the biggest shareholders.

We have said that their primary purpose is to provide support for development and they will do this by lending money or making grants to projects within their remit. These agencies are by definition political bodies, since their executive bodies will be composed to a large extent by political appointment, but they are not intended to further the interests of any individual member but rather to work together towards common aims. Later we will look at the EIB and one of the things we will see is how the management is put together with a pyramid structure of the highest level political appointments being on the Board of Governors, and then filtering down to a Management Committee that is most involved in the day-to-day running of the agency as a bank and investment fund. However they always have to remember that they are public bodies and are therefore highly accountable so we tend to see that when they come to use the financial markets they do so in a very open manner, doing very high-profile deals and spreading their business amongst many different market participants.

WHO ARE THE SUPRANATIONAL AGENCIES?

There is a reasonably small group of these agencies that we tend to see in the markets, although some far more than others. The most prolific borrower by far is the EIB, although the World Bank is often called the best credit in the world because of the breadth of its ownership. We are going to take a quick look at these major agencies, but in Appendix D we look in a little more detail at the EIB as an example of the sorts of ways in which these supranationals will use the markets.

The World Bank

This is probably the most famous of the supranational agencies. It was established in 1944 coming from the famous Bretton Woods meeting in New Hampshire that set the groundwork for stabilizing the financial system following the Second World War, and also established the International Bank for Reconstruction and Development (IBRD) to enable post-war reconstruction and development. From there it has grown to an agency whose primary objective is to alleviate world poverty. The World Bank Group itself comprises two main development institutions, IBRD and the International Development Agency (IDA). Then there are three other branches to the model, the International Finance Corporation (IFC), the Multilateral Investment Guarantee Agency (MIGA) and the International Centre for the Settlement of Investment Disputes (ICSID). Very briefly these institutions focus on the following:

IBRD – provides support to public and private projects in poor and medium-income nations

IDA – provides support to the very poorest level of countries

IFC – this institution is involved in project finance and the development of financial market infrastructure through making available a range of investment products and advisory services to help develop these and allow access to domestic and international financial markets

MIGA – an investment guarantee agency, in which they insure eligible projects to enable international investment

ICSID – an arbitration service set up to facilitate settlement of investment disputes.

Each of these is an autonomous institution, focusing on different types of development project, but all belonging to the World Bank Group and collaborating to provide a full suite of services working towards the common goal. They share a group of shareholders, although not every shareholder is a member of every institution. For example, San Marino is only a member of the IBRD, whilst Germany is a member of all. This shareholder community is a group of 186 countries globally. Any country member of the IMF is allowed to become a shareholder of the World Bank and their allocation of shares is based on their economic status, with the largest economies taking the largest stake, which obviously commits them to the most capital. With these shareholdings come voting rights, again on a proportional basis, so the largest countries will have the most influence on the organization. When the World Bank was first created its share capital was $10 billion dollars, consisting of 100,000 shares of $100,000 nominal each. Today the share capital consists of $189.9 billion, of which $11.5 billion is paid-up capital and the other $178.4 billion available on request to meet debt obligations. The World Bank has never had to call on this additional capital but has always been able to service its debt from revenue and refinancing. So we can see from this the support behind the agency contributing to the triple A rating.

The main purpose of the World Bank and its affiliates is to support both private and public development on a global basis. They can do this by making loans, and offering interest-free credits and grants, along with guarantees to projects that are acceptable to the agencies. To do this they need to raise funds and this is why we see them as borrowers in the financial markets.

European Investment Bank – EIB

This supranational agency is owned by the countries of the EU and focuses most of its attention on development projects in and around this region. For many years it was seen as second to the World Bank in terms of market presence but the past years have reversed that perception. EIB is by far the largest borrower, raising nearly twice as much as the

World Bank in 2009, and with a larger capital base. As we will see with all the agencies their mission will be very similar, to support their specific regions, and the EIB does this by providing financing to public and private projects. Their work is not exclusively in Europe as they all sponsor projects in other areas but to a lesser extent. Similar to the World Bank the EIB consists of two core institutions, the bank itself and the European Investment Fund.

European Bank for Reconstruction and Development – EBRD

This is a broader based European agency, owned by 61 countries, predominantly European but also including Australia, New Zealand and Japan, along with the European Union and the EIB. A very young agency, it was only established in 1991 as a transition bank, following the fall of the Berlin Wall. When we say a transition bank we mean that this agency was set up to help economies moving towards democracy, a very specific political agenda, which differentiates it from other development banks. The EBRD invests primarily in the private sector and is the largest single investor in Central and Eastern Europe. It provides loans and trade finance and will often work with regional financial institutions to make credit available in the region. Following the recent Financial Crisis the EBRD has been actively recapitalizing banks that it considers fundamentally sound but that have been affected by the liquidity crisis, so taking a very hands-on approach in the financial infrastructure.

Inter-American Development Bank – IDB

The Inter-American Development Bank (IDB, also known as IADB) is the agency for Latin America and the Caribbean. As with the previous agencies it carries a triple A rating owing to its ownership structure, with 48 countries being members of the bank and the US being the largest single shareholder accounting for 30.01% of the capital, and the 26 borrowing member countries of Latin American and Caribbean holding 50.02%. The other 19.7% is held by the other 21 nonborrowing members, major countries such as the UK, Japan, Germany and others. The US is also a nonborrowing member. As with the previous agencies it provides financing through loans, grants and guarantees and operates two investment arms, along with the bank's structured and corporate finance department, these being the Inter-American Investment Corporation and the Multi-lateral Investment Fund, both focused on different types of project for investment.

Asian Development Bank (ADB); African Development Bank (AfDB)

As their names would suggest these are both regional development banks, and as with the IDB they comprise a membership of local and major international countries, promoting development in their regions through loans, grants and guarantees. Whilst not wishing to undermine the uniqueness of the economic situations within their regions, from a financial market perspective what we see with these agencies are internationally owned and capitalized entities and it is on that basis that the top-quality ratings are assigned when they issue senior debt which makes them very much the same as the other agencies we have already looked at. This is why we can put all these agencies together into one big, supranational pool with the distinguishing features really being how often they access the markets.

SUPRANATIONALS AS BORROWERS IN THE FINANCIAL MARKETS

From the World Bank Group the IBRD and the IFC are the two names that we will come across in the market; the IDA is funded by donations from its members since its remit is to help the very poorest countries. Both the IBRD and the IFC work not just with poor countries but middle-income countries as well. As we said the IFC focuses on pro-viding investment and financial services to the private sector, helping to build the private infrastructure to aid the development of the region. They focus a lot on small to medium-sized firms (SMEs) providing a broad range of financial instruments to them, not just loans but equity fi-nance and risk management products. The IFC is the smaller borrower, with $25.66 billion outstanding debt in the market as of June 2009, whilst the IBRD had at the same time $110 billion. Both of these are regular borrowers, the IFC has issued a large USD bond every year since 2000, and in 2009 the IBRD issued $44.4 billion debt, mostly (76%) in US dollars but also in 17 other currencies. The EBRD, whilst being a relatively small borrower, is nonetheless remarkable for the currencies it uses. Whereas the World Bank will borrow in many currencies and then turn them into US dollars using derivatives, the EBRD likes to borrow in local currencies of its projects when possible, and so in 2009 we saw them issuing in Russian Rouble and Romanian Leu to fulfil some of their needs. They are not large borrowers, borrowing a modest €4.9 billion in 2009. This is not too dissimilar to the levels raised by

IDB and ADB, both of whom raised around $9 billion, and the AfDB comes in as the smallest borrower, raising less than $4 billion. To talk of billion dollar funding as small is really only about relative size. These borrowings are dwarfed by the €80 billion taken from the markets by EIB in 2009, and yet they were successful with all of their deals just showing that the markets have a good appetite for supranational debt.

Another characteristic of the supranational agencies is their commitment to supporting local markets. We have spoken of the EBRD raising money in local currencies to finance specific projects, but as well as this the supranationals will often use local markets for infrastructure purposes as well. By doing this they hope to encourage investors and other issuers to follow suit. For example, the ADB was the first supranational to issue in the domestic markets of Australia, China, India, Korea, Malaysia, Philippines, Taipei and Thailand. Then in 2009 it issued a bond in Chinese Yuan so really promoting its regional markets. Not surprisingly the main currencies for all of these agencies will be US dollar or euro (although the AfDB has raised 32% of its funds in Japan), and in these well developed markets they tend to issue large global deals in the most straightforward structures, but then also use innovative structures to diversify their risk in terms of interest rate, and potentially increase their investor base through the use of these alternative structures. We have seen these agencies issue many structures in fixed rate, floating rate, with payments linked to other indices such as stock indices or inflation measures, and others.

Considering the purpose of these agencies it is not surprising that they will also try to raise money from socially responsible investors (SRIs). These credits would typically fall within the mandate of SRIs because of their overall humanitarian objectives, but beyond this the agencies have issued bonds linked to specific areas of concern. For example, there have been a number of deals where the agency has pledged the proceeds raised to be lent to specific projects such as water, climate awareness, etc. This is fulfilling a twofold purpose: raising the necessary funds and also highlighting specific actions of the agency.

SUPRANATIONALS AS INVESTORS IN THE FINANCIAL MARKETS

These agencies also have an important role to play as investors in the market. They rely heavily on the money that they have raised to finance their projects but they are obliged to keep funds in reserve to cover them in the event of non repayment of the loans. Also, for grants that are made there is no repayment so the agencies have to have a way to generate income so that they do not use all of their capital and effectively bankrupt themselves. One of the ways in which they do this is by taking advantage of their top-quality credit ratings. With this rating they can borrow at very low cost and if they then retain some of these funds, which they must as reserves, they will reinvest them in slightly lower credits and make a spread profit: the difference between their funding cost and their investment return. This is an important source of revenue as well as being part of the risk management strategy of the agencies. The World Bank, for example, runs a portfolio of over $75 billion, on behalf of themselves and some other public entity customers. They tend to be very conservative investors, normally preferring not to take very long maturity risk on their books, and liquidity is important to them in case they need to sell the assets to cover a need from their core business. Some of the agencies will specifically run trading books, bonds that they buy with an intention to sell for a profit, and long-term investment books, with bonds they intend to hold to maturity. Obviously the Financial Crisis has not left these investors totally unscathed. They were large buyers of asset-backed securities, specifically mortgage-backed securities, and, of course, these assets have been severely affected by recent events. At the time the agencies were buying these securities they would have seemed perfect, rated as top-quality but paying higher returns because the timing of the cash flows was less certain than on an ordinary bond, they fitted perfectly into the investment portfolios. However the falls in value that have affected these bonds have naturally affected the profitability of these portfolios. This illustrates the risks that can accompany even the most cautious investments.

One other area in which we see these institutions is in the derivatives market, particularly the swaps market. As we have already said, a lot of the issues brought to the market by these borrowers will be transformed into another interest basis or currency and this happens by attaching swaps to the issues.[1] Considering the size of some of the deals that these issuers bring to the market, often multibillion dollar deals or equivalent,

---

[1] An interest rate swap is a derivative contract where one party pays an interest rate on a notional amount to their counterparty in return for an interest payment made on another basis. The classic structure would be where one side pays a fixed interest rate and the other pays a floating one. The swap can also be across currencies, the same structure with one side paying out interest in one currency against receiving interest in a different one.

and the frequency with which they issue, it is not surprising that they are a major counterparty. Indeed the World Bank says that it carries out $25–35 billion of derivative transactions every year. These derivative deals will not be undertaken for speculation but purely as part of their risk management strategy, which, again, will be very conservative.

All in all this group of institutions plays a large and influential part in the financial markets and we are likely to see them in both the long end of the market and in the money markets on a regular basis.

So to summarize in Text Box 19.1 we illustrate how we are likely to see these supranational agencies in the markets.

Box 19.1 Summary of Supranational Agency Activity in the Financial Markets

Their role in the markets:

- Supranational agencies will be actively seen as issuers in the market, often issuing very large, benchmark deals.
- They are also significant investors in the market, with a conservative investment approach, focusing on very good quality debt.
- They are intermediaries in as much as they may raise money on behalf of their development customers, and the World Bank will manage funds on behalf of customers as well.

The markets in which they are most active:

- They will be very active in both money markets and FX. They typically tend to hold quite a few money market assets for liquidity, particularly treasury bills.
- They will be very active issuers in the long-term debt markets in an exceptional range of currencies and structures. They also use these products as their main investments, so all in all they have a very large presence in the market.
- Equity is not a market in which they would have a natural place, except in the private equity markets of their development customers.
- They are very large users of derivatives to manage the large risk exposure they have from their capital market borrowings, particularly since they actively target using a wide range of currencies and structures, but are likely to use specific currencies for their development projects.

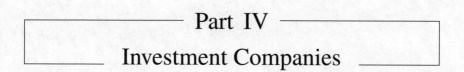

Part IV
Investment Companies

20

Introduction

In this section we are going to look at the business of investment and the companies, and divisions of banks that carry out this business. In the Introduction we described this part of the market as the *buy-side*. This is because if we think of the definition of disintermediated financing that we looked at right at the beginning, seeing how funds flow from those with surplus to those looking for money, these investment companies will be the ones with access to the excess funds that they are looking to place in the market by buying the investment products. We are going to look at different types of Investment Company, both in terms of their sources of funds and how they decide to invest them. These two things are inextricably linked: different sources of funds are likely to have different requirements in terms of the sorts of risk to which they can be exposed and the returns needed. We are not going into the mathematical intricacies of portfolio management – as always our focus is on the business, so we will look at the different types of investors, their motivations for being in the markets and some of the processes they will need to go through to ensure they invest these funds appropriately.

One thing we should deal with straightaway is the difference between investment management, fund management, portfolio management and asset management. Essentially they are all the same. Under each of these titles used in the markets the underlying process will be the same, to invest money in financial products for investment. The reason we use the various different expressions is often to describe where the money has come from. For example, someone running a mutual fund in a bank, a form of collective investment scheme, *might* be called a fund manager. Someone looking after the financial assets of a corporation *could* be called an asset manager. Someone managing investments on behalf of individual customers *is sometimes called* an investment manager, and so on. The reason we have had to say *might, could, sometimes* is because there is no rigid definition of when one term should be used over another. You may well find that in one firm the department looking after collective investment schemes might be called the asset management department, whilst in another it is the fund management department. Often a bank will use several of these titles to define the different types of investment management happening within the firm. The trickiest of these titles is portfolio manager, as this has a common use beyond financial markets. An example of this is someone managing a group of research projects in a bio-technology firm who will typically be called a portfolio manager, as indeed the title is often used as part of the organization of project management in many firms. However it is also used in the financial markets and whatever the title that is used the core duties and responsibilities remain the same.

WHERE WE FIND INVESTMENT MANAGERS

As we have said, and we will see later, we can find this function in many different sorts of institution, sometimes managing other people's money – their customers' – sometimes managing the firm's money. Firstly we will take a quick look at some of the main places where investment management is located and start to get a feel for how it fits into the business model of not only a standalone investment management company, but also as part of a bigger organization.

Banks

This is typically an important business division of the banks, especially the universal banks. Logically we can say it fits most comfortably into investment banking, but if we think about the commercial and retail banking flow we can also see how that would bring in natural customers, both retail and institutional. To offer either money management or collective investment schemes is a natural addition to the offerings that banks can make to complement the core business of lending money and taking funds on deposit. Since there could be potential conflicts of interest the bank has to take care to safeguard this department using Chinese Walls, which we discussed earlier when we looked at the corporate finance departments in banks. Taking this a step further, some banks have even created independent companies, in which they are the sole or major shareholder, to carry out this business. Clearly there will be a link in terms of introducing clients etc., but when it comes to managing the investments there should be no charges of collusion if the bank and the investment company operate independently. We will look further at these investors in the section on Traditional Investment Managers.

Independent Companies

Whilst many of us may buy and sell financial instruments, in market terms we are only collectively significant, not individually. However there are a small group of individuals who run investments on a wholesale basis. Clearly these will often be high net worth individuals (HNWIs) that we discussed in the section on Private Banking. The issue here is the amount of time it takes to actively manage money. If the individual is managing their money alongside their primary business they are quite likely to need the help of a professional fund manager, or a private banker to help with the flow of this business. If they are managing money as their primary business then they are likely to need to incorporate, quite often to achieve tax efficiency, and so we have that crossover from individual to independent company. We have seen a lot of crossover at the end of the 20th century and the beginning of the 21st century, as fortunes have been made – and lost – as a result of the technology boom and also in financial services. When we look at hedge funds we will see that a number of them were created by very success- ful ex-employees of financial firms. Once the crossover has been made many of these new companies expand their business by managing not just their own money but other people's as well. We define this group of investors as independent because they are not affiliated to a bank, but we should not necessarily underestimate their size. Whilst many of them can be small, such as individuals or small unlisted companies, we can also find large, listed corporations in this area. A spectacular example of this is Warren Buffett's Berkshire Hathaway whose revenue in 2009 was greater than that of JPMorgan Chase and not far below the biggest bank in the US, Bank of America.[1] There are also companies that do not choose to accept other people's money for management – an exam- ple of this might be a family trust. . This is where a fund is structured to manage the wealth of a group of related, normally, Ultra-HNWIs,[2] and is a long established practice. For example, the Guinness family first created a family investment trust back in 1886. Whilst typically these funds do not look to attract investment from outside the 'family' group, they will very occasionally develop into more mainstream invest- ment management firms. This has been the case with the Guinness and Rothschild families who have both developed beyond managing purely their own wealth to open public funds, which are, as at 2009,

---

[1] Forbes 500, 2009.

[2] For a definition of this see the chapter on Private Banking.

majority-owned by family members, but the bulk of the family trusts remain private vehicles for investment.

So the world of the independent investment manager is very diverse with a range of structures and size that provide a lot of variety in the investment market. We will look at some more examples of these in the sections on Traditional Investment Managers and Hedge Funds.

Investment Divisions of Corporations

Once again we are going to have to be quite careful in our use of terminology here because when we are talking about nonfinancial firms their primary investment will be in their core business, not the financial markets. However if we look at many of the biggest multinationals we will often find a financial investment manager, managing some or all of the financial assets of the company, and we will sometimes also see this in smaller companies, although economies of scale may make it more efficient for firms of either size to outsource this task to professional money managers. However if a company does decide to manage money in-house then this investment manager will often sit within the structure of the treasury department and will manage the portfolio in the same way as any other money manager. The funds that they are managing could be the long-term financial assets of the corporation, so would be invested to generate long-term return for the firm, or they could be short-term financial surpluses, such as money from a disposal that is not needed immediately within the infrastructure of the company but could be 'earmarked' for an acquisition or corporate development investment at some time in the future. If this is the case then the priorities for investment will change. The investment manager will still be looking for return but will also need to balance this against liquidity to ensure the funds are available when required. This is the sort of strategy employed in corporate treasury all the time, whether they are managing excess cash or managing their borrowings: the cash flowing into and out of the company is inextricably linked to the business model of the firm and this has to be the primary driver for managing both funding and investment. This is very different from how the bank and independent investment management companies and divisions will operate. For them, the business is the money and not a direct by-product of another activity, although, as we will see, how they build portfolios will have to be influenced by expected inflows and outflows, although the link is less direct.

Another example of a money managing division of a corporate, at the high end of the scale, is Promark Global Investors, a money management arm of General Motors. This division was managing nearly $25 billion in 2009. Some 80% of this was General Motors pension fund and other assets, but the rest was money of other corporations taken under money management. The division is now a business unit that has transformed itself into a professional money manager using its in-house expertise to generate more revenue. This is not the most common model, although we have looked at it already in the chapter on Supranational Agencies, when we saw that the World Bank has also developed a similar strategy.

Insurance Companies

Since we are looking at divisions of corporations it is worth introducing here the insurance companies, who will often run large investment management divisions, and are also massive suppliers of funds to the other investment management companies. We are going to look at these in more detail later because the business of investment is crucial to their being able to perform their core business. Without careful investment of insurance premia they will not have the funds to pay out against claims, so we will see that these are some of the most sophisticated investors that we find in the marketplace.

Agencies

In the previous section we looked at various government and government-related agencies and again we saw by looking at their models of business how active they must be in the financial markets both as borrowers and investors. These agencies will have investment managers whose job will be to invest the funds at the best possible rates for the acceptable risk. With the supranational agencies we saw that the acceptable risk was actually very low risk, but other sorts of agency can take higher risk, depending only on the internal restrictions and any external ones such as legislative ones. These agencies are generally investing public funds so tend to have a high level of transparency. They may also have particular economic or political requirements on them, such as a requirement to buy bank securities to support the financial system, or to place a certain percentage of their funds in domestic instruments to support the economy. This will compromise the process of investment management on a purely theoretical basis, but in practice all it does is to redefine their universe of investment. If the fund managers know they must work within these frameworks they will alter their asset allocation accordingly. When we look at Sovereign Wealth Funds we will take a look at how an agency of this sort might be structured and how its investment criteria may be defined.

SOURCES OF FUNDS

All of the above are the sorts of firms and departments that can be involved in investment management but we should now look at where the actual money comes from, their potential sources of funds and how it comes under management. This money will basically arrive into these firms in one of two ways, by the funds being given to an investment manager to manage on the clients' behalf, a *managed portfolio*, or by the client buying into an investment package produced by the firm, a *collective investment scheme*. We will look at the second of these in a bit more detail in the next chapter but firstly let's take a look at the idea behind managed portfolios. These funds can be anything from a company's reserves to a pension fund, an individual's wealth and various other sources. There are two ways in which the firm can take the money: on a discretionary or nondiscretionary (or advisory) basis. If the funds are given on a discretionary basis then the investment manager agrees a strategy with the client and works out a set of parameters, but they make the actual investment decisions and act on them autonomously. In a nondiscretionary account the investment manager makes recommendations, also based on agreed strategy and parameters, but leaves the final decision-making to the client.

The choice of investment route to take – whether to allocate funds to a fund manager or to buy a collective investment scheme – is, to a certain extent, dictated by the source of funds, although with large investors we are likely to see a combination being used. The following are some of the major sources of funds that we see in the market and form a large part of the bedrock on which the industry is built.

Individuals

Whilst we as individuals may well be net borrowers we are also very likely to have some form of savings. Whether these savings translate into a source of funds for investment management will depend on the time horizon we have for our savings, our required return and also the extent of our familiarity with the financial products. If we choose to just leave any excess money we have in our bank current accounts these funds will simply become part of the bank's overall liquidity and so we will not see them within this market. However if we decide to place our funds in an investment product, like a mutual fund or unit trust, then our funds will become part of this market. For most retail customers the natural route will be to place our funds in a collective investment scheme. If we have enough money to invest that we reach a firm's criteria for placing it directly with an investment manager, then we will be classed as, at minimum, mass affluent, but most probably we will be high net worth. These criteria will differ from firm to firm, as we shall see, but will be based partly on the cost of providing this service. This will have a knock-on effect on the return to the investor. The whole idea of the collective investment schemes is to pool small amounts of money into sums which are more acceptable in the market and so can benefit from economies of scale. As we have already discussed the mass affluent sector of the market is a growing area. When we defined HNWI we spoke of these individuals as having a certain level of net investable assets, so basically they were net investors. In the mass affluent world the individuals may actually still be net borrowers, for example, they may have mortgages on their homes that they will be servicing from their incomes, but at the same time as having this long-term debt, they may also have cash to invest that they choose not to offset against the loan. To take funds directly under management some firms may require minimum deposits of say, £50,000 or $100,000 although for some it will be less than this, and for some it will be considerably higher. In other words there is no set barrier; this is determined by the company and their target markets, not by any regulation of the marketplace. Part of the driver for determining these levels will be dictated by how tailored the investment portfolio will be – the more tailored, the more time-consuming, therefore the more expensive. When funds are placed with an investment manager there will be fees to pay, which is why for smaller sums of money, in relative terms, the collective schemes will be the most cost-efficient.

Of course at the other end of the spectrum we find the HNWIs and par-ticularly the Ultra-HNWIs. When we spoke of these earlier we said that, for many of them, managing their wealth was just a part of their activities and it is this group that is actively targeted by the investment manage-ment firms for their managed portfolio business. It is worth making sure we are clear about the distinction between investment management and private banking, since this is where we see the two worlds collide. In the chapter on private banking we described a premium bank service, where the customers were offered bank accounts, investment advice, tax planning, or whatever financial services they should need. One of those services may well be to have their money professionally managed. This is not the job of the private banker; this is the job of the investment manager. So, it could be that a customer of a bank's private banking department may well also become a customer of their investment management department either by placing funds in a managed portfolio or buying investment products. One more thing that private banking can offer is anonymity. If the customer does not want to be identified to the fund manager then the private banking department can stand as an intermediary with all cash flow transactions taking place through them, with the client identified by a private banking account number. Similarly the customer may not want to buy the investment products or services of the bank with which they conduct private banking, and this is not compulsory. The private banking service is an advisory function, not a money management one.

So as we can see from this, whilst investment flows from individuals, in all forms, are a major source of funds for this part of the industry, they are not the only source, as we will discover below.

Corporate Money

When we spoke about the investment management divisions of corporations we gave an example of a company with excess funds that they could invest in the financial markets. This is certainly one source of funds that can be given to an investment manager, and there are actually investment funds, such as money market funds, that are targeted at exactly this kind of cash flow, offering not just a good rate of return but also the sort of liquidity that would normally be available from direct money market investment. Another important corporate source of funds, though, are the ones that General Motors chose to manage in-house, their pension funds. These are often seen as the crown jewels of corporate investing and are competitively fought for by the major investment managers. If you look at any of the big firms you will see that they all claim to manage the pension funds of the biggest companies, and this reflects the fact that quite often these funds will be divided amongst more than one investment manager so as to benchmark performance. Sometimes the company will even retain a portion of the fund in-house as a further check. In 2009 the global pension market stood at \$23 trillion in the 13 largest pension markets that accounted for 85% of pensions, which equates to about 70% of GDP, so we can see that this is a significant investment market and one the investment companies will fight for. At its highest point this percentage of GDP was 76% but at current levels it is still a more than significant percentage. Even if a fund is managed in-house there is still a lot of potential business for the investment management industry as many of the assets will be invested in funds (indirect investment) as opposed to direct investment. So the money will still flow into the industry by buying these collective investment schemes managed by the investment management companies.

State Money

Governments are another major source of investment funds in various different ways. We have spoken earlier in this book about long-term reserves manage by central banks on behalf of the government and these reserves will need to be invested. When we look at Sovereign Wealth Funds, we will be able to take a closer look at this. On a less long-term basis there can also be cash flows such as tax receipts. Given that most governments are net borrowers it may sound strange to say that tax receipts can be investment funds, but again it is all about timing. Money cannot just sit doing nothing, it must always be made to work, so there can be patterns of short-term investment actively managed by some of the central banks on behalf of their governments. Some are more active than others, using things such as money market funds to achieve the best results over even very short time horizons, others concentrate more on cash management, using inflows to offset outgoing balances, but as a whole this is a cash flow that can show itself in the market and can be highly significant in value.

Away from this, we will see government agencies again popping up in the market, and once more we need to think about pension funds. The 10 largest pension funds in the world are all state-owned, with the largest being the Japanese Government Pension Investment Fund. This has assets of over \$1 trillion equivalent, and 90% of this fund is managed by external fund managers, overseen by an internal investment board. So clearly there will be a major source of funds coming from parts of the public purse.

Charitable Foundations and Endowments

It is quite easy to overlook this part of the market until we stop and think about the size of funds sitting out there waiting to be invested. As an example, Harvard University has the largest endowment fund, a value of $26 billion as of June 2009 – and this is after a 27% fall over the financial year. This fund is managed in-house by Harvard Management Company whose intention is to gain maximum return for the fund to finance the educational and research activities of the university. Its investment strategy is very long-term as the aim of endowment funds is generally to generate income to finance projects as opposed to using capital. There are many endowment funds attached to universities, corporations, charities and, once again, these funds will need to be invested. Whilst it is traditionally said that a 60/40 equity/debt portfolio is the normal portfolio for a fund of this type, giving potential for long-term capital appreciation through the equity component whilst generating income through the debt, many of these endowment funds are now run much more actively and can be quite innovative in the structures they put into their portfolios. This is a double-edged sword because whilst this means they can achieve higher than average returns it also means that they became the sort of investor that carried large exposure to the asset-backed security market, which as we have said many times was one of the major contributors that led to the Financial Crisis.

So with a quick look at these various sources of funds we can get an idea of how diverse the investment market can be. We have spoken of funds that are basically invested permanently in the markets and others that are left there for only short periods of time. We have conservative investors, like pension funds, and others that may be willing to take on 'riskier' exposures in return for income. This is why it is important that, when funds are placed in the hands of an investment manager, they pay attention to the source of these funds as this will give insights into how the money should be appropriately invested.

In the next chapter we will take a look at the basic processes of investment management and start to get an idea of how this can be put into practice but in Text Box 20.1 we have a summary of how this group might collectively be seen in the financial markets. We have put this together collectively to underline that their job is intrinsically the same. The differences we will see will typically come from shifts in emphasis, with maybe one group being more active in derivatives, or another group being predominantly in fixed income. But in terms of the bigger picture of how they fit into the infrastructure the following will essentially apply to all:

Box 20.1 Summary of Investment Company Activity in the Financial Markets

Their role in the markets:

- Investment companies are technically seen as issuers in the market by using capital market structures to raise funds, such as OEICs issuing shares. Really, though, this is just a vehicle to enable the funds to be listed on exchanges and therefore achieve a level of transparency or liquidity. Lots of these firms are private companies and so they will sometimes use the equity market to raise funding, and occasionally we will see them issuing debt in the markets to raise funds for their corporate purpose.
- It is as investors that they are most commonly understood and actively seen.
- They are intermediaries in as much as they form the link between the owners of the money, the stakeholders and the market. This intermediary relationship is a long-term one, though, with them taking responsibility for the funds over a long time horizon after they are placed in the market.

The markets in which they are most active:

- They will be very active in both money markets and FX. These funds can be multi-currency, so leading to FX exposure, and they will normally all have an element of cash reserve which will need to be invested in the money markets. We also have specialist funds, the money market funds, that invest exclusively in money market products.
- Long-term debt and equity are their natural homes. Whether a fund invests more in equities or debt will depend on its objectives. As a rule of thumb, an investor wanting capital appreciation and the ability to take significant credit risk will go to the equity market, whilst those looking for capital safety and income will look to the debt market. Obviously these markets are far more sophisticated than this, and offer a wide range of products, but at the end of the day the investors need to understand the risk tolerance and return

---

requirements of the funds they are managing and this will drive their asset allocation decisions.

- As a group they are quite heavy users of derivatives for risk management, although less so than we saw in the last part of this book, Quasi-Sovereigns and Supranationals, who we said were large uses for risk management. This is because this group is one of net investors and on the whole investors hedge their positions far less than borrowers. There will be some investment companies that will use derivatives for investment, but the biggest group of these will be the hedge funds for whom derivatives form an intrinsic part of many of their strategies.

21

Basic Structure of Investment Management

Since we have now looked at some of the types of firm that carry out this business and their sources of funds we are going to look a little more at the processes that go into it. We will take a look at how a firm might be organized and what are the key responsibilities of the investment manager so we can have an understanding of how this works as a business within the financial markets.

Obviously whenever we try to talk generically about anything we have to be aware that one size does not fit all. We have already seen this in the first couple of sections of this book when we spoke generically about banks and then went on to speak about the different banking landscapes in several countries. In investment management our differences will not be driven so much by differences in location but more by differences in size, and yet again, sources of funds. However, having said this, the basic tasks and responsibilities need to remain the same; the differences will tend to arise in organization.

When money comes into an investment management firm this money is entrusted to them and their duty is to look after these funds, invest them appropriately and account for them to the owner, the stakeholder. We have already said there are two main routes by which the funds will be allocated, either into a collective investment scheme or into a managed portfolio. Depending on which route is taken the process for fulfilling these core duties will be different. In both cases, though, the funds will be allocated to a fund manager or managers whose responsibility will be to find the best investment, and there will be others whose job it is to track and monitor the funds. This latter is part of the administration side, and is something that can either be managed in-house or outsourced. We will talk more of this later.

COLLECTIVE INVESTMENT PRODUCTS

If funds are placed in a collective investment product then it is the investment management house that is the one that has already determined how the money will be invested and the stakeholder has only to decide whether this vehicle suits their purpose or not. The fund will be created in principle and in legal form before it receives any money so that when the product is marketed potential investors will be given the information they need to make an informed decision. This will include telling them about:

- the structure of the fund
- any restrictions on potential buyers
- the investment strategy
- the expertise of the firm in running this type of fund.

This information is normally carried in a prospectus which is a key sales document for the fund.

Structure

There are various structures that can be used for these investment vehicles. Below are some definitions of the most commonly used types that we will see, although we are going to encounter different names in different countries. However these definitions are of the most common structures and the most commonly used expressions:

Open-Ended Investment Company (OEIC) – this is also known as an Investment Company with Variable Capital (ICVC). This vehicle is created as a company with shares being issued as money is placed into the fund, and then being cancelled as money is taken out. It is open-ended so there is no limit to how much money can be placed within the fund; it is continually open to new investment. The assets in which OEICs can invest will include predominantly equity and debt, but they can also invest in other assets such as property and even other funds so creating a wide range of potential products all using this structure. The fund is run by a board of directors and the shareholders generally have voting rights attached to their shares. Traditionally OEICs have one single price, the asset value of the fund. However nowadays there are some that employ dual pricing, a bid and an ask, a price at which the shares would be cancelled and one at which they would be sold. Clearly if we have two prices then we will have a difference, a spread, between the two and this spread represents an administrative cost.

SICAV – this is another open-ended form common in Western Europe, particularly in Luxembourg, Spain and Switzerland, and is comparable to the OEIC. There is also a closed-end form, a *SICAF*, which has a limited number of shares available. A closed-end fund means that the fund will close – not accept any new investment – once it reaches a certain level of subscription. The SICAV structure is often used as an umbrella, with a number of funds being issued by the company under one main programme. For example we could have a SICAV that was to invest in European equity, so there could be a range of funds such as French blue-chip stocks, Dutch high-tech stocks, Emerging Eastern European equity etc. There can also be different share structures within the funds, with some, for example, being targeted at retail investors and some at institutional, so the product overall becomes as flexible as possible.

Mutual fund – this is the US version of the OEIC and SICAV, but predates them by several decades. It is also an expression that is often used as a generic one to describe a collective or pooled investment vehicle. As before these can be either open or closed-end funds and they can also issue different shares within the fund, although often these relate to expenses and distributions rather than limiting investor groups.

Investment trust – this is another share-based investment vehicle. They are closed-end funds and tend to carry quite strict controls on how the fund can be invested. A good example from the US is the large market for Real Estate Investment Trusts (REITs). These funds have to be at least 75% invested in property, with at least 75% of their income also deriving from this source through rents or interest from mortgages on the property. They also have to distribute 90% of their income to the shareholders as dividends. So we can see the structure is very prescriptive and the funds will normally have trustees overseeing their composition to ensure they meet the requirements. Since investment trusts are closed-end we can often see an unusual situation in that their value as listed securities often differs from the net asset value of the holdings (NAV), more commonly trading at a discount to the NAV rather than at a premium. This means that the sum of all the shares in the fund can be worth less than the assets held, which really makes no sense. This is a result of supply and demand but is an anomaly in the market that can reflect badly on the fund and its management. So to counter this many managers try to control these movements by having a share buy-back scheme in place. If the price of the investment trust falls to a level that is deemed too low then the company itself will buy back and cancel shares to support its price level.

Unit trust – this is a different sort of structure from the share-based systems above. With the unit trust structure investors in the fund receive a certain amount of units representing the value of their investment. The fund is open-ended so units are created and dissolved as money moves in and out, but unlike the structures we have looked at so far all income on the fund is retained with the investors being given more units, as opposed to being paid out in dividends. To give an example of how this works, if we take a fund with $1,000,000 invested by 10 investors they may receive 100,000 units with a value of $1 per unit. If the fund then makes a 10% absolute return the value of the fund is now $1,100,000. This value is translated to the investors by increasing their unit holdings, giving each of them a holding now of 110,000 units. An equivalent structure often seen in French speaking parts of Europe is the *Fonds Communal de Placement (FCP)*.

It is the investment management company that decides which of the structures is the most appropriate for their target market, bearing in mind any restrictions or incentives, such as the ability to make a certain structure tax-efficient for potential investors. Whilst we said at the beginning that differences in this part of the business are not driven so much by location we do have to bear in mind the response of individual country regulators to the need to protect their markets, particularly retail investors. For this reason there will be differences in the structures according to the locations as some regulators will apply more stringent restrictions than others. The job of the investment management house is to know these restrictions and also to be aware of opportunities. Sometimes an investment management house will create a new structure for a specific purpose or customer. This was the case in 2007 in Germany when the German bank HSBC Trinkaus created a new vehicle specifically targeted at a German pension fund, the Nordrheinische Aerztversorgung (NAEV), which actually worked together with the investment managers to create the structure of the fund to suit its requirements. This was created under the structure of a German *spezialfond*, a structure that is limited to institutional investors, and which can be created for one investor, as in this case, or for a group of investors. This fund took advantage of a change in the law in 2007 that allowed institutional funds to be created in a very different way from retail ones, giving them far more freedom in investment and with fewer restrictions on investment product and limits.

Restrictions

We have already touched on this but it is important that any product offered for sale will be legally acceptable. The spezialfonds mentioned above are a good illustration of this, funds that can only be sold to institutional customers, not retail. So again before the fund can be launched the firm will need to decide, along with the structure, where would be the best place to list the fund and to be aware of any selling restrictions this might bring and incorporate this into its target audience and its marketing.

Investment Strategy

This is a crucial part of the process because collective investment schemes are created to pool investor funds to give more efficient access to the market. The downside is that if the investor opts to buy one of these funds they give up the ability to make specific investment decisions. So it is important to let the investors know how the funds will be invested. If a fund advertises itself as being a UK-based (sterling) Asian equity fund should we expect to see the fund investing in UK banks? Well, the answer is maybe we should. The fund is an Asian equity fund but that fund will also need to keep some of its assets in cash, so it is very likely to use deposits or money market products of a UK bank to place these funds. The big question that should be asked is how much is 'some'? Whilst 10% might be acceptable, would 90% also be acceptable? The investment strategy should set out how the fund will be invested: the geographical area; types of securities to be used; use of derivatives for risk management and/or risk creation; target for return (if this is applicable); and may even include a projected portfolio breakdown. It also has to explain any particular risks that the fund might encounter as well as carrying legal disclaimers on performance. Beyond this it will also provide information on the fees the investment management firm will be taking from the fund for its services. All of this is to give the investor insight into how the fund will be operated and the kinds of risks they can expect the manager to be taking and returns they are expecting to achieve.

Expertise

Since an investor would be abdicating responsibility for their investment decisions to an investment manager it is important that they know something of their expertise. This is often done by benchmarking similar funds against one another. Generally we look at these returns over a given time period and there are several services in the market that offer these comparisons. This is quite easy for the more common funds, but obviously more difficult for the more esoteric investment universe. The specific individual fund managers working on the funds will tend to be allocated according to their specialism, so any one fund may have a number of fund managers involved in running it depending on the breadth of the fund. The fund manager in charge of each part of the fund will normally be named and their biography will include details of their experience. Again this is about establishing credibility and there are some investors who will follow fund managers as they move around the market. Other things that tend to be considered are the quality of the research of the firm and its ability to administer the fund – although this is less transparent and is often, probably wrongly, considered less important.

All of this is the sort of information that should be included in the prospectus for the fund that is used to inform and attract potential investors and help them to make an informed investment decision.

UCITS – UNDERTAKING FOR COLLECTIVE INVESTMENTS IN TRANSFERABLE SECURITIES

It is worth mentioning this set of European directives that were first adopted in 1985 and were intended to allow pan-European selling of collective investment schemes. In order to be UCITs compliant the funds had to be open-ended and invest in transferable securities. The intention was to create a single European market with a single regulator and a level playing field for all the European UCIT compliant funds. However this was over-ambitious for the time as marketing rules in the various countries really made this impossible. The early 1990s saw negotiations on a revised plan, UCITS II, but the member states were unable to agree on how far this should go and so eventually the directive was abandoned. Then in 1998 negotiations began again, leading to UCITS III being adopted in 2001, with firms being given until 2007 to ensure their funds would be fully UCIT compliant. The reason for this five-year introduction was because UCITS III introduced some quite broad changes to the market. It was divided into two parts, the first looking at the management of the fund, and the second the actual composition. For the management side the UCITS III compliant funds can be sold anywhere in Europe under a 'passport' scheme, with a simplified prospectus that would be easily understood and accessible to all. On the investment side the funds would be classified as *sophisticated* and *non-sophisticated*. The latter would be traditional funds invested in securities. Sophisticated funds could be very different. Apart from just investing in securities these funds could also invest in derivatives and other asset classes, such as commodities or real estate, and they can also invest in other funds, a strategy of indirect investment whereby they are creating funds of funds. They could also use different investment strategies such as taking short positions[1] as well as long ones within the portfolio. A major proviso is that the investor cannot be exposed to greater losses than their investment and that the fund manager will have to provide the regulators with detailed risk management proposals.

UCITS IV is the latest development, approved in 2009 for implementation in 2011. This is intended to further streamline the process and allow potential cost savings. For example, under UCITS IV there would no longer be a need to produce a prospectus, despite everything we have been saying about its usefulness. Instead this would be replaced by a two-page Key Investor Information document that will put more responsibility onto the investor to research the firm themselves. Similarly funds could also be set up under a cross-border 'Master Feeder' organizational structure, like we saw in our description of SICAVs, whereby assets can be pooled for a number of funds. This is a structure that exists at national level, but under UCITS IV would be allowed at a cross-border level across Europe. Probably one of the most significant features is the 'Management Company Passport' that would allow the investment managers to sell funds across the EU without having to have individual national administration in place, and also for funds to be managed across borders, with a management company in one EU country being allowed to manage a fund domiciled in another. These changes may not be so visible to investors but will make it much easier for funds to run efficiently and also to merge, which is no bad thing as the market is very fragmented with many funds which are too small to achieve the best economies of scale and so are not run as cost-effectively as others. These are exactly the funds that could potentially benefit from changes in the rules on mergers. This directive has not been uniformly

---

[1] A short position is one where the fund manager sells a risk, such as a security, that they do not yet own. At some point they will have to cover the position by buying it back, but the trade was made in the belief that the price of the position will fall. If it does they will then be able to buy it back at a cheaper level to close it out and so make a profit and conversely will lose if the price rises. In the meantime there are well-developed markets to facilitate the 'borrowing' of securities in the interim, which, of course will have to be returned when the position has been closed out.

welcomed and it remains to be seen how the market will cope with the administrative challenges that are bound to come about as these changes are introduced.

As of September 2009 the European investment fund industry comprised 52,715 funds of which 36,588 were UCITS compliant, with a net value of €5,157,294 million ($7,553,949)[2].

MANAGED PORTFOLIOS

If the firm is managing a portfolio on a customer's behalf then the investment process will be a little different from the one we have just seen for the collective schemes. Before the portfolio can be created it is important that the investment manager understands the objectives of the stakeholder. A customer looking to have their funds invested to generate high income flows will need a very different portfolio from one looking for long-term capital appreciation. So the manager cannot even begin to build the portfolio without understanding these objectives. They again also need to be aware of any regulatory restrictions. Pension funds are a good example of this, although restrictions will vary from country to country. For example in Australia pension funds have essentially no limits on what they can invest in, whilst in Korea there are limits or restrictions on pretty much everything except domestic bank deposits. So again the investment management firm would need to be aware of these restrictions and ensure the portfolio adheres to them.

Once the investment manager has a good idea of what the fund is trying to achieve and any restrictions then they can start to build the criteria for the fund. These criteria will form the basis for asset selection and allocation within the portfolio. In order to be efficient these criteria will tend to be quite generalized and what sounds like a highly tailored solution is often one that can be replicated for a number of customers. However this is being sold as a tailored service so if the customer has a particular investment request that will always be incorporated within the investment plan.

Once the criteria have been established the portfolio can be built up by the manager looking for assets that fit within the criteria and start to look for the best mix of risk and return.

---

[2] EFAMA, 2009.

BUILDING AND RUNNING THE PORTFOLIO

Whether we are talking about a managed portfolio or collective investment scheme the process of building and running the portfolio will be the same. In each case the aim is to find the best possible combination of assets that fit within the framework of the fund. Depending on the size of the portfolio this can be a lengthy process, and sometimes a fund will not be fully invested for many months. During this time the money will still need to be invested but typically this will be in the money markets or possibly very liquid securities such as government bonds so that these short time horizon investments can be liquidated as the longer view assets become available. Investment managers are not like traders; they are not trying to find investments to hold for a short time to make relatively small capital gains. Their perspective is far more long-term so we would not expect to see them trading excessively on the portfolios. This is called 'churning' and is not a practice that has much validity in investment management except, possibly, for hedge funds for certain of their strategies. However fund managers are not immune to market movements so when the value of one of their assets changes it can alter how it fits within the portfolio. If a price rises then there could be another asset out there that fits the criteria yet gives a better return so it makes sense to trade out of the first asset and buy the new one. This may look like trading but is really portfolio management as it should always be undertaken with the view of the whole portfolio in mind. The manager is also going to have to think about hedging the portfolio, managing the risks that are in the assets, typically using derivatives to do this. Depending on how the fund is created this could mean managing interest rate risk, credit risk, currency risk, and since the level of protection put into the portfolio will affect its potential performance, they often have to make very strategic risk management decisions. Sometimes this decision will be helped by a house strategy: for example a blanket decision to hedge all currency exposure whilst leaving the risk of individual assets to the discretion of the manager.

The firm will also have to make sure that they can manage the investments after the trades have been made. They need to take responsibility for the safekeeping of the assets, which in practice will most commonly mean tracking them through the various central depositories in which the securities will be held, the bank accounts in which funds will be kept, ensuring that all transfer of ownership takes place efficiently, any expected payments duly received and/or made and the client's accounts updated accordingly. All of this is part of the settlement and custody process that forms part and parcel of fund management, although as a series of functions it may be that they are kept in-house but alternatively they can be outsourced. The funds that have been invested belong to the customer, so the firm has to provide reports and valuations to show how well the investments are faring. In some firms the investment manager has to justify every single trade so that, if necessary, the firm could prove that the funds were being managed with optimum care. This comes in the wake of some high profile court cases, notably amongst them the 2001 case between Unilever and Mercury Asset Management (MAM) (at the time of the case owned by Merrill Lynch before being sold to Blackrock Investments), in which Unilever accused MAM of negligence for not sufficiently supervising a young investment manager who they claimed managed their pension fund in too risky a fashion. The case was ultimately settled out of court, but at the time attracted a lot of publicity and attention – and more claims of mismanagement against MAM. In the normal course of events the investment management firm will produce an investment report on a periodic basis for the stakeholders, be it daily, weekly, monthly or whenever, whilst internally the managers will be monitoring values and trade flows continuously.

As we have mentioned they will also have to deal with cash flows into and out of the funds. Many of the assets will produce income, interest payments on debt, dividends on equity, and these cash flows have to be both collected and allocated which means keeping track of stakeholder values at all times. This can be particularly onerous for the collective investment schemes, but is absolutely necessary as these income flows represent part of the value of the funds. This is why many firms outsource this administrative part of the business and there is a thriving industry for funds administration. One of the advantages is that this does not need to be based in a financial centre, just as long as there are good internal communication lines. In Europe, Dublin is a perfect example of how this can work with many banks and other companies setting up fund administration businesses in the city to take advantage of lower costs rather than being, for example, in London. In fact the business expanded so rapidly that the firms had to expand beyond Dublin to other locations across Ireland to find the workforce to meet the demands of the growing business. Similarly other cities in the UK, such as Edinburgh, Birmingham, Belfast, have all attracted this type of business from the UK investment industry, although it is not necessary for the administration of the fund to take place in the same country as the fund managers are located. It is perfectly possible to have a fund managed in Paris but with the administration taking place in Mumbai. Just as long as there is an efficient flow of information then theoretically the two tasks, whilst inherently linked, can be treated as separate entities and so the decision on where to carry out these administrative tasks will lie within the firm.

So, all in all, everything about this business of investment management centres on trying to achieve the best acceptable returns for the stakeholder and controlling the whole spectrum of risks associated with this, not just the obvious market risks of running financial positions. Understanding the responsibilities that come with managing other people's money is really key to creating the processes that mean we will have as few court cases like Unilever and MAM as possible.

22
Traditional Investment Managers

We have now looked at some of the institutions that run investment management business and some of their sources of funds, so in this chapter we are going to focus on the most common group of commercial firms, the professional investment management companies. We are going to look at who are some of these firms, their owners and their expertise, so that we can get a sense of the sort of companies and products available on the market. We are not going to pay too much attention to the hedge funds at the moment, as they are covered in a separate chapter, since they have an interesting approach to this investment market. Instead we are going to focus on the more mainstream companies and products so that we can see the range available on the street and consider their importance to the financial markets.

The business of investment management has been around for something like 150 years. Probably one of the earliest investment management companies still in existence is the Scottish American Investment Company Ltd, which now forms part of Bailey Gifford, a UK-based investment firm. The 1920s saw the beginnings of some of today's major names, such as Wellington Management and John Hancock of the US, companies that in their 90-year existence have grown to be amongst the largest in the world. In 2008 global assets of the fund management industry totalled over $96 billion asset value, including funds held in money market funds.[1] This was down by 17% on the previous year, but this had followed five years of continuous growth. The chart in Figure 22.1 shows the breakdown of the sources of these funds:

The US is by far the biggest contributor to funds under management, accounting for more than 50% of the pension, insurance and mutual funds, and almost half of all funds under management, with Europe being not far behind.

In the next chapter we will look at insurance companies, as they contribute in two ways to this industry: one, as a major source of investment funds, and, two, as an investment manager in their own right.

---

[1] IFSL Fund Management, 2009.

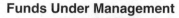

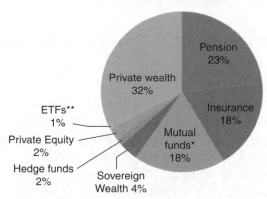

Figure 22.1   Sources of Investment Funds

*Mutual funds is used as a generic expression for collective investment schemes
**ETFs (Exchange Traded Funds) are a form of tracker collective investment scheme that we will discuss below

One area that is expected to see growth in funds under management in the coming years is Asia, particularly Asia ex-Japan, and, probably not surprisingly, China seems to be showing the most signs of long-term growth potential. Whilst China's public funds have been actively targeted by the fund management companies over the past few years their private institutional funds have been less visible, being predominantly managed in-house, but this is a trend that may change, following the model of the public funds and relaxing of restrictions by the Chinese regulators.

INVESTMENT MANAGEMENT IN BANKS

When we looked at the business of banks we saw that often amongst their core businesses we find investment management offered as a service to their customers. As we said in the last chapter the banks have to take care to show that their investment management divisions are separate from other areas of the bank, in particular their trading divisions. This is because of the very real potential conflict of interest. Both the traders and the investment managers work for the bank, so their primary responsibility must be to the bank. However the investment manager also carries a large responsibility to the stakeholder of the funds that they are investing, the responsibility to manage the funds fairly and efficiently. Given all the discussions that have been taking place about desegregating banks and a potential return to a Glass-Steagall-like regime in banking, the topic of whether investment management should also be separated has arisen. Partly this is due to a fall in income in the post-Financial Crisis period, that made people re-evaluate what had previously been thought to be a business model that would make pretty consistent, fee-based rather than risk-based income, but falling asset values, and fees related to this, have proven this to be untrue. We do have to remember that this is a very competitive business, particularly for the institutional funds, which have actually shown that they can be quite surprisingly mobile, with the institutional stakeholders constantly evaluating and benchmarking the fund managers to whom they have outsourced money management. There also seems to be a trend to increasing the spread of managers, particularly following the high-profile fall of houses like Lehman Brothers, to avoid the complications that arise from being a customer of a failed bank.

Whilst the large, international banks should be very well placed to attract global funds in actual fact there is a strong nationalist tendency when it comes to placing funds under management. These banks find that, despite their best efforts, the bulk of their funds come from their home markets so their global networks are not really being exploited to their best advantage. This explains many of the cross-border acquisitions we have seen as the banks buy investment companies based in their target markets to build up their presence and help develop their relationships with clients overseas. It is interesting that global banking brands need to do this which is a characteristic that differentiates banking and financial markets from other global industries such as cars and soft drinks!

In January 2010 a new investment management partnership was formed with the creation of Amundi Asset Management, a joint venture between Crédit Agricole and Société Générale, two French banks who would traditionally have competed for business. Instead by joining forces their aim was to create economies of scale and, working with other partner banks and investment firms, to create a global offering across all sections of the investment management business from institutional to retail, from traditional to alternative investment products. This model of cooperation could become more common in the future as the market is seeing a period of consolidation, following the acquisition of Barclays Global Investors (BGI) by BlackRock, and the probability that more bank asset management divisions may be separated from the banks and sold into the private, or semi-private, sector.

NON BANK INVESTMENT COMPANIES

The non bank part of the market is a large and thriving area, ranging from small firms with only a few million dollars under management, to firms like Blackrock, which since the merger with Barclays Global Investors in December 2009, found itself with $3.2 trillion in assets. This is more than twice the size of the second largest investment manager, a bank that specializes in asset management and related services, State Street. BlackRock is an independent company, although its share ownership in 2009 was nearly 80% in the hands of three banks, Bank of America, PNC Financial Services Group and Barclays PLC, none of which had a majority holding, and with Bank of America being the largest share-holder with 34%. BlackRock had previously acquired Merrill Lynch Investment Management, a Bank of America company, which explains the legacy share ownership from this deal. The other 20% holding of the company was by individual and institutional investors through its listing on the New York Stock Exchange. Another interesting structure is that of Vanguard, the US-based Investment Company with, at end of 2009, $1.3 trillion in assets, making it the fifth largest non bank-owned Investment Company. Vanguard is neither publicly traded nor owned by a bank or other private shareholders; instead it is owned by its funds, of which it has more than 200 internationally. This then is a cooperative structure such as we have seen with the cooperative banks. These independent companies do not have to answer questions about conflicts in interest as their business is exclusively managing money on behalf of clients, and servicing this industry, but their potential flaw lies in their very independence. If we have said that the industry saw a downturn due to a fall in asset value and associated fees this has to affect the independent investment management companies as much as the bank owned, and in terms of relative size then most of them must be more vulnerable to failure than a large, full-service bank. We have certainly seen this in 2008 and 2009 in the hedge funds part of the industry. This is an issue that, once again, the regulators have to monitor carefully. Investment management is predominantly a very regulated part of the market, at all levels from the management of the firm, to the management of the product, to the distribution networks employed to sell the investment

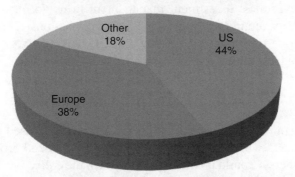

Figure 22.2   Sources of Funds by Geographic Location

products to the retail investors, although much has been made of the regulatory status of hedge funds, that we will discuss shortly.

INVESTMENT MANAGEMENT PRODUCTS

As we said in the last chapter there are two ways of managing money, through a managed portfolio or within a collective investment scheme. As we saw earlier, the US is the largest source for these funds, but Europe combined is not that far behind. In 2009 the geographical breakdown of funds was as shown in Figure 22.2.[2]

There are two styles of investment management, *passive* and *active* management. Passive management is designed to have the minimum amount of movements within the fund as the money is invested to replicate and therefore track an index. Active management focuses on trying to outperform the market by investment selection. These are very different styles of investment management and there is always much debate about which produces the best results. It is in active management that we come across the superstar fund managers, the individuals who seem to be able to choose the stocks that will outperform the market. Some names, such as Warren Buffett, spring to mind as being particularly successful, although none of these are infallible. It is also quite difficult for a stakeholder, particularly an institutional stakeholder, to pin too much importance on an individual when it comes to choosing where to place their money as you cannot rely on individuals staying with one company

[2] EFAMA, 2009.

or even within the industry. Even Warren Buffett will have to retire one day! However most investment management firms do make it known how long they retain their managers, and will use long retention rates as a marketing tool, as they can show track records that are attributable to the managers in-house at the time.

CHOOSING THE PRODUCTS

Whichever the style of investment management being used the investment managers will need to employ all sorts of financial products, and possibly others, to build up their portfolios. On the collective investment side they will offer a range of products defined by market, risk level or management style. The job of the investment manager is to build and run these funds according to the criteria set out.

Market

Some funds can be based around a geographic location and/or a particular asset class. For example you could have a Japanese equity fund or European fixed income fund. Whilst the assets will be denominated in the currency of the market, the fund itself can be denominated in any currency, although if this is the case the investment manager will need to manage the currency exposure as well as managing the assets.

We have mentioned money market funds and these are a particular type of market fund that invests in short-term, highly liquid securities and money market deposits. These are supposed to be very safe instruments where the value of the fund should never fall below the nominal amount of the fund's share, the par value, because the maturities are so short. If this does happen this is called 'breaking the buck', and we first saw this in 2008 with a fund that had held a large exposure to commercial paper (short-term debt) of Lehman Brothers at the time of its collapse. Unfortunately following this all the top US dollar money market funds went on to break the buck and so the Treasury had to step in and guarantee these funds for one year, and the Federal Reserve Bank had to put into place liquidity arrangements for them. Following on from this, and after the maturity of the guarantee, in January 2010 the SEC[3] adopted new restrictions on maximum maturities, liquidity and holdings, amongst others, designed to make these funds safer. They also gave the

---

[3] Securities and Exchange Commission.

Funds by Product Type

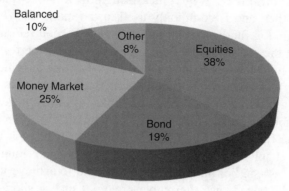

Figure 22.3   Investment Funds by Market

fund manager the ability to suspend the fund if its value falls below the par value and then, if necessary, redeem the fund to avoid there being a run that would further excessively devalue it. The fact that the SEC took these measures is a reflection of the importance of the funds in the market, since the US money market funds were holding $3.5 trillion in assets in 2009.

Aside from single market funds there are also balanced funds that invest across the range of equity and debt, both long and short-term.

Figure 22.3 illustrates the breakdown of funds,[4] showing the dominance in equities, although a growing portion in money market funds.

Target Return

Targeting returns is inextricably linked with the risk of the assets in the fund. If a fund is established as a blue-chip fund it will be investing in the biggest, typically the safer, credits in the market. For example, a blue-chip equity fund will generally invest in the stocks which have the highest market capitalization, a measure of value based on looking at the price of the shares relative to the number of shares in the market. Conversely a high yield fund will invest in riskier assets with the aim of achieving a higher return for taking on the greater level of risk.

Measuring return can be done on either a relative or an absolute basis. A relative return is when you benchmark a fund against another fund

---

[4] EFAMA, 2009.

or an index. Obviously you have to compare like for like, as much as is possible, but this gives a way of measuring how well one fund performs against another, and is commonly used in the markets. What this can show us is that a fund can look to have made a good return but if this is less than the return on the benchmark then it has performed badly. Similarly a fund can lose value and yet still be a star performer if it loses less money than its benchmark. Everything is relative. An absolute return fund takes a different perspective and looks to always make a positive return without reference to a market benchmark. In order to achieve this aim the fund may have to use different management techniques. In the last chapter we mentioned that most funds are long only, they simply buy assets. For an absolute return fund to achieve its objective they may well have to use alternative strategies such as short-selling and using derivatives for investment. Clearly this is taking us into the land of hedge funds that are good examples of absolute return funds, and we will discuss these further in the next chapter.

MANAGEMENT STYLE

As we said, we can find both actively and passively managed funds. The latter are often called tracker funds as they will track a known index. Sometimes the fund will literally buy all the constituents of the index in the same proportion, directly replicating it; others will use more compli-cated financial modelling to derive a range of products that will still track the index without exactly mimicking it. Clearly there will be very little reason to adjust these funds unless there is a change in the index, and these adjustments are often generated by software, not human beings. The actively managed funds are ones where the investment manager decides how to build the fund and takes responsibility for running it, adjusting as they feel fit and appropriate. As we have implied passive funds tend to rely heavily on technology, with automated trading, and can therefore be run very cost-efficiently after the initial investment. According to Standard & Poor's mid-year report for 2009 40.95% of actively managed US domestic equity funds outperformed their bench-marks over a five-year period, and over the same period in the fixed income market no sector of the US fixed income fund saw more than 25% outperforming their benchmark, except emerging markets. In fact of the 13 market sectors studied by S&P seven of them saw less than 10% of active funds outperforming passive so it would suggest that in that year the passive model was more efficient than the active.

One of the reasons that the BlackRock and BGI merger was such a good fit is that BGI specialized in passive funds, whilst BlackRock specialized in active, so there was very little crossover, in terms of product, between the two companies and a great way to expand their offering.

Exchange Traded Funds – ETFs

There is also another product, called an Exchange Traded Fund (ETF) that is another form of tracker fund. These are normally open-ended funds that are initially sold to authorized investors, large institutions, and are then available to be bought and sold on the secondary market by anyone, including retail investors, since they are listed on exchanges. This means that we actually have a sort of hybrid instrument between open and closed fund; as the fund is not strictly increased or decreased on demand, these actions are limited to the authorized investors, and for others they need to buy and sell the funds on the secondary market within the Stock Exchange on which it is listed. Whilst ETFs do not necessarily have to be tracker funds, in practice most of them are. They are a reasonably young product, dating back to 1989, but in that time they have become an important part of the investment landscape.

These traditional investment managers are the most visible forms of the commercial investment management business, exhibiting the core trait of managing other people's money. This is an interesting part of our market, and one in which we are likely to see changes and consolidations over the next few years.

23
Hedge Funds

So far we have looked at the role of traditional investment management, but now we are going to take a look at an alternative style of investment management, that employed by the hedge funds. These investment managers work with a different investment model using a broad range of instruments and strategies. They tend to attract a lot of attention, in good times because of the returns they make, and in bad times because they can fail, therefore risking investor funds. This comes about from the combination of assets and strategy, which are designed to maximize performance. We could say that this is the aim of all investment management, which is true, but it is all about how this aim is achieved. Hedge funds also attract attention because of their regulatory status – or rather their perceived lack of regulatory status. They often appear to fall through the cracks of regulation, not being treated in the same way as the main body of investment management because of the structures they employ. The hedge funds will insist this helps them to achieve the returns they seek, but the regulators are considering what can be done to bring these firms more into the mainstream and so under stricter regulation. The Finance Bills going through the US Senate and House of Representatives in 2010 both include provisions for tightening regulation on the larger hedge funds, calling for them to be registered and to open their books for public scrutiny. Whilst the bills may differ in precise content, they agree in intention so it is highly likely that some form of hedge fund registration will be brought into the market. In Europe the Alternative Investment Fund Management Directive proposed in 2009 went further, calling for registration of larger funds but also imposing limits on borrowing and pay, and these restrictions would also apply to non EU funds wanting to market to EU investors since they would have to register with a local regulator. This is a politically very sensitive issue, contested by the US and within the EU the UK. However, since the UK and the Czech Republic seemed to stand alone in their objection to these proposals it is very probable that the Directive will be adopted.

In the aftermath of recent events hedge funds have been criticized for exacerbating the Financial Crisis due to the size of their trades and the fact that they will take short positions as easily as they take long ones. So, when the banks were at their most vulnerable hedge funds were seen to be shorting their equity making the situation even worse for them. Many countries, the UK, US, Germany and France included, imposed bans on short selling in 2008, and Germany did so again in May 2010 in the aftermath of the Greece crisis, although Japan did not join in imposing this general ban. To be fair to the hedge funds, though, part of the reason they were seen as aggressively selling at the period of the Crisis was to put their assets into cash as they were experiencing many redemptions, investors wanting to remove their investment from the fund, and also just to protect capital in such a volatile market – a conservative investment management strategy. However when market commentators want a scapegoat the hedge funds often seem to fit the bill.

HISTORY

The first hedge fund was set up in 1949 by Alfred W. Jones who had spent the previous few years studying the markets and market performance. He started his fund with $100,000, $40,000 of which was his, and decided to employ a technique that he believed would give the best chance of beating the odds in investment. The technique he used was to become a classic strategy for hedge funds, long-short strategy. This involved taking long equity positions in the fund in the normal way, but then selling short other stocks in order to hedge the risk on the longs. So the net positions were both long and short in different risks.

To show an example of this if you take a long position in Volkswagen and an offsetting short position in Peugeot your position can have any of the following nine outcomes:

1. Volkswagen goes **up** – you make a **profit**
   Peugeot goes **down** – you make a **profit**
   The best possible outcome
2. Volkswagen goes **down** – you **lose**
   Peugeot goes **up** – you **lose**
   The worst possible outcome
3. Volkswagen remains **flat**
   Peugeot remains **flat**
   You make neither profit nor loss
4. Volkswagen remains **flat**
   Peugeot goes **up**
   You lose

5. Volkswagen remains **flat**
   Peugeot goes **down**
   You make a profit
6. Volkswagen goes **up**
   Peugeot remains **flat**
   You make a profit
7. Volkswagen goes **down**
   Peugeot remains **flat**
   You lose

In all of these first seven outcomes you make or lose depending on the movement, but the crucial thing is that in each case the two equities have moved in a different pattern, either one going up and the other down, or one moving and the other not. The interesting outcome happens when the equities move in the same direction:

8. Volkswagen goes **up**
   Peugeot goes **up**
   You win if Volkswagen rises more than Peugeot
9. Volkswagen goes **down**
   Peugeot goes **down**
   You win if Peugeot falls more than Volkswagen

It is these last two outcomes which are the true arbitrage trade. Ideally the fund manager finds assets that are positively correlated with one another, and so should move in the same direction, but the expertise of the trade is in determining which will move the most. This is very simply put, and there are plenty of variations, but it goes to illustrate how Jones was spreading risk, since if you had taken an outright long position in Volkswagen you gain if the share rises, and lose if it falls. However with this strategy you can gain regardless of what happens to Volkswagen as long as you have the relationship you expect.

In 1952 Jones converted his company from a straightforward partnership to a limited partnership fund and, working with several other investment managers, he created the first multimanager fund. It was in the 1960s that Jones and the other investment managers came to public view, in particular the levels of return that they had achieved on the funds using Jones' strategy. This marked the beginning of a boom in this industry and the time when the description hedge fund was coined to describe what is basically a hedged strategy. In Jones' mind his was a conservative investment strategy that he felt could outperform straightforward risk investing, and yet this part of the industry is today considered by many to be highly speculative. This is to do with how hedge funds have evolved, adopting new strategies that may be less easy to understand and also the business model can, in some cases, involve the fund in losses greater than the sum of the investments. There have also been a few spectacular scandals surrounding hedge funds.

Quantum Fund

This was the hedge fund established by George Soros, the famous trader, speculator and fund manager, and his partner Jim Rogers, a fund that at one time was the largest hedge fund in the world. It was also the vehicle through which George Soros was famously said to have taken on the central banks in 1992. This was at a time when the European currency markets were coming under a lot of scrutiny and criticism for the workings of the Exchange Rate Mechanism (ERM). This was the precursor to the introduction of the euro which bound the currencies of the European Union that had joined the system to trade within bands from a starting point, being the one at which they had entered the system. This was intended to limit volatility and ease the way for combining the currencies into one at the end of the century, and presumed that the entry level would be a fair market rate. Unfortunately many thought that some currencies had joined the System at the wrong time and therefore had unrealistic levels from which to try and peg their market movements, the UK amongst them. Things came to a head in September 1992 when, following a few attacks on some of the less high-profile currencies, such as the Swedish Kroner, the market, with apparently Soros' Quantum fund at the forefront, took on the Bank of England by aggressively selling the UK pound. It is said that Soros sold short the total value of the hedge fund – and won. The UK government ultimately took the UK out of the ERM and Quantum reportedly made a multibillion dollar profit on the deal. This was not Quantum's only high-profile foray into the currency markets as just five years later Soros was publicly blamed for leading an attack on the Malaysian Ringgit, leading to the currency losing 50% of its value. A lot of the impact of these trades is caused by the size of the trade, a size that the market, in this case represented by the central banks, found difficult to cope with.

Tiger Management Corp

As an example of what can happen when trades go wrong, the year 2000 saw a couple of big downturns for the industry. One affected the

Quantum funds, when the fund had to be restructured following a string of losses in the high-tech equity market. This followed a bad period for Quantum as they had already had to close one fund in 1998 when Quantum Emerging Markets had to be closed after losing one third of its value following a fall in value of the Russian Rouble, so having to restructure again on the string of more losses in the market was difficult for them and damaging for their reputation. In 2000 Quantum was still the biggest hedge fund in the world, but confidence in the whole sector had been knocked not just by this but by another event in the same year. This second example of how things could turn against these funds was the closure of all the funds of Tiger Management Corporation. Tiger Management was a very high-profile fund company founded by Julian Robertson, and they closed all their funds in March 2000 following a period of troubles, most notably highlighted by the fact that the fund held a very large position in US Airways, a failing company, that proved to be the wrong investment. So we can see that whilst these funds can make exceptional returns they are also potentially vulnerable, and this vulnerability is highlighted even more by Long-term Capital Management.

Long-term Capital Management (LTCM)

This was a fund created by a group of extremely successful traders at Salomon Brothers, led by John Meriwether, who left the bank to form the fund, along with a former Vice Chairman of the Federal Reserve Bank, David Mullins, and two top economists, Myron Scholes and Robert C. Merton. The latter were famous for their work on option pricing, and became Nobel Prize winners for Economics. In 1993 the fund opened with $1.25 billion of investment. Its basic structure was an arbitrage one, a model that involves dealing in products from related markets, such as between asset classes, interest rates etc. Basically the fund was looking for investments that were relatively out of line. In very simple terms, using analytical techniques they looked for when instruments moved away from their perceived fair value and would then buy or sell accordingly. They also ran a very highly leveraged model which meant they only had to generate a small margin over their cost of borrowing to translate into large profits. So all was set for a stellar fund, and in the first years the fund did achieve typically good returns, averaging around 40%, and with assets growing to about $120 billion. However within five years it was on the brink of failure and needed intervention from the Federal Reserve Bank to broker a bailout with its creditors. The problem this time lay in the fact that the market did not behave as the mathematics expected it to. We are talking about the same period of time that brought down Quantum and Tiger, and the formulae that LTCM were applying essentially followed the logic that things would return to a 'normal' scenario. For example it believed that if volatility was high then it would lower and that increased differences between values in related markets would return to their status quo. It also believed that the prices of assets had to move incrementally and did not jump. Unfortunately, whilst these things may be fundamentally true they were not being seen in the period leading up to 1998. Added to this was the fact that the fund kept a relatively low capital base, in order to increase its leverage, and we had the situation that market losses led to the fund needing to be bailed out. This took the form of a $3.65 billion loan fund put together by a consortium of 14 banks, and brokered by the Fed to prevent its failure. This move has been much criticized, because within two years the fund had repaid its debt and then liquidated in 2000, so it has to be questioned whether the bailout was necessary on a number of grounds. Firstly, there was an alternative: a consortium consisting of Warren Buffett's Berkshire Hathaway, Goldman Sachs and AIG offered to buy out the managing partners of the fund for $250 million and recapitalize it with $3.75 billion. This deal was not attractive to these partners as they would have lost their jobs and most of their investment, and so they rejected the consortium's offer and hung on to see what the Fed could broker for them, an outcome that proved ultimately far more attractive. Secondly, the Fed's action could have set an unnerving precedent that has shown itself again in the recent *financial crisis*. Strictly speaking LTCM was not really any of the Fed's business and so it should not necessarily have been involved. It chose to become involved though because it feared the failure of the fund would cause intrinsic damage to the financial system owing to its size and influence: the 'too big to fail' concept again. We can hear echoes of this action in 2008 when the Fed brokered a deal to sell the failing investment bank Bear Stearns to JPMorgan Chase for similar reasons.

Hedge Funds in the Twenty-first Century

The Financial Crisis had a significant impact on the hedge funds, with, once again, losses for many funds, but even more significantly major outflows of investment. We do need to put this into context, though,

Table 23.1   10 Largest Hedge Fund Managers

	AUM $ bn
Bridgewater Associates	38.6
JP Morgan	32.9
Paulson & Co.	29
D.E. Shaw Group	28.6
Brevon Howard	26.8
Och-Ziff Capital Management	22.1
Man AHL	22
Soros Fund Management	21
Goldman Sachs Asset Management	20.6
Farallon Capital Management	20
Renaissance Technologies	20

because during the period from 2000 until 2007 the industry grew year on year from an estimated size of around $400 billion to nearly $2.2 trillion.[1] It is hard to get precise figures in this market as it is not very transparent and not subject to the same reporting requirements as other investment companies that we have looked at, but what is beyond doubt is the magnitude of the drop it experienced in 2008 as it fell to around $1.5 trillion, a fall of some 30%. Table 23.1 shows a list of the 10 largest hedge fund managers in January 2009.[2]

We also saw a number of hedge funds having to close on the back of these redemptions and falling asset values, with the smaller funds being particularly affected. The industry also suffered another loss of confidence on the back of situations like the scandal involving Bernie Madoff, who whilst not running a hedge fund, did invest in funds of hedge funds. But more than anything, people have likened the lack of transparency in the hedge fund sector to the lack of transparency that allowed Bernie Madoff to carry out his fraud. However confidence appears to be quite easily restored as despite many anticipating that 2009 would be a bad year for hedge funds, we saw the markets rebound and once again witnessed these funds producing great returns. The HFN Hedge Fund Aggregate Index showed the highest level of performance since 2003, at +19.44% for the year. The centre of the hedge fund industry is in the US, with Europe, particularly the UK, in second place. Asia is relatively small in terms of hedge fund management but is increasingly important as a source of stakeholder funds, and in 2010

---

[1] IFSL estimates.
[2] Institutional Investor, January 2009.

there are certainly firms looking to increase their exposure in this region, with these firms being both Asian and international.

An interesting by-product of the Financial Crisis is the impact it has had on the leverage of hedge funds. At its peak in 2007 the funds carried about 165% of exposure against its assets, meaning that for every $1 it had it took on $1.65 of risk. In 2008 this figure slumped to under 110%,[3] meaning the funds are taking less leveraged positions, a pattern that still appears to be employed in the market, although whether this is by strategic decision or force of circumstances, as lending to them has tightened, is not known. Likely it is a combination of the two.

INVESTMENTS AND STRATEGY

The fees charged by investment managers running hedge funds tend to be higher than more mainstream funds. The managers typically charge a percentage of the profits from the fund as well as a standard administrative charge. This performance fee can be as high as 20% although many investors have renegotiated fees in the light of recent developments. You may have noticed that when we spoke about the various funds involved in the scandals affecting this part of the market we actually named individuals, something we have not done in any other chapters of this section. This is because the individual fund managers play a different role in this part of the market. Typically they are equity holders of the firm, often using their own funds at the start-up of the firm. The track records of the individuals will also play a large part in attracting funds which is why the individuals can become so high-profile. There may also be a limited number of direct investors in the fund, and traditionally this has been the case. In the US this investor base is limited to less than one hundred investors to avoid the fund coming under a different form of classification and regulation. This is one of the reasons the funds of funds have become so significant for hedge funds. This is a way to extend investment within the funds from other sources, such as retail investors, without having the investors placing money directly. To give an example of this, investors in a hedge fund could be high net worth individuals, but they could also be other investment firms, including ones that are running collective investment schemes. So an investmenet management company creates an investment vehicle, such as an OEIC, that takes in funds from, say, the retail market and then invests them in a

---

[3] IFSL estimates.

series of hedge funds. In other words they create a fund of funds. Whilst the retail investor might not be able to invest directly in any single hedge fund, by placing their investment in the fund of funds structure they are able to gain exposure to this sector. From the hedge funds' point of view they are expanding their potential investment base as these 'fund of fund' managers bring to them investment that they would not otherwise be able to access.

In the last chapter we discussed the difference between relative and absolute performance, and hedge funds will typically look for absolute return. In order to achieve this there are various different styles of investment management that they are likely to employ, and below are examples of some of the most common.

HEDGE FUND STRATEGIES

Directional

This is the most common style of hedge fund management. The fund determines what to buy (or sell short) based on a view, whether that is a view on an economy, a currency, a sector or individual securities. Once the investment decision has been made the trade will be put on and this is when we might see the investment manager hedging the position with a long/short strategy. Often they will aim to be market-neutral, where a long position has an offsetting short, and they will make profit just as long as the price of the long position increases more than the price on the short position meaning that the profit made on the long more than offsets a loss made on the short, or vice versa.

Arbitrage Funds

These funds are also known as relative value funds. Their basic concept is to look for anomalies in pricing between related assets. For example, they could buy a currency in a spot market, the market for immediate settlement of the trade, and at the same time sell the currency back in the forward market, for delivery on a future date. If the market has priced these two trades correctly then the price of the forward should be equal to any net return that would be made if the funds were placed in the market in the intervening time, but often the market misprices deals because of the pressures of other factors such as supply and demand, and so a gap might open up. This is the sort of gap that would be identified by the hedge fund and they would then trade on this. Sometimes they will trade on expectation that gaps will open up or close down, and as we saw earlier sometimes this does not work, so this is not a foolproof investment strategy.

Event Driven

These are funds that trade on the back of specific events, such as mergers. If a potential takeover is announced a typical trade would be to buy the shares of the potential acquisition and sell short the shares of the buyer. This is based on the idea that the bid is normally at a higher level than the current trading price of the target stock, and so will rise if the bid is successful. The price of the bidder may fall as the cost of the acquisition has to be factored, but even if this share price rises, which would mean a loss against the short position, it is unlikely to rise as much as the target, so still giving a net profit. Of course this could be wrong, so again this is a risk strategy.

Algorithmic Trading

Hedge funds are generally very technical, whether that is through the way that they apply mathematical formulae to define their strategies, or analysis of individual assets or markets. Therefore it is no surprise that some funds employ quantitative trading strategies where they use computer programs to monitor market movements and patterns and dictate high frequency trades. The funds will often invest in supercomputers and copious amounts of market data to have both the optimum information and ability to manipulate this. This is an area of the market that is still developing with the use of increasingly sophisticated technology and analysis.

REGULATION

There is no single set of regulation that covers all hedge funds globally. In some countries they can only be open-ended as, for example, in Spain or France, whilst in other countries they can be either open or closed-ended. In some countries they can only invest in financial assets and derivatives, whilst in others they can invest in any other assets as well, and in Switzerland they can invest in anything at all except physical commodities. In the US, hedge funds can only be sold to accredited investors, those with a very high minimum investment, typically be-tween $250,000 and $25,000,000, owing to their legal status. This, though, has been challenged in 2010 with the advent of Bernett Capital Management's Bernett Diversified Global Fund. This has been estab-lished by lawyer Sarah Bernett with a minimum investment of $1000, on the basis that the law actually does allow a lower threshold as long as the investor is informed. It will be interesting to see if this marks a sea-change in the US industry. In Europe there are some countries that impose minimum investment criteria, such as Italy with its €250,000 limit, and other countries, such as Luxembourg, where there are no limits on investment and the funds can be freely offered to the public.

All in all, as you can see just from the above examples, we have a very mixed bag, but this may change. In April 2009 the G20 finance ministers announced proposals for overseeing all financial institutions, including hedge funds. This is the first time that this group has been universally included amongst the key financial institutions. The intention would be to have a single regulator, the Financial Stability Board and there would be global standards on matters such as disclosure, organization and business controls. This would be a massive change for the market and so the industry is waiting to see if, and how, this would come into being.

Prime Brokerage

Finally, we should say something about how the hedge funds raise the money to actually create their highly leveraged portfolios. Obviously they will borrow directly from banks but they are also large customers of the bank in the prime brokerage market, which will often incorporate collateralized lending. Prime brokerage is actually a suite of services offered by banks to their customers like hedge funds, including taking custody of their securities, arranging lending and financing transactions against these, arranging for them to borrow securities to cover short positions and generally providing operations support to enable the firm to focus on investment management. Increasingly they are also offering a service known as capital introduction, whereby the bank can arrange introductions, without recommendations, to potential investors in the fund. All of this obviously carries a cost but many hedge funds, particu-larly the smaller ones, find that it is a cost-efficient way to manage their business.

In terms of how we see the hedge funds in the market they are likely to be active in all the various financial instruments. When they trade it is quite often in very large size, so they can have a very big influence on the markets. We have said that the market is over $1.5 trillion in size, which is small by comparison with some of the other investment markets that we have come across in this section, but we should also remember that because of their leveraged style of investment we will see these funds trade in the market in even greater size and their presence is so significant that they are often blamed for causing structural market movements.

Part of the allure of hedge funds is the way in which they look at the market, which can be very different from the traditional investment managers and the banks themselves. To a certain extent we can see a 'cat and mouse' game going on as the market tries to understand the thinking of these managers and anticipate their next move. Considering how famous this sector is for its lack of transparency the market as a whole spends a lot of time trying to analyse its movements.

24
Insurance Companies

The insurance industry and the financial markets are very closely linked. When we look at the business model of insurance we can see how the financial markets are necessary to enable them to literally have the means to meet their commitments. Beyond this, though, the expertise that comes from their industry has allowed them to develop further in the markets, building up investment business not just on their own account but for their customers and in some cases even going so far as to establish their own banks.

The insurance industry has been around for hundreds of years, with the first insurance company starting up after the Great Fire of London in 1667, known as The Insurance Office. The company insured houses and other buildings and to help protect them they established their own fire department. Pretty soon other insurance companies started up and, following the same model, they also had their own fire departments which led to a few problems. If a fire broke out all the various fire departments would attend but would only put out the fire if the property was insured by their company. Since this was sometimes hard to determine the fires could continue burning whilst the competing companies tried to find out whose customer, if any, the property belonged to. So to counter this the insurance companies started to give their customers something to hang outside their houses to show that they were indeed a customer, and so speeded up the identification process, however this did nothing to improve the ridiculous situation of having multiple firefighters. Eventually a single fire department was established for the city, leaving the insurance industry continuing to grow in a more focused way and gradually expanding the services it offered from property damage to include theft and then onwards towards the many products we see offered today. The oldest still existent insurance company is Royal & Sun Alliance of the UK, which dates back to 1710. Today, of course, insurance is a far-reaching global industry, with the UK having the biggest share of the market, followed by the UK and then Japan.

THE BUSINESS OF INSURANCE

Insurance is all about transferral of risk. If you take out car insurance the insurer will guarantee that if you have an accident you will be financially covered for the value of your car, so that if it is written off you will receive the cash value. Therefore you are transferring the financial risk of the car's value to the insurer. Naturally the insurer will charge you for taking this risk, and this charge is called the premium which is the amount you pay for taking out an insurance policy. This is where the financial markets have to come into the picture. This premium has to do certain things: it has to be a value that could cover the losses if a claim were to be made, and yet it also has to be attractive to consumers, particularly in the competitive market of the 21st century. When we talk about the premium covering the potential loss this has to be looked at on a probability basis. What is the likelihood of the policyholder making a claim? If we are talking about car insurance this will be affected by things such as the age of the policyholder, their experience of driving, where they live, all of these factors combining to create a risk profile that then equates to a probability of claim. The other part of the equation comes from investment income. The insurance premium is paid upfront so this is a cash flow that can be invested and this investment income will form part of the fund needed to cover any outgoings. Insurance companies are highly regulated and are expected to keep good levels of solvency. We saw from what happened with AIG, the largest insurer in the world, that we can again come across the 'too big to fail' phenomenon, with the US government feeling obliged to bail out the company for fear of the consequences of its failure across the financial system, so we can expect to see even more attention paid to the liquidity and solvency of insurance companies in the future. We look more at what happened to AIG in Appendix E.

To give a sense of the size of the industry in Table 24.1 there is a list of the 10 largest insurance companies in 2009, by market value.[1]

The insurance industry is divided into two core businesses: life and health insurance, and property and casualty (known as P&C or General). Most of the companies above are full-service, offering not only both sorts of insurance but also a range of financial products, including savings vehicles, asset management and even banking. Generally the large companies will operate on an international basis but

---

[1] Forbes, 2009.

Table 24.1 10 Largest Insurance Companies

		Market Value ($ Billions)	Country
1	American Intl Group	$172.24	United States
2	AXA Group	$66.12	France
3	Allianz Worldwide	$65.55	Germany
4	Manulife Financial	$50.52	Canada
5	Generali Group	$45.45	Italy
6	Prudential Financial	$39.70	United States
7	MetLife	$37.94	United States
8	Aviva	$33.10	United Kingdom
9	Munich Re Group	$30.99	Germany
10	Aegon	$26.40	Netherlands

will typically tailor their offerings according to the local market, once again bearing in mind any local restrictions on the business they can carry out. They will also create combined products, for example whole life bonds, which are long-term savings schemes with embedded life insurance policies. By doing this they draw on their expertise and use this to expand their product range. In 2008 global insurance premiums amounted to $4.27 trillion[2] so we can appreciate why this is such a major source of investment flow for the financial markets.

The companies themselves will generally be structured as one of the following:

- Proprietary insurer – the company takes a joint-stock corporate structure either listed or privately owned.
- Mutual (cooperative) insurer – a member-owned structure with policyholders being the members of the society.
- Government insurers – there are a number of government insurers, some of whom we have seen already in relation to banks and financial markets, such as the FDIC in the US.

Most insurers nowadays are proprietary but if we think back to the section on Friendly Societies in the chapter on Banking in the UK we came across that link between banking and insurance again when we spoke of the largest friendly society, Liverpool Victoria, whose primary business seems to be offering insurance products under the friendly society cooperative structure. In Japan the life insurance companies, a major group in the financial markets, were traditionally set up as mutual

---

[2] Swiss Re, 2008.

societies until the 1960s. At that time only four of these companies were proprietary; as of 2008 34 of the 41 companies had now demutualized.

TYPES OF INSURANCE AND PORTFOLIO PROFILES

When the insurance companies are investing these premiums they need to find the best mix of investments to generate the returns needed and suit the liquidity profiles of the policies. Obviously the business is not run on a policy-by-policy basis but we will be able to see characteristics in the nature of their business which will explain why we see the mixes of financial assets that are typical of the two sides of the industry.

LIFE INSURANCE PRODUCTS

More correctly these should be called assurance products as they *will* pay out. Insurance policies will pay if a claim is made against them, which may or may not happen, assurance policies will pay out when a claim is made. Life assurance will definitely pay out because one day the policyholder will die. The three main types of life insurance are:

- Whole of life – a policy that covers the holder for their lifetime and pays out on death.
- Term life – a policy with a fixed maturity to it. The policy will pay out on death but will expire with no payment on maturity date. These policies are sometimes offered as part of an employee compensation scheme, with the maturity date being the retirement date of the employee.
- Endowment assurance – a policy that pays out in the event of death or on a fixed maturity date. It differs from whole of life because it effectively includes a savings element to it for the policyholder, as it will make a payment and unlike term life will not expire worthless to the policyholder.

Each of these is a long-term product with expected payout dates being calculated according to life expectancy, location, health factors etc. We called this part of the business "life and health" as the insurance companies will often offer further other health-related insurances from the same division, drawing on their expertise in pricing life insurance, life expectancy etc.

The portfolios carried by these life insurers tend to be very large, so even when we speak about small percentages of investment we need to put this into context. For example, in the US, the largest insurance market in the world, their share of the net annual premium income is around $1.1 trillion, and they have assets of $1.2 trillion in P&C insurance, and $3 trillion in life insurance. So even if we are talking of 1% of the assets held by life insurance companies this would equate to $30 billion, a far from insignificant amount.

Given the profile of their business it is not surprising that the life insurance portfolios tend to be very top-heavy on debt, typically around 71% of their investment. This is because debt, particularly bonds, carries a high probability of repayment and therefore gives the insurance companies the safety they need in terms of protecting their capital, especially if the bonds are held to maturity, which in a long-profile fund is likely to be the case. Whilst government debt would give them the highest level of safety it would also give them the lowest returns, so they would typically carry more corporate bonds than government debt, with quite a broad range of credits although tending to weight the portfolio towards holding more of the better quality debt. The insurance companies were quite badly affected by the recent Financial Crisis, with large falls in the value of their portfolios, particularly their holdings of structured securities like the asset-backed bonds. However to a certain extent these funds can ride out fluctuations in market values, just as long as the debt makes all of its payments and matures. Clearly the revaluation numbers will look as bad for the insurance companies as anyone else which can definitely have a knock-on commercial effect – again as we saw with AIG – but it is receiving the cash flow that is crucial to make the portfolios work for their investment purpose. Aside from long-term debt the life insurance portfolios will have to hold a proportion of their money in cash, as in deposits or loans that can be immediately recalled for repayment. This part of the portfolio will typically not realize too much income, so again we are seeing insurance companies increasingly placing some of their cash holdings in money market funds to try and boost the return.

The next largest asset class after debt will be equities. Equities carry a lot of advantages: they tend to be liquid and carry the potential for large capital gains, but against this they also carry the potential for large capital losses. The life insurance companies tend to invest in the better names in the market, quite often the companies with the largest market capitalization, but even these are not immune to failure, and if this happens then the shareholders will be the ones to suffer the most. This is why the equity part of the portfolio tends to be quite actively managed, with the investment managers often setting strict limits on acceptable losses to try and limit the downside within the fund. They do this by using what are known as stop-loss orders, where they put a standing order into the market to sell the shares automatically if the price drops to a certain level, and also by using derivatives such as options, which are effectively taking out financial insurance policies.

Aside from these core financial assets the fund will invest in various other things, such as real estate, which has always been popular with the life insurance companies, particularly commercial real estate, and an increasing part of the portfolios are now being invested in funds. An advantage to investing in funds is that the risk is diversified, so you can invest in a fund that buys higher risk instruments or uses a higher risk investment strategy, and yet the overall risk level of the fund will be less than the sum of the individual components because the exposure is not to just one credit or instrument but to a whole range. So the probability of every single investment failing is relatively low, even if the risk of one single one failing is very high.

PROPERTY AND CASUAL INSURANCE PRODUCTS

In this group we are going to come across a lot of the insurance products that we will use every day but also lots of one-off insurance contracts. For example, this group of products will include car, house and travel insurance – products that we are all likely to buy and which will typically be the bread and butter business of the insurance companies, although these policies are often not just on a retail basis but also on a commercial basis, insuring, for example, a fleet of lorries for a transport logistics company. Alongside these we can find more specialized products such as marine and aviation insurance, both for pleasure and commercial purposes, where the risk profiles and sums insured are very different from, say, the average family car. Thinking along the business lines we can find a whole range of financially related insurances, including director insurance, public and professional liability, and then further into the financial field we can find insurance on specific assets or groups of assets, as we have seen with the government insurers, but also the non federal insurer of credit union American Share Insurance. Then there is event and catastrophe insurance – whether this is insuring a village fair against bad weather or a city against a natural disaster, the industry can cover both. Not surprisingly 2005 saw the record year for payouts on catastrophe insurance in the US in the wake of Hurricane Katrina, when the industry paid out $62.3 billion. Although in 2008 it also paid out $27 billion, and again Hurricane Ike accounted for a large percentage of this.

Given the broad range of types of policy coming under this umbrella we can immediately get a feel for one of the most glaring characteristics of this set of exposures: uncertainty. With life insurance we know that death is a certainty; the key issue is when. With this group of insurance we have no such certainty. We do not know if someone will crash their car, whether it will be a good hurricane season or a bad one; these are the sort of uncertainties that make cash flow prediction so difficult. This part of the business depends a lot on probability modelling, but at the end of the day we know we are going to need a good level of liquidity in the portfolios to manage this risk.

So, when we look at the breakdown of assets, we are still going to see that the investments are top-heavy in the debt side, although a little less so, in general, as the portfolios take in more liquidity through cash and equities. Similarly they tend to hold less real estate as this is not a liquid asset group so does not lend itself to a portfolio that may need to be liquidated quite quickly. When we look at the breakdown we do not see massive differences in the percentage values, but this is because of the size of the investments. As we said before we are looking at around $1.2 trillion of assets. Again a 1% shift in overall investment is a considerable change in liquidity profile.

INSURANCE COMPANIES AS FINANCIAL FIRMS

We have already said that some insurance companies offer products beyond pure insurance and this has caused some significant shifts in their business models. A natural progression was to offer long-term collective investment schemes, often with embedded life insurance, because if we think back to endowment assurance the cash flow on these policies will mimic that of a fixed maturity savings product. So, to offer a solution that combines a saving element with purchase of the insurance policy makes sense. From here, though, some insurance companies, like MetLife and Allianz, have gone on to build up their banking business. This tends to focus on retail business, and again offers savings products, but this time the maturities can be short-term, for example taking in call deposits. They will also offer loans, both home and consumer loans, sometimes through subsidiaries, such as MetLife Home Loans, a specialist division of the bank. Segregating the business in this way is all part of the risk management profile of the company as a whole. The net result, though, is that we have a company that starts to resemble the retail business of the full-service banks and the insurance company has another source of cash flow that can be invested to bring in higher returns, as we have seen before.

It is not only in the retail markets that we see the insurance companies active in the financial markets; we will also see them in the wholesale markets doing more than just investment. Insurance companies can be issuers of debt, either just on their own full faith and credit, meaning that the debt is not secured against any particular assets of the firm, or by issuing asset-backed securities. In spite of what we have said about the need to maintain liquidity, the bulk of the firm's investments will be held long-term so these assets can be used to generate more income by being used to collateralize securities. The insurance companies can be very creative, using all potential cash flows to reduce the cost of borrowing that can then be reinvested in higher yielding markets. Sometimes these higher yielding markets will be derivatives rather than securities, so, for example, we see the insurance companies as very active players in credit derivatives, to the delight of the banks, as they are often looking for end investors to take the risk of these deals away from them. We therefore see these institutions very actively in the markets where they tend to hold an influential role and are keenly sought as counterparties by the banks.

Some insurance firms will also offer asset management services to other institutional and individual customers. Once again we are looking at the idea of building on strength, and if these insurance companies are managing their own large-scale investment portfolios, with all the costs involved in doing so, then to some it makes sense to extend the business model into a commercial venture. This is exactly the same logic we saw in the earlier chapter when we spoke of family trusts and corporate pension funds expanding into offering investment management as a source of fee-based income.

REGULATORY ISSUES

Not surprisingly insurance companies are strictly regulated, often by the same regulator as the banks. The buyers of insurance rely on their being able to meet their commitments if a claim is made so there are various rules in place to try and ensure this will happen and a lot of work has been done in recent years to try and bring this more into line with the level of bank regulation. A lot of this focuses on the solvency of the firm as this is seen as a key risk in the market. The insurance companies have

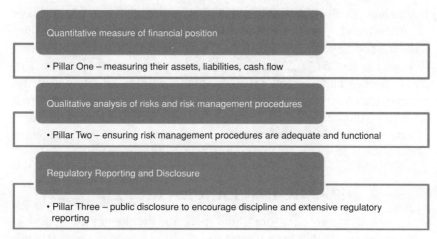

Figure 24.1 Solvency II

to measure their ability to meet their customer claims and they will use a range of ratios to do this and to report to the regulators. These would include:

- loss ratio – a measure of total losses against premium income;
- policyholders' surplus – the amount of excess funds they hold above the legal requirements;
- yields on their investment;
- investment income against invested assets;
- increases or decreases in premium income;

and more. There is also another European Directive coming into the market for the insurance industry called Solvency II that uses a three-pillar approach to regulation. This effectively makes the companies focus attention on their cash flow and ability to generate income to make claims, by setting minimum capital requirements, whilst also having in place the mechanisms to appreciate and manage the financial risks arising, and report to regulators and make full disclosures. The idea of full disclosure is to ensure that the companies take public responsibility for their positions and so encourage prudent management of their funds.

It is expected that Solvency II will be implemented in October 2012 and Figure 24.1 illustrates this 3-pillar approach.

REINSURANCE

The insurance industry is built on the idea of spreading risk and one way in which it spreads the risk on its policies written is by transferring that risk to another firm, the business of reinsurance. This way the insurers are effectively insuring themselves and spreading the risk around the industry and beyond a single firm. There are different ways in which this risk can be shared. One common form is a proportional basis, where part of the risk and consequently part of the premium, are retained by the primary insurer and a proportional amount of both is then transferred to a reinsurer. Another is a non-proportional basis, which where the insurer effectively buys insurance to protect themselves for claims above a certain level. This is very common in catastrophe insurance.

ISLAMIC INSURANCE – TAKAFUL

It is worth mentioning one final part of the insurance industry, Islamic insurance that we referred to briefly in the chapter on Islamic Finance. When we looked earlier at Islamic banking we saw that this was established to allow the practice of banking under Shari'ah law, and so the same is true of the insurance industry. In its mainstream commercial form insurance would not be acceptable as it contains too many uncertainties, but the market has developed an Islamic version which is gaining much popularity. Aside from the risk elements of insurance, according to Islamic law insurance should not really be necessary as people are meant to help one another in times of need, but these days there is a growing acceptance that as the world has developed this may not afford enough protection. So there is a growing acceptance of *takaful* insurance, and not just in Islamic communities. As we said earlier it is based on the idea of mutuality with members contributing sums that are pooled to cover 'claims', and then any excess profits are shared between the members and the organization. Unlike mainstream mutual insurance companies a certain portion of the contribution is deemed to be a donation, which covers the requirement of helping one another, and then any claims that are made will be covered by the pool, to which all have contributed. So whilst the donation element is not akin to the standard cooperative structure the idea of the claims coming from the pool is similar to the claims being covered by the assets owned by the members. So whilst not the same there are similarities. In takaful insurance though, the amount paid in and the amount that will be paid out are known amounts since any amounts not paid out in claims will be redistributed to the members of the group and the institution running it, so profits are not retained, as is the case with the mainstream insurance firms.

The insurance industry is a major component of today's financial markets. We have seen the size of their investment portfolios and the amount of annual income generated into this industry, which again translates into a financial market exposure. For this reason, as we have said, some have developed their business to grow beyond their core purpose to become financial services firms, and take an even more active role in the markets, as well as introducing another dimension of competition to the traditional investment managers and banks we discussed in the previous chapters.

25
Sovereign Wealth Funds

A sovereign wealth fund is a government-owned fund whose purpose is to invest money from various government sources. The two big classifications of source are wealth coming from exports of commodities, particularly oil, and non commodity sources, such as foreign exchange reserves. The IMF has identified five potential purposes for these funds:[1]

- stabilization funds – intended to provide protection against fluctuations in the economy, particularly those caused by changes in the value of core commodities, such as oil;
- savings funds;
- reserve investment funds;
- development funds;
- contingent pension reserve funds.

These purposes are not discrete; there can be overlap in the purpose depending on the situation. For example we saw several SWFs injecting capital to banks during the Financial Crisis, with the intention of helping to stabilize the financial situation, whilst that would not have been their original primary purpose. Generally speaking the funds are run independently and do not get involved in macroeconomic policy, except in times of particular need. In 2010 there were 55 sovereign wealth funds, with some countries such as China and the UAE having multiple funds – indeed the UAE has seven funds with different sources and purposes. Table 25.1 is a table of the top 10 SWFs by assets in 2009.[2]

At the other end of the spectrum are funds with less than $500 million, such as the Mauritian National Fund for Hydrocarbon Reserves, so as with all other areas of investment management we again have a large range of size and corresponding levels of activity. The total size of these funds by assets is in excess of $2.5 trillion. Given the size of the largest of these funds we must realize how they can impact the markets, particularly if they are investing in domestic markets that may not be

---

[1] Sovereign Wealth Funds – A Work Agenda, 2008.
[2] Sovereign Wealth Institute, 2009.

Table 25.1   10 Largest Sovereign Wealth Funds

Country	Name of fund	Assets ($ bn)	Source
UAE – Abu Dhabi	Abu Dhabi Investment Authority	$627	Oil
Norway	Government Pension Fund – Global	$445	Oil
Saudi Arabia	SAMA Foreign Holdings	$431	Oil
China	SAFE Investment Company	$347.1	Non commodity
China	China Investment Corporation	$288.8	Non commodity
Singapore	Government of Singapore Investment Corporation	$247.5	Non commodity
Kuwait	Kuwait Investment Authority	$202.8	Oil
Russia	National Welfare Fund	$168.0	Oil
China	National Social Security Fund	$146.5	Non commodity
China – Hong Kong	Hong Kong Monetary Authority Investment Portfolio	$139.7	Non commodity

that large and able to absorb large volume without disturbing the overall balance. Another potential problem we have is that not all of these funds are very transparent, and so sometimes we do not know how they are invested, so we may not be able to immediately understand movements if they change their portfolios. This is quite serious given the size of some of these funds and therefore this situation is changing, with more of the funds becoming transparent and giving the market a better idea of the sorts of assets in which they invest.

There are two main structures used for creating the SWFs: one, to form an independent legal company, e.g. Dubai World, and two, to just create a subdivision of the government's overall holdings, a pool of defined assets. This second group will generally fall under the jurisdiction of the Ministry of Finance or the Central Bank.

Dubai World

If we take a look at Dubai World we see that this is a SWF that was established in 2006 under the corporate structure as a holding company for various investment businesses, Sovereign Wealth Enterprises (SWEs). These enterprises are investment vehicles owned and operated by an SWF. In the case of Dubai World the holding company operates 10 SWEs in various businesses: transport and logistics; dry-docks and maritime; urban development; energy and natural resources; and investments and financial services. Dubai World has hit the headlines several times over the past years, such as with its acquisition of the British company P&O in 2005 that had management contracts for six major US ports. This gave rise to panicked fears of security issues and a series of legal wrangles, with Dubai World ultimately agreeing to sell P&O's US operations to AIG. More recently they hit the headlines again in November 2009 when they asked for a six-month standstill on debt becoming due for payment and sent the financial markets into turmoil. This is not the sort of headline we are accustomed to seeing accompanying SWFs, but it does highlight the sort of difficulties that can arise with the range of investments that these funds will make. As of 2010 Dubai World is looking at a range of options to reschedule and restructure its portfolio, including potential asset sales and negotiating with creditors for a $22 billion debt restructuring, including potential rescheduling and/or exchange debt of one SWE for another.

Kuwait Investment Authority

Staying in the same region we have an example of the SWF structure established not as an independent company, but simply as a fund, a pool of assets, with the Kuwait Investment Authority. This fund was originally established in 1953 so is very well established in the markets, and holds some equity investments dating back to the 1960s and 1970s. The fund has a small number of SWEs, including a minority holding in the Kuwait China Investment Company, with these SWEs being set up as specialist agencies in specific sectors, such as property. The overall fund itself is an oil-based one, intending to translate the volatile returns on oil exports into a steady growth pattern for future generations (the savings fund) and managing general reserves (the reserve investment fund). It is one of the most transparent funds, making regular reports on activity to the Kuwaiti parliament, and has small holdings in many domestic and overseas companies, without the intention to ever take majority positions.

China – State Administration of Foreign Exchange (SAFE) and China Investment Corporation

We must talk about the Chinese SWFs as they have had a major impact on the markets in the past decade. There are two entities, both of whom are involved in managing China's extensive foreign exchange reserves, standing at \$2.399 trillion in December 2009. These funds are SAFE Investment Company, based in Hong Kong, and China Investment Corporation (CIC). Together they hold about \$636 billion in assets. Much more is known about the assets of CIC than SAFE, but what is known is that both have very significant holdings of overseas assets. CIC's assets stood at around \$288.8 billion at the end of 2009, but there were also reports in December 2009 that the fund may receive an extra \$200 billion which again would greatly change its investment profile. The fund owns six SWEs, the largest being Central Huijin Investment Limited that makes equity investments in domestic financial institutions. Another SWE, the Stable Investment Corporation, invests in money market products and was one of the largest investors in the Primary money market fund we discussed in the previous chapter. These funds have taken such significant holdings in overseas assets that they have drawn much regulatory attention. Their scope is global but some of their most high-profile investments are in companies such as Citigroup and BlackRock.

INVESTMENT AND INVESTMENT STRATEGY

Obviously we cannot say there is one blanket definition of how these funds are managed, but there are a few common characteristics we can see. If we ignore the strategic domestic investments for development purposes, and any investments the funds need to make in response to exceptional economic events, we are left with an industry that invests in a broad range of financial assets. The larger funds will often comprise both in-house and externally managed funds, quite often using different external investment managers in order to be able to benchmark performance. These investment managers will be given the funds to manage on both an active and a passive basis, meaning that the overall fund has a mixture of individual and broader market risks. It is often said that SWFs have a higher risk tolerance than many other funds as they are running portfolios where liquidity is definitely secondary to return, so they will often look further along the risk spectrum in order to achieve the higher returns.

Santiago Principles

The IMF estimates that the SWFs hold around 30% of all foreign assets held by sovereigns and that the size of these assets could top

$7–11 trillion by 2013. In 2008 the International Working Group of the Sovereign Wealth Funds (IWG), a group of 26 countries all of whom have SWFs, met in Santiago, Chile, and agreed a series of 24 principles for regulation, investment and governance of these institutions (see Text Box 25.1).

Box 25.1 Summary of Santiago Principles

1. The SWFs should operate within a sound legal framework.
2. There should be clear definition of the policy purpose of the SWF.
3. Any impact of the SWF's activities on macroeconomic policy should be closely monitored.
4. The source of funding should be disclosed and there should be clear policy on withdrawals and expenditure.
5. Statistical data should be regularly provided to the owner countries for inclusion in macroeconomic reports.
6. There should be sound governance and clearly defined roles and responsibilities within the organization.
7. The owning country should set the objectives, appoint the governing board and oversee operations.
8. Governing bodies should operate in the best interests of the SWF and have authority to do so.
9. They should be able to operate independently to carry out objectives.
10. Accountability should be clearly defined in legislation, charter, constitutive documents or management agreements.
11. Annual reports and financial statements should be prepared in accordance with national or international standards.
12. There should be annual audits of the same.
13. Professional and ethical standards should be defined and disclosed.
14. Dealing with third parties should be supervised and based on economic and financial grounds.
15. Overseas activities should be carried out in accordance with the host location's regulatory framework.
16. There should be public disclosure of the governance framework and objectives as well as proof of independence.
17. Relevant financial information should be disclosed to encourage stability in financial markets and promote trust.

18. Investment policy should be clear and defined and in line with portfolio management principles.
19. Investment decisions should aim to maximize risk-adjusted returns based on solid financial and economic decision-making processes.
20. They should not take advantage of privileged information or inappropriate influence when competing with private firms.
21. When investing in equity the SWF should exercise ownership rights in keeping with maximizing investment return.
22. They should have a risk management framework in place.
23. Asset and investment performance should be reported to the owning country to defined standards.
24. The process of adhering to these principles should be monitored by the SWF.

These principles are voluntary but their adoption is intended to reassure the markets on the conduct of this influential set of investors.

In terms of the assets typically bought by the SWFs, these cover very much the whole range of financial instruments, from equity, both public and private, to debt, both long and short maturity, through to the use of alternative investments, including commodities, derivatives, real estate and investing in funds. Naturally they will be large users of foreign exchange as they build multicurrency portfolios. So all in all we are likely to see this investor group in all of our major markets, and many smaller and emerging ones, as they tend not to be geographically bound but can invest wherever they choose. Some funds, like CIC, actively look for investment in specific geographic areas such as Africa, which is not the most mainstream of investment regions, but if it can clearly offer the fund the types of return it is seeking and at the same time increase the fund's – and by default the country's – visibility and presence in the area then it could well be an investment worth considering for these funds.

Part V
Traditional Non Bank
Intermediaries

26

Introduction

In this last section we are going to look at a group of intermediaries that play an important role in providing liquidity to the financial markets. Essentially these are intermediaries that assist liquidity by bringing together buyers and sellers. Strictly speaking many of the institutions that we have already discussed would be classified as nonbank intermediaries. Hedge funds, insurance companies, even building societies, are examples of this as they act as a form of intermediary in the market and do not have (full) banking licences. In this book, though, we have grouped things according to their core business model in financial market terms, and so we have covered hedge funds and insurance companies under the banner of investment management, and we have discussed building societies under banking. This reflects how we see these organizations in the financial markets. However there are some firms that have not fitted neatly into this structure and these are the firms we want to take a look at here.

In this section we are going to look at two sorts of broker, agency brokers, also known as stockbrokers, and interdealer brokers (IDBs). These two sorts of firm bring together buyers and sellers of financial products, securities, currencies, commodities, derivatives, a whole range depending on the organization, but they differ from one another primarily in their customer base. The agency brokers will deal with a range of customers from institutions down to retail, whilst the interdealer brokers only deal with wholesale market participants. So since their target markets are very different the liquidity they bring to the market will operate on different levels.

The other group that we will take a quick look at is the venture capital firms. These are intermediaries in a different way. Their focus is on raising money for firms in need of funds. Put starkly, it is hard to differentiate from other banking functions that we have discussed, but most of the venture capital firms are independent of banks, and will actually rely on the banking market as one of the sources of funding, along with the investment companies that we have been discussing. We will see that the venture capital company acts as a very hands-on conduit for these funds, with a particular specialism in start-up and turnaround projects as opposed to day-to-day financing that is the core business of corporate banking, or even the emphasis on raising funds for the more traditional type of borrower covered by the Corporate Finance departments in the banks.

Whilst we are defining these as nonbank financial intermediaries we have to remember that in the 21st century banks have a very broad reach and we will see that many of the agency brokers and venture capital groups are once again going to be owned by banks. Sometimes they will be divisions of the bank, sometimes independent subsidiaries but wholly or majority-owned. This will not be true of interdealer brokers that must maintain independence from the banks to enable their particular business model to work efficiently.

Once again the regulation of these firms has been a hot topic. Being nonbank they have typically been less stringently regulated although really this must depend on the markets in which they operate and the specific roles they fill within that market. On the whole, we should not say that they are unregulated firms, either on an institutional or an individual basis. If an employee of an agency broker is giving advice to customers on the securities markets then they will have to be approved as registered representatives of their firms. If a venture capital firm is running a venture capital fund then they will be regulated as an investment firm. However we have already said elsewhere that there is a move amongst the G20 to create a single uniform regulator for all financial market institutions which will bring this group of firms more firmly under the spotlight.

27

Inter-Dealer Brokers

Interdealer brokers (IDBs) are firms that provide liquidity in the whole-sale markets by matching buyers and sellers from amongst the "professional" market participants. The expression "professional" is one that we commonly use to define sell-side functions as opposed to buy-side, which we often refer to as the clients, but essentially we are focusing on firms willing to show prices to the market. In some markets this will mean that they only deal with the market-makers in the market, in other markets where we do not have the formalized market-maker structure – which in the 21st century is actually most markets – they will deal with the largest players, the price-makers, most commonly banks but some other nonfinancial institutions. So this group is not in competition with any of the other types of institution that we have looked at in this book. They occupy a unique position, and their competition is with each other and advances in technologies which help the transparency and efficiency of trading within the market that could ultimately make them unnecessary. For this reason these IDBs tend to have invested heavily in technology to ensure that they are the ones providing the means for trade execution and transparency.

Sometimes this group of intermediaries is a bit more difficult to understand because their contribution to the financial markets is less intuitive than the services offered by the other institutions we have looked at. Their role centres on the infrastructure of the industry, making it work by enabling the trades to happen efficiently and by allowing the dealers to spread risk. To understand the role of the IDB we need to be clear in our heads about how trade flow works, in other words how our financial products go from buyers to sellers. Probably in the ideal world the most efficient (and cost-efficient) way would be for end buyers and sellers to transact business directly (see Figure 27.1):

Figure 27.1

The seller of the financial product, say equity or debt, sells directly to the buyer with no middleman. The only problem with this is that these two parties may not know each other and may not know that the two sides of the trade are in the market, so the deal would not be executed. This model really only works if we can guarantee that all potential sellers will be aware of all potential buyers, and vice versa. This is why we have spent so much time looking at banks and other dealers, like the sales and traders in the banks who also fulfil this function of matching buyers and sellers. So a typical model could be as depicted in Figure 27.2:

Figure 27.2

So now we have a model where there is a dealer sitting as an intermediary. Again this works perfectly as long as the dealer has both the natural buyer and seller, but if they do not then the risk of the deal sits on the books of the dealer. This is what trading is all about but to limit this risk we have to impose constraints on the dealers so it makes sense for them to keep their trading books as fluid as possible. This means that pretty much as soon as they take on a position they will be looking for how to reverse it, in this case to find a buyer. As we said ideally this will be another customer, another end buyer, but more realistically the dealer is likely to spread the risk of this trade into the market by dealing with another firm. So, as shown in Figure 27.3, we end up with:

Figure 27.3

Already we have double the number of participants in this chain and we have not mentioned IDBs. So where does the IDB fit into this picture? Well sometimes the two dealers may not want to deal directly or do not have the time to find one another. The IDB is there to act as this link, putting them into the chain by providing the buyer, in this case, from the dealer market (see Figure 27.4).

Figure 27.4

So here we can see the function of the IDB, to put market dealers together to facilitate the trade. The IDB provides an additional level of liquidity. Some markets can be very fast-moving meaning that the time it takes to find another dealer to unwind the position could be the time it takes to go from profit to loss. So, the IDB helps to speed this up. They can also provide anonymity: it could be that the dealer that is buying has no idea of the identity of the dealer that is selling, and, of course, vice versa again. This protects the two parties from sharing too much information about their business. We keep talking about the competitive nature of this industry and using processes such as this helps to protect information that we do not want to share being disseminated around the market and so is an important part of why we choose to use the IDBs. Of course it is equally as important that the market can rely on their integrity. It may seem strange that we have gone from an original model of two participants to one with five, but again if we are truly realistic about how the market works before we "match" an end seller with an end buyer there may be lots of trades between market participants before the financial products find their ultimate home, so it is not really a stark case of just adding in layers. The IDBs offer a service that the market needs or they would not still exist in the 21st century when we are looking at reasonably mature financial markets.

METHODS OF EXECUTION

There are two main models of executing these trades, voice broking and electronic broking, and sometimes the IDBs will use a combination of both.

Voice broking is where you have an individual, the broker, whose job is to talk to market participants and get them to give bids and offers in the financial products to the broker. These bids and offers are normally known as "firm", which means the dealers who have given them will commit to buy or sell at these prices until the broker is told otherwise. The broker then calls other market participants and will show them the prices to see if they are interested in dealing. Whilst they are talking to the market they will also try and get more bids and offers to add to their portfolio of offerings. This method hinges on the brokers having good contacts within the market, and many of the brokers are long-established and well connected which is how they are able to build up a portfolio of potential trades and traders with whom they can deal.

Electronic broking is where buyers and sellers post bids and offers on an electronic marketplace. This lends itself to the more standardized markets, such as government bonds. The system will typically display the highest bids and the lowest offers that have been input, on an anonymous basis. When a dealer sees a price that they like and they want to deal on they simply accept the price that is quoted on the system and the price display mechanism then becomes a trading system. These systems can be very sophisticated, because in some markets participants will only be able to deal with one another if they have sufficient credit lines and limits for the type of transaction, so the system must be able to accept this information, although responsibility for managing these controls, for example making sure they are up-to-date, must lie with the trading house, not the IDB. The broker screen will show the highest bid that the broker has been given, and the lowest offer, on an anonymous basis, along with the amount that can be dealt at this level. Naturally these prices will not necessarily, nor indeed typically, have come from the same dealer. When a bid or offer is matched by more than one dealer this is known as *joining the price* and the deals will then be executed in order of when the price was given, with the first price-maker taking priority, then the second, etc.

Electronic broking systems have definite advantages over voice broking systems, not least the speed of execution, but also the integration of price display and trade execution means that there tend to be fewer trade errors when deals are carried out in this way. On the downside, though, cutting out the personal contact may also mean cutting out the value of the broker's experience and contacts. So, as we said, in some markets the IDBs use a combination of the two, so that the dealers can deal directly with an electronic system or talk to a broker, as they choose. Often they will take the latter route when they have a large size to trade, or a more difficult product that they want to buy or sell, since this could involve the broker negotiating with the other market participants on behalf of the anonymous price-giver. There are also some electronic systems that mimic this by allowing the users to input comments, requests for bids or offers, as well as pure price discovery.

When a deal is executed the names of the buyer and the seller may still not be revealed between them. Some broker trades are executed on a totally anonymous basis, meaning that the seller sells to the broker and the broker sells to the buyer. The broker has to make a fee for carrying out the deal and this will be incorporated in the price at which these two trades are done. They will buy from the market at a slightly lower price than they sell. The two deals will be executed as close to simultaneously as possible, since the markets are continuously moving. Again this is why an electronic system can be preferable to a voice one. Sometimes, though, the names of the two dealers will need to be revealed as the actual deal must be carried out directly, such as money market borrowing and lending, and this has an impact on credit lines. In this case the trade is executed on a given name basis. This means that when the deal is actually struck the broker discloses the names, steps out of the picture and the two parties deal directly. The broker will still need to receive their fee for matching the counterparties so this will be invoiced, normally to be paid either by both parties or by the dealer that accepted a price offered by the broker, depending on the trade.

As we have already mentioned, the integrity of the IDBs is very important: the market must trust that they do not run positions themselves and that when they say that they have bids and offers that these values exist and that deals can be traded on these prices. The IDBs that have the most prices and ones that are most actively changing and so reflect the moving market will tend to be the ones that attract the most trades. Unfortunately in December 2009 the SEC found that ICAP USA, the US subsidiary of the UK-based IDB and one of the largest of these companies, had been feeding false values into their electronic systems to attract the attention of dealers. These prices were flashed onto the screens and then removed before participants could deal on them but they contributed to creating a false impression of the market. This was a really serious matter as the markets rely on this broker data as being the most accurate overview of where the market itself is actually trading. These price feeds will be bought, and analysed by many to determine trade flows and patterns, so having false data appear really compromised the integrity of not just this one firm, but potentially led us to question the market as a whole. To represent this seriousness the SEC obliged ICAP USA to pay $25 million in repayments and penalties.

IDBS AND MARKET COVERAGE

The last few years have seen a lot of consolidation in this sector leaving a group of about five major international brokers:

- ICAP
- GFI
- Tullett Prebon

- Tradition
- BCG/Cantor Fitzgerald.

Obviously there are others that specialize in domestic markets, such as Shorcan, a broker in the Canadian government bond market, but given that this has limited international involvement Shorcan is very much a domestic broker purely by dint of their workflow. The big five above operate in the major international markets and so have a more international presence. Tullett Prebon can trace its roots back to 1868 when Matthew Marshall founded Marshall & Son, a broking company in London, building up an expertise in FX broking. The company we have today is the amalgamation of a number of famous broking houses, including Prebon, Tullett & Riley, Tokyo Forex Co., Charles Fulton & Co. and Liberty. All of these amalgamations have created an IDB that now trades well beyond its original roots in FX to cover not just currencies but interest rates, equity products and derivatives on many things including energy and property, amongst others. BGC Partners, Inc. is another interesting one: it was originally part of Cantor Fitzgerald, an IDB founded in 1959, but over time Cantor Fitzgerald adapted its business model to move beyond broking and start to take proprietary positions and in 2004 it separated out its voice brokerage business forming BGC, and it then concentrated on building up sales and trading and investment banking activities in the markets in which it used to offer IDB service, and beyond. Cantor Fitzgerald is now a primary dealer. As a firm, though, it still offers broking services in very different markets: environmental and alternative energy, radio frequency spectrum and tower/rooftop and emerging coverage resources – a very different set of market products but leveraging on the company's experience of running broker markets and developing these models to adapt to new and changing markets.

This last example shows just what a broad range of coverage these firms can have. In pure financial market terms we will see them actively involved in the core cash markets of currencies and interest rates. Equities have never traditionally been a major source for IDBs because they are exchange-traded and so their liquidity is limited within a confined environment; however there are opportunities for them in some of the emerging markets and in equity-related products. Away from these they will trade energy, commodities, structured securities, any products that have a sufficient volume of trading to create broking opportunities.

Traditionally the OTC markets[1] have been a more lucrative area for this group, where the benefits of their assisting liquidity can easily be seen. The brokers are also quite active in credit products, both cash and derivatives. Again these brokers are naturally more active in the OTC derivatives than the exchange traded ones and it is in the OTC markets that there can be a need for their liquidity matching. Interestingly, though, in 2010 we are seeing some blurring of the lines between these two market models as more and more market trades, particularly OTC derivatives, are being settled via a central clearing counterparty,[2] but this serves to help the IDB as it removes any concerns that the market may have with dealing with these firms as counterparties.

As well as broking trades these companies can also offer ancillary products such as market data and analytical software. The brokers have a particular view of the markets and their data feeds can be used for providing a perspective on wholesale executed trades that will often be used in, for example, algorithmic trading systems.[3] So we can see that starting from a basically simple business model these companies have developed, through keeping close links and expanding their coverage to follow market trends, they are now, in some cases, creating more full-service ancillary businesses to continue their theme of servicing the markets. In all cases, though, they have had to respond to changes in the market with the knock-on effects of changes in how and with whom they will conduct business, and in their own competitive environment.

---

[1] Over the Counter.

[2] A central clearing counterparty is one that will stand in the middle of all the trades on a given market. This means they take away the counterparty risk from the market participants by substituting themselves as counterparty in every deal being cleared through them.

[3] We spoke about these systems in the chapter on Hedge Funds in the previous section.

28

Agency Brokers

An agency broker is an institution most commonly seen in the equity markets. This is because the role they play is most suited to an exchange market rather than an OTC market. One of the key differences between these two trading models is that only members can transact business directly on an exchange market. This does not mean that non members cannot buy or sell the products that are traded on them, only that they will need to use a member to actually do the deals within the market on their behalf. This is why these agency brokers actually came into existence, to provide this link and are really a legacy from when the functions of market-making and servicing customers were separated on the exchanges.

We have spoken earlier of exchange-traded and over-the-counter (OTC) markets, and equities are typically traded on exchanges, as opposed to FX, which is always an OTC market, and bond markets which are normally OTC. Derivatives are a mixture of exchange-traded and OTC products. As we have looked at how our various financial institutions have come into being we have often seen a largely simultaneous development of banking and equity markets, one a market for borrowing and lending, the other a market for raising capital. At an early stage we started to see exchanges developing for this capital side of the market, an example being in Bruges in the 13th century, where commodity traders took to meeting in a specific house of a man named Van der Burse, to transact business. This is the very beginning of how exchanges developed as a known meeting place for interested parties to meet and carry out business, in other words to join in with the exchange. Then at the beginning of the 17th century, in 1602, we find an actual stock exchange beginning to operate in Amsterdam when the Dutch East India Company issued the first shares to be traded exclusively on this exchange. Then at the end of the same century, in 1698, the London Stock Exchange also began trading when John Castaing began listing and trading shares at Jonathan's Coffee House in Change Alley in the City of London. From the beginning we saw this idea of members in use in the market. Obviously it took a while for the exchanges to formalize themselves but certainly by the end of the 19th century we had well-established equity markets based on this model of membership.

Since these markets began with physical exchanges we can actually also understand how these agency brokers, or stockbrokers as they are also called, evolved. The members came together to transact business but they needed to bring in trades from non members, and so we started to see a division where some firms would concentrate on bringing in the business, liaising with customers, advising them on what to buy and sell, whilst others concentrated on trading, and so we have the stockbroker and market-maker structure. If we look back one hundred years we could see this as a very clearly defined distinction, but in the 21st century it is less clear as the markets have evolved. If we take the UK as an example, traditionally the two sides of the business were known as stockjobbers (market-makers) and stockbrokers. The two functions were mutually exclusive and the companies that carried out this business were independent of one another. In 1986 this changed with the *Big Bang*. This was a sweeping change in the structure and trading practice of the London equity market. With *Big Bang* the London Stock Exchange moved from a floor-based market to a screen-based one, so allowing easier access to the market and increasing the possibility of who could become members. Up until then foreign membership had not been allowed but with *Big Bang* this changed. The market also started to gradually move away from being market-maker driven towards being order driven. The terminology and definition of the members also changed. Rather than having stockbrokers and jobbers, with the two roles clearly distinguished, instead we moved to a model of agency brokers and broker dealers; the agency brokers were the equivalent of the stockbrokers, intermediaries between clients and the market, but broker dealers were not a straightforward name change for stockjobbers. Instead broker dealers are a combination of the two functions, firms that execute business on behalf of their customers but also on their own account, and making markets where required. This was such an important change that actually it could potentially have meant that the traditional small agency brokers would just cease to exist. Now they were put in direct competition with the larger firms offering both sides of the business. They did not disappear, though, and are still in the markets today, which means they must have some competitive advantage to offer that we will look at a little later.

This model that we see in the UK is one now seen in most major markets, the big exception being the US market where we still have floor markets, such as the New York Stock Exchange (NYSE) and until recent times this market has been dominated by market-makers, known as Specialists. However this is changing. In the 1980s there were 50 Specialists; in 2010 there are five, now known as Designated Market Makers (DMMs):

- Bank of America Specialist
- Barclays Capital*
- Kelloggs Specialist Group
- Spears, Leeds and Kellogg Specialist
- Getco LLC**

*In January 2010 Barclays Capital acquired LaBranche & Co.
** In February 2010 Getco LLC became a DMM, a particularly interesting development as GETCO are a major global screen-based proprietary trader, renowned for high frequency trading.[1]

So we are seeing the change in this market as well as more business moves to the complementary electronic trading systems and away from the DMMs.

If we look at Bank of America Specialist we can see an example of how one firm offers the full service that creates the competition for the pure agency broker. Clearly through this particular part of the business they carry out market-making for more than 400 companies, yet through Bank of America Merrill Lynch, and in particular parts of the wealth management business they acquired through the merger with Merrill Lynch, they now have a broad customer base for traditional stockbroking, offering advice and execution to a wide range of customers, all under the Bank of America Merrill Lynch brand. So they can effectively carry out both sides of the business.

The business of the stockbroker, then, is to offer investment advice and execution to their customers. These customers will be either individuals or institutions, with some houses specializing in one type of customer or the other, whilst others cover the whole market in terms of customer base. These firms can also specialize in broad markets, and even in sectors within the markets. It would seem that the firms like Bank of America Merrill Lynch would have an advantage over the smaller more specialized firms as, being broad-based broker dealers, they carry inventory of their own that can be offered to customers, meaning they

---

[1] High frequency trading is just what it says, a system of trading that involves making numerous trades based on small movements in the markets. It is a product of algorithmic trading systems and tends to be dependent on good technology to monitor the market moves.

can sometimes offer slightly better prices than those transparently seen in the market, so there must be another way to differentiate these firms. Yet again we are looking at a very competitive market, coupled with the fact that since it is exchange traded it is also very transparent with delayed pricing easily and freely available to anyone through a number of roots, not least of all the exchange's own web sites. Even premium data, such as trade logs, is often commoditized by the exchange and sold in reasonably priced packages. When it comes to looking at the value of the companies listed on the exchanges again we find that all the fundamental data about the companies, their filed accounts and so on, are public records, so again they can be easily accessed by all market participants. This being the case, it makes it difficult to understand how the firms can differentiate themselves from one another, let alone how a small firm can make itself competitive against the larger, full-service ones. So this has to be based on what the firms can offer into the market and how they offer it. In other words we are looking for some sort of value-added service. Since it is not really going to be in the actual pricing of the product, nor the availability of the information, it has got to be linked to how these things appear and are used by these market participants. Essentially there are three key areas that this can focus on: expertise and research, execution and cost.

Expertise and Research – the Advisory Service

Many of the agency brokers will build up an expertise in either a specific market or even more than that a particular area of the market. One way in which they have become very successful is by bringing access to foreign markets. When we looked in Part II at Banking in Japan we spoke about the Japanese Securities Houses that were so influential in international markets in the 1980s. These Securities Houses were originally agency brokers that then became broker dealers, and ultimately, as in the case of Nomura, went on to gain full banking licences. Originally, though, they built up their reputations overseas by bringing access to the Japanese equity market to Europe and the US, and then grew to become members in these foreign markets having shown their expertise in areas such as research and valuation. Another interesting example of this concerns the UK's oldest still existing stockbroker, Hichens, Harrison & Co., since 2008 acquired by the Indian financial services group Religare Enterprises and now renamed Religare Hichens Harrison. This is interesting because it shows how such an acquisition can be a two-way street: Religare bought an old established firm with a strong presence in the UK markets in both agency broking and corporate advisory, so giving them a presence in the UK market and a UK customer base. This UK acquisition added to their growing global equity portfolio encompassing locations in Asia, US and now Europe, giving them a truly international presence and product range. So as well as sustaining the traditional UK product this acquisition also gives the company a new outlet for offering Indian equities and market research, one of their core domestic products, as well as products from their other international acquisitions, giving an international portfolio of offerings. So in the best of acquisitions they are able to effectively increase their market memberships which allows them to offer a complementary but not conflicting product range.

Equity valuation is a very data-intensive and somewhat subjective area and often the firms that tend to specialize in markets or sectors will have built up an expertise in research that will be used as one of the ways to attract customers. It can be a useful model for managing resources if a firm can present itself as an expert in say, high tech stocks, and its research is often its way of highlighting this expertise. This research should be independent opinions, and in the institutional market this is a very important point. The market has not been without scandals in the past where firms have been accused of using research as a way of promoting stocks in which they held large positions, as we spoke of earlier, and so the independence of the research is of paramount importance. For retail investors the research will often be their primary decision-making tool and so many houses personalize this, making a great play of the names of the analysts and commentators to build up customer loyalty to a name that has given them profitable trading suggestions.

Agency brokers rely heavily on building strong relationships with their customers. In the chapter on private banking we spoke of the relationship between the private banker and their customer, and in this part of the business we see a similar relationship with the agency broker building up a relationship with the customer in order to ensure trades are routed through their house. On the individual market most customers tend to deal with only one firm, but on the institutional market there will normally be more than one key relationship, although on both sides if the relationship is an advisory one then the broker will be assessed not only on the quality of their recommendations but also with the quality of their recommendations. It is not unusual for people working as agency brokers to be paid on commission so it is in their interest to build up long-term relationships to build up revenue flows.

Execution

We have just mentioned advisory service but not all customers want to have this relationship – some are looking purely for execution. This is when the company's technology comes into play, making the most efficient link between the customers and their order books. In the 21st century great strides have been made in encouraging online transactions as opposed to telephone ones that are obviously more expensive for the firm. Of course if all the trades were automated then the role of the individual broker would cease to exist, so the business model at the moment incorporates some of each. Once again we can see how easily the smaller pure agency brokers can lose out to their larger competitors on this part of the business as they have no obvious market advantage to offer. The value added will come from the technology, not from expertise in valuation or relationship building. Typically their technology budgets will be smaller than the large broker dealers. However we have one interesting development in this part of the market which involves Sungard, the technology firm. Sungard is a member of all the US exchanges and the largest European ones, so becoming an agency broker in its own right, and one that sees substantial market share. Sungard's business model, though, is somewhat different. Rather than targeting the buy-side customer, as do all the other agency brokers and broker dealers, instead they target the other agency brokers. Their competitive advantage comes from two things: one, their technology for routing orders etc., and two, their membership of numerous exchanges. What they can offer is efficient access to a range of markets so allowing their customers, the other broker dealers, to also access these on behalf of their end customers. Again the large broker dealers will have multi-market memberships, but for the smaller agency brokers this may not be commercially viable for the amount of trades they have. If they choose to use Sungard as their conduit, though, this gives them access to this broader range, also under one technology umbrella. Sungard is careful to point out that using their service is not dependent on being their technology customer but there will probably be mutual advantages to a system designed specifically with this model in mind. This is an interesting variation on how we typically view agency brokers and maybe this is what we need to continue developing this whole business model.

Cost

Cost is the final way in which all the market participants strive to differentiate themselves. In the past we had fixed fee structures in the markets, but as markets have developed so these have become more flexible. Agency brokers rely on the fees they charge to their customers for accessing the market on their behalf, and yet there is a lot of pressure on these fees coming not just from the competition of other companies but also from automation of the market. In markets which are less automated fees have to be higher, but as internet trading has become a more generally accepted model so fees have been able to fall. Advisory service, though, is a premium priced product, so in many cases the firms will have multilevels of fees depending on customer type, service and volume. Agency brokers do not necessarily set out to be the cheapest means of accessing the market, for some they can actually be relatively expensive. In this case, though, what they are doing is emphasizing the additional value added they bring over pure execution service. So, if the market values, for example, their research and recommendations they still seem willing to pay for the service.

This whole group of intermediaries actually causes a few problems for us in understanding why they still exist in the 21st century. On the one hand they seem unnecessary since there are enough full-service firms that carry out their function. However the fact that they do exist suggest a couple of things in the way the market perceives them. Firstly, it would appear that as long as they can offer some value-added service, whether it is advisory or execution, the market is big enough to allow this sort of competitor. So their existence hinges on this value-added aspect. Secondly, though, there may also be an issue of diversification. If you are an investment company and you run your bank accounts with a certain bank, then place funds under management with this bank, and then trade securities with this bank, you are building up a lot of exposure. Even if we substitute three bank names for one, we still have a lot of exposure to the banking system, and recent events have shown us how systemically vulnerable this sector can be. So maybe the market needs to have the alternative, the non bank agency broker to help to diversify this risk away from the bank sector.

29

Venture Capital Companies

Venture capital is the business of financing business propositions that may be too risky for traditional bank lending or capital markets. This risk may come from the fact that often we are dealing with start-up companies, with no track records or reputations on which to start to build an assessment of the risk. Or it may come from a company that needs restructuring and so may already be carrying debt from the traditional lenders but now needs further funds to turn the company around. The venture capital firms quite often tend to specialize either in financing companies at a certain stage in their lifecycle, such as at the start, or maybe within a particular industry, depending on how the firm itself is resourced. People working in a venture capital firm will generally either be business and finance experts or industry experts since both sides of the equation are generally needed to ensure that the project looking for investment is viable. They have to have a good understanding of what the company is trying to achieve in order to understand its viability before they can risk capital within the firm. Some very well-known names including Starbucks and Ebay were initially financed with venture capital and went on to become great successes.

We can see how the idea of venture capital is closely tied with our descriptions of the birth of investment and merchant banking, when these banks grew up from their roots in trade. We also noted that the development of many banks was tied to developing railroad networks in the 19th century. It is from this sort of background that the business of venture capital also grew up, with financing for projects such as the railroads coming not just from banks but from the wealthy families of the 19th and early 20th centuries, those that had the large pools of money and, for some, an appetite for a somewhat risky investment. From this developed venture capital companies, the two earliest being the American Research and Development Corporation (ARDC) and J.H. Whitney & Co., both established in the 1940s. J.H. Whitney is still in existence and very active in this market. The name of ARDC is very apt as it really highlights what this sector is about. As we said venture capital aims to provide finance for small and medium-sized firms

(SMEs), based on value decisions on the viability of the company, its products, its research, looking at the companies in an in-depth way, and often taking a very hands-on approach to the firms in which they invest. This is another way in which they differ from banks. They will often provide entrepreneurial support to the firms they are financing, obviously to protect their capital investment, but this can go as far as putting management (or interim management) in place to help the firm achieve its objectives. A good example of this came in the UK in 1999/2000 when BMW was looking for buyers of the UK car company the Rover Group. The company was nearly sold to the venture capital group, Alchemy Partners, who announced plans for focusing on a specific brand of the business, the MG sports car, and developing further lines in the sports car market-space that would lead to closure of the major domestic car building plant. This was not a popular bid and received a lot of negative attention in the press and eventually Alchemy's bid failed when another bidder entered the market; finally the company was sold to another consortium, Phoenix Venture Holdings. This consortium was formed by individuals with a more specific knowledge of not just the automobile industry but specifically the Rover Group. In the end they did not make a success of the company and raised a lot of concerns about the way in which it was restructured that led to an official inquiry being ordered by the UK Secretary of State for Trade and Industry. We could wonder whether in this instance a firm with more of a venture finance background rather than such an industry-specific one would have done a better job, but essentially these are the two models that drive venture capital: that of the generalist operation, evaluating all projects on a value basis with limited pre-knowledge of the sector and the company's positioning, and the companies that focus on a specific sector bringing depth of understanding of the market to their projects. Ideally, of course, you want both, which is why we have some of the specialists that we referred to earlier.

The venture capital companies are intermediaries as their role is to provide the financing for these SMEs. Venture capital is a long-term investment, although generally venture capitalists will be looking to release their investment in five–seven years. They take a very disciplined approach to managing the investment, often setting interim targets to measure the progress, and they can be seen as quite brutal in the way they will close down an underperforming enterprise in order to salvage as much of their investment as they can through a sale of assets. If the project goes according to plan they will be looking to sell the company, either as a private equity deal or by taking the firm public on a stock exchange, to realise the return on their investment. So if we think about some of the things we said concerning investment companies in the previous section, some of whom had held investments not just for years but for decades, then the horizon of five to seven years does not seem that long, but it is long-term by the definition of financial market debt. Really though, whilst these companies are typically taking an equity stake in the firms in which they invest, the net result comes across as very much a hybrid. From the very beginning it is known that they will be looking to divest their holding so, as with a debt investment, there is something of a fixed maturity to the investment.

The venture capital firms are typically limited partnerships and the capital they need is raised through the creation of venture capital funds. These funds will normally be closed-end so that investors cannot demand immediate liquidation. The bulk of investors in these venture capital funds will be institutional, the likes of insurance companies, pension funds, endowments, who are willing to sacrifice liquidity and take on greater risk in exchange for higher returns. If these investors are investing in a fund then this is a second-level investment, they are not directly investing in the projects but in the diversified fund, thereby spreading the risk again, as we have seen before in the previous section of this book. These funds are typically run by professional investment managers who will build up the portfolios according to risk and return criteria, as well as investment criteria relating to geography, industry sector, etc. This means that a venture capital company can and often will run numerous funds according to its expertise.

There is a lot of variety in the market in terms of how different countries allow different structures for these funds, a situation we have seen so many times before. To give some examples of this, in Austria the main vehicle for venture capital investment is an equity corporation called a Mittelstands-finanzierungsaktiengesellschaft (MFAG) which is a tax-advantaged structure created to encourage investment in SMEs. So the Austrian market shows itself as keen to develop this type of investment through this tax-efficient structure. In Denmark the funds also typically use the private company structure but this time there are no specific regulations for venture capital funds and so there are no particular tax advantages to encourage investment. Finland's method of encouraging investment comes through the common use of the limited partnership structure, but with a clause that says the partners have to have the right to liquidate this partnership after 10 years, giving an efficient exit route. So we can see that across the markets there will be a variety of structures and incentives for investment in this part of the market, which actually goes to show how important the regulators believe it to be on a very intrinsic level. The UK has the largest venture capital market in Europe although this market is far smaller than the one in the US. To give some perspective on this, in 2009 the UK saw 264 deals, France was the only other European country that came anywhere this figure, whilst the US saw 2489 deals.[1]

It is not unusual for venture capital investment to be leveraged, so these companies will also be customers of the banks, which begins to explain why banks will sometimes have their own venture capital departments – that and the profit potential of this business. When a bank makes a loan to a venture capital firm they are making it based on an assessment of both the project and the venture capitalist so we are likely to see that the well-known established firms such as J.H. Whitney will often be better placed to raise additional financing than newer companies, but the track record of the venture capital company will be carefully monitored, looking not just at ultimate outcome but also at the processes used within the firm. On the whole this is a part of the industry that shows itself to be very disciplined.

Probably not surprisingly 2009 was not a great year for venture capital. In Europe investment was down by 41% on 2008, in the US a fall of 31%. These falls were not just in the overall amount invested, €3.2 billion in Europe, $21.4 billion in the US, but also in the number of deals.[2] Certain sectors like technology saw a big fall in investment, but bearing in mind the economic environment this should not really be a great surprise, as clearly the economic climate has a large impact on start-ups and firms that are looking for help in restructuring and refinancing. This is an important area, though, particularly in times when banks have been more restrictive in lending and companies have had to look at alternative sources. Typically these sorts of borrowing companies will be too small, or too risky, to access the mainstream financial markets, the alternative to bank lending. Yet interestingly, using this structure they will actually be accessing the same investor funds (pension funds, insurance companies etc.) that will invest in listed equities, bonds etc., but from the investors' point of view through a safer, diversified structure. To these investors venture capital provides an alternative investment vehicle, and

---

[1] Dow Jones Venture Source.
[2] Dow Jones Venture Source.

it is the role of the venture capital companies to form that link between this group of those in need of funds and those with funds to invest.

In terms of what we can see in the market from the activities of these venture capital enterprises, there is a whole range of possibilities beyond the financing raised by the venture capital firm itself. Not surprisingly we will see equity deals, both public and private, as often being the end result as the company in which the venture capitalists have invested reaches fruition of the project. We can also see these projects in the debt market, for example through leveraged loans. These are loans made to the enterprise itself, which will typically be a poor credit. To reflect this situation these loans will generally be higher yield, higher risk instruments, but, to mitigate some of this risk, will contain covenants that can enable the lenders to force early repayment if the borrower does not meet its targets in terms of maintaining liquidity or even profitability. These loans can be crucial to the borrower as they provide another important source of funding and also start to build relationships within financial markets that can be maintained as the business builds and the credits improve. From the investors' perspective it is another source of return, again that balances risk against return, so whilst not suitable for all investors they have had a lot of support over the past decade.

Conclusion

Throughout this book we have looked at a broad range of financial institutions, from the major full-service banks through to small boutique firms such as some of the venture capitalists. This diversity is one of the things that make the markets so interesting. At the end of the day, though, the market has room for these various types of firm, indeed the market needs them to ensure the efficient flow of funds that has been the main theme dominating everything we have looked at. We have looked at firms that have fulfilled the functions of issuers, investors and intermediaries, and have considered the different structures they can take. In many cases it is these structures and their purpose that have dictated how we see them in the market. For example, commercial banks with their constant need for liquidity are likely to be the biggest players in the money markets, insurance companies with their need for safe investment will be large players in the government bond markets, and so on. We have taken an international look at the markets, looking at institutions in all of the major centres to reflect the international nature of the markets. Whilst some of these institutions will only be found in their domestic markets it is interesting to note how the structures appear across borders even if the institutions themselves do not.

We have said so many times that this beginning of the second decade of the 21st century is likely to herald some key structural changes to the financial markets on the back of the Financial Crisis. This really cannot be overemphasized. It is very easy to have our attention diverted by returns to profit, bumper bonus payments, healthier markets all round (or nearly!), from the reality that this crisis fundamentally shook not just the markets but also the global economy. The scale of the government bailouts of banks and other financial institutions was unprecedented and not something that can easily be replicated. Therefore it is crucial that everything possible be done to prevent a recurrence. Of course this is easier said than done, and this is why there is so much debate on how best to proceed towards achieving this. Remember also that these changes are being conceived from a point of weakness, a point where we are seeing a lack of confidence not only in the system of financial markets but even in the governments themselves, with fears of developed countries within the eurosystem being unable to support themselves. This is far from ideal but we do not work in an ideal world.

In the final part of this book we have a series of case studies to look in a little more detail at some of the big events that have shaped today's financial landscape. These are the events and firms that are likely to be at the forefront of everybody's thinking as so many consider how to develop our markets in the 21st century. Not all of these appendices will be focusing on the bad things, indeed we will look at the EIB as an example of a supranational agency that has been a great success story in financial market terms, but we would be naïve to think that we can consign the bad stories to the history books. Their influence, and in many cases the cost of their failures, will be with us for years to come.

Appendix A

The Financial Crisis – Six
Months that Changed Investment
Banking

All through this book we have spoken about the Financial Crisis and the impact it has had and is continuing to have on the markets in many different ways. We now going to take a brief look at what actually happened and how the very infrastructure of the market changed with the failure of two of the big names, Bear Stearns and Lehman Brothers, that we have had to reference so much, and the impact this had on other banks and their positioning within the market.

If we look at the environment in which the financial markets were operating at the beginning of the 21st century one of the most striking things we will notice is the low interest rates that we saw on a global basis. If we look at Table A.1 we can see a comparison of the key interest rates in the US (Fed funds rate), the UK (base rate) and Japan (basic discount rate and loan rate):

Table A.1 Interest Rates
2000–2003

	1st Jan 2000	1st Jan 2003
US	5.43	1.94
UK	5.50*	3.75
Japan	0.5	0.1

*The UK actually raised its interest rate on 13 January 2000 to 5.75%.

As we can see over this three-year period there were substantial falls in these interest rates. By the time we reach 2003 we were focusing a lot of attention on Japan with its near zero interest rates, and believed then that this was as a situation particular to Japan and not one that would be emulated in any of the other major currencies. This was particularly true as we saw the Bank of Japan struggling to find the means to stimulate their economy further once they had reduced rates to these levels. In

Europe the euro was still a very young currency and the European Central Bank (ECB) had said from the very launch of the currency in 1999 that their policy was to promote low interest rates with the minimum of central bank intervention. So in this environment we saw a well-documented increase in borrowing to take advantage of these low rates that many felt were only temporary and this was to form part of the cause of the mortgage crisis that would show itself a few years later. However there is also another significant impact of low interest rates that in turn had an effect on the markets – the lack of investment return available. In this book we have looked at a lot of different institutions and have dedicated a whole section to the professional investors, the likes of pension funds and insurance companies. When we spoke of these investors we always bore in mind their need to balance risk against generating return, and for many we said that their largest portfolio holding by asset type was in the debt market. Well, here is where the problem lies. With such low interest rates in the short end of the market even long-dated bonds were not giving very high returns and so many of these investors were forecasting shortfalls in their required returns. This can be particularly serious if you are something like a pension fund that needs to build up a certain reserve to meet your pension commitments, particularly if you are locked into defined benefits,[1] which was often still the case at the beginning of the century. So we have a market which is hungry for return and a market condition that was not meeting this requirement. Is it really then a surprise that the market started to focus more attention on redesigning itself to take advantage of opportunities that may be there, such as looking at derivatives for investment return and maybe borrowing to increase the size of an investment portfolio, and so operating a more highly leveraged model? This was certainly part of the picture we were seeing painted as we moved on into the 21st century.

If we think about these two strands, the impact that we have just identified on borrowing and investment coupled with the development of the markets we can see how both sides of the market are affected as the decade continues. In the middle years of the decade we started to see interest rates rise as the economic situation began to change. Borrowers who had maybe over-borrowed affordably in the low interest rates were now facing higher costs and yet the market did not contract, borrowing continued, particularly dangerously mortgage borrowing, fuelled by the banks' continuing willingness to lend even in the sub-prime mortgage

---

[1] This is where the pension fund had committed to paying a certain level of pension, typically a percentage of final salary, commensurate with the number of years payments had been made.

market. This is dangerous because it makes the banks very vulnerable to a fall in the property market, which could well be the final nail in the coffin, a fall that inevitably eventually happened. On the side of market structure the market had been developing at a pretty much unprecedented pace, which in itself can always be dangerous. As new products were created, such as increasingly complex derivatives, and structured securities which embedded these derivatives, it was clear that it was sometimes difficult for our valuation tools and techniques to keep pace with this development. Assumptions were made about value which in time proved not to be true. An example of this is in valuations of the credit of mortgage-backed securities,[2] again particularly the sub-prime ones. Many of the valuation techniques used related them to classic credit models whereas in fact these credits behave quite differently, as we were to find out. The problem was that we did not have the right data to make some of the underlying assumptions that were being fed into the valuation models. This is not the first time this has happened and it will not be the last. It is unfortunate that market conditions were about to play such a large part in bringing these anomalies to light in such a dramatic way. Often when the maths is wrong there are losers in the market but not in such a broad and visible swathe that we were to see over the next few years. We had had a bit of a warning just a few years earlier with Long-term Capital Management,[3] a hedge fund brought to the brink of collapse and in need of government help in arranging a bailout when some of the assumptions being used to run the fund, assumptions that were driving the mathematically based trading models of the fund, proved to be ill-founded. Then again with the collapse of Enron in 2001, beneath all the fraudulent transactions, there was also an issue of valuation. Ideally these scandals should have suggested caution, a slowing of the development of the markets, but for many reasons, including the need for return as well as the more commonly stated greed of the market participants, this was not to stop the momentum of the market.

At one point Enron was a top counterparty in many financial markets, not just the energy markets where you would expect to see their name. These markets included credit derivatives, a market in which Enron believed they could value credit risk better than many of the banks. This is why they became so involved in this market, acting as a major counterparty and contributor of prices to the trading systems in use at the

---

[2] We have looked a little at these structures in the section on Quasi-Sovereigns in the chapter on Agencies.

[3] See the chapter on Hedge Funds for a little more about this.

time. It was interesting to see how quickly Enron traders were snapped up by banks after the fall of the company, with one bank in particular taking on a whole team of credit derivative traders, as a testament to this. This idea of an alternative perspective on value from that commonly seen in the market was a belief also held by AIG, and by some of the hedge funds, so the fact that there was so much disparity in how to value these products should again have been another warning signal. This was particularly true when we saw how happy non banks were to step into the market and take on large positions of risk from the market dealers, essentially the opposite deal to the one more traditionally seen whereby the bank takes risk from its non bank customers. The trouble was that the banks needed these counterparties. Without them you have two choices: first, to just pass the risk around the market, from bank to bank, rather like a ticking time bomb, and secondly, to not do the trades, which is clearly not going to happen. The market knew this, as did the regulators who encouraged the banks to hedge the risks and not keep these trades on their balance sheets. As we saw products created that on paper were safe products, certainly judging by the top quality ratings assigned to them by the credit ratings agencies, lots of market participants, both on the buy and the sell side chose not to ask too many questions about what was behind these products. Instead everyone focused on the commonly perceived risks and the return, which was often very attractive, and if they fitted into, say, a fund manager's criteria they were happy to buy them and reap the rewards. So to a certain extent it seems that the market may have closed its eyes to warning signals that were blatantly blinking in front of them.

One last comment we should make about the nature of the market leading up to the crisis was how big it had grown, not just in the number of transactions being executed, but also in the amount of money being put into these riskier products. Since we have said that more investors were running leveraged portfolios this means that the amount of investment funds in the market is being artificially buoyed by borrowed money, and borrowed money does not have the same almost infinite profile[4] of investment funds. So we have a different set of time constraints on the fund managers in which they need to not just turn a profit, but turn sufficient profit to cover the funding costs and still generate return. Remember we had been talking about a low-interest rate environment

---

[4] Investment funds are normally left in the market indefinitely. Whilst there will be individual movements into and out of a fund the fund will continue to exist, hence the definition of the funds as being infinitely available.

but as rates were to rise this became more difficult to achieve. So we started to see a more aggressive trading model being applied particularly by some of the hedge funds, often doing very large deals, market-moving deals, in order to ensure they saw the movements that they needed. Again this flies in the face of true value as the price moves are brought about more by market sentiment and trading restrictions than by analysis of the core market risks and values within the instruments or contracts.

So we arrive at 2007 and the cracks are beginning to show quite deeply in the global economies and in the financial markets. As the economies slow down more attention starts to be paid to these risks. As we said, we had been used to a market of falling rates and good liquidity, but as rates start to rise so liquidity starts to come under some pressure. Then as underlying default rates start to increase on mortgages, with repossessions rising, people begin publicly questioning values on some of these securities and derivatives. This then has a knock-on effect on willingness to lend.

The other trend that was going to influence events was was the bank consolidation that we had seen over the past decade. Banks like JP-Morgan Chase and Citigroup were increasing their balance sheet size by aggressively buying up banks in other regions and sectors, and so we started to appreciate the value of a large balance sheet, saying that these banks were more solid because of their balance sheet size – the idea of 'too big to fail' that we have spoken so often and in particular in the section on Banking. By contrast the investment banks, the likes of Merrill Lynch, Lehman Brothers, Goldman Sachs, had light balance sheets. If we join the dots and say that large balance sheets = safety, then light balance sheets = '?' (at best uncertainty; for some this was defined as weakness) and so people started to question the viability of these names in the 21st century market. The second you start to think this way it must affect your willingness to lend to these institutions, and so we start to see credit tightening for this type of name. This certainly was not the first time this had happened to these investment banks over the previous 20 years, but again this time a raft of circumstances were conspiring against them. Not only was credit tightening for these names but we also saw it begin to evaporate for even the big, solid names, as people became increasingly concerned not just with balance sheet size but the quality of assets still on these balance sheets. As the market turned against sub-prime mortgages we saw credit lines being reduced to mortgage lenders, commercial banks, insurance companies – so many of the major financial institutions – leading to the central banks and market regulators having to step in to try and normalize the market, often by taking abnormal steps such as bailing out Northern Rock in the UK. We also saw the failure of some of the hedge funds, some of the most highly leveraged investors in the market, amongst which were two owned by Bear Stearns, with the bank itself falling victim to a liquidity crisis in the summer of 2007. This caused even more nervousness in the market.

A key problem with this is that as the rest of the market seeks to minimize the risk to themselves so they increase it for the victims of such a liquidity crisis. Even though Bear Stearns did not go bust in 2007 their reputation was much damaged, and many of their customers and trading counterparties started to distance themselves. This had an impact not just on liquidity but on profitability both of which made the bank appear less safe. By March 2008 the bank was in the grip of another liquidity crisis and was then faced with the visible signs of the markets concerns. One was in the price of Bear Stearns CDS,[5] which are used to buy protection against the name defaulting. Effectively the buyer of a CDS will be buying protection against the credit defaulting and this price more than tripled over a six-week period from February to March, until the market for the product completely disappeared with no one willing to take on the risk at any price. Then Goldman Sachs famously sent an e-mail to customers showing their concerns. In the derivative markets it was not uncommon for participants to transfer the names on OTC contracts and the e-mail concerned this practice. For example, if you wanted to get out of a contract you could find another counterparty to take your place, as long as they were happy with the counterparty's risk. In this e-mail Goldman Sachs informed their clients that they would probably not be willing to enter into one of these substitutions if Bear Stearns were the counterparty. This e-mail was leaked and the market understood by it that Goldman Sachs no longer had faith in Bear Stearns as a counterparty risk and so this sentiment was picked up by others in the market. This was on 11 March, pushing Bear Stearns deeper into a liquidity crisis, and on 14 March they announced that they were to receive funding from JPMorgan Chase, backed by the government, a move that seemed to everyone to really be a back-door way of the government bailing out the bank. Bear Stearns was an investment bank, not a commercial bank, and as such we would not have expected the central bank to bail it out. Central banks have a close relationship with commercial banks because of the issue of depositors' funds, but their exposure to investment banks was minimal. So the fact that the Federal

---

[5] Credit Default Swaps.

Reserve Bank (the Fed) was willing to be involved, firstly in this funding line, and secondly in brokering a deal to rescue the bank, says more about the state of the market than anything else. On 16 March, a Sunday, a deal was agreed whereby JPMorgan Chase acquired Bear Stearns for $2 per share. Along with this they agreed to honour the bank's trading obligations, including derivative contracts, to ease market concerns. A year previously shares in Bear Stearns had been trading at $170 so the price of $2 raised a lot of eyebrows. Since this acquisition there has been much discussion about the way the deal was arranged and the price paid. This seems to have been a private transaction, negotiated quickly to avoid the bank's collapse, but meaning that no other firms had a chance to bid and so find a consensus market value. This is in stark contrast to the situation with Northern Rock that we look at in Appendix B, where the need to follow disclosure guidelines prevented the Bank of England from finding a speedy buyer for that ailing bank and ultimately led to its nationalization.

Had Bear Stearns been the last casualty of this crisis we probably would have accepted the deal and the price paid far more easily, but as it turned out March 2008 was the beginning of one of the most traumatic six-month periods the markets have seen.

After Bear Stearns the market started to worry about which other banks were as vulnerable and amongst the banks coming under the spotlight were clearly all the investment banks and naturally this caused their funding to become even tighter; this spread further around the market. However the next major bank failure was not an investment bank but instead the California-based Indy-Mac Federal Bank, the second largest bank failure in US history,[6] which failed in July 2008. This was the same period during which the two federal agencies FNMA and FHLMC were coming under close scrutiny and rumours started circulating about possible bailouts for them, an event that happened in September when the agencies were placed under government conservatorship.[7] These events made an already nervous market even more nervous and so the liquidity crisis continued, and even started to spiral, making it increasingly difficult for the stronger banks to fund themselves, let alone the weaker ones.

Another of the banks in trouble during this period, Lehman Brothers, suffered a change in its fortune when rumours circulated that a potential

---

[6] The largest to date had been the failure of Continental Illinois in 1984.
[7] See the chapter on Government Agencies in Section 3, Quasi-Sovereigns.

buyer for the bank was around in the form of Korea's Korea Development Bank. This caused the share price of the bank to rise, a sign of optimism as the markets considered the implication of the cash this acquisition would bring to the bank, but this came to nothing. Over the next couple of months rumours of potential deals involving just about every investment bank were circulating in the market. One such was about a merger between Morgan Stanley and Wachovia, as ill-fated as that would have been given that by the end of September Wachovia itself had been sold to Wells Fargo, to prevent its failure and it is unlikely that a merger with Morgan Stanley would have done anything to avert this. During August the price of funding became even higher, despite the efforts of the central banks to help the market by increasing money supply, and so we reach September and this is where we see some monumental changes in the market.

In September we saw several key events: Merrill Lynch's acquisition by Bank of America; the Japanese banking group Mitsubishi UFJ taking a 21% stake in Morgan Stanley; the biggest ever US bank failure with the collapse of WaMu (Washington Mutual), dwarfing IndyMac Federal Bank and Continental Illinois; the first bailout of insurance company AIG; and, of course, the collapse of Lehman Brothers, all within a few weeks. It is the collapse of Lehman Brothers that caused the most fundamental structural change in the markets as this time we did not see the Fed intervening to save the bank despite the bank and the market's pleas for it to do so. The bank filed for bankruptcy on 15 September, following a weekend in which it made public its dire situation and prompted the International Swaps and Derivatives Association (ISDA) to allow an exceptional Sunday trading session to allow people with derivative exposure to the bank to try and manage their positions in an orderly fashion. Banks also offered short-term funding to allow the bank to wind down its operations and potentially find buyers for various parts of the business, even if a single buyer for the whole could not be found. They were joined in this by the government offering to swap some of the bank's poor assets for financing but stopping short at a bailout. Despite these measures the shockwaves were profound with liquidity tightening even further, particularly as the extent of the market's exposure to Lehman Brothers came to light, and fears abounding that this would not be the last high profile failure – which it was not.

With Bear Stearns and Lehman Brothers gone, and Merrill Lynch merging with Bank of America, this left only Morgan Stanley and Goldman Sachs as the last of the major investment banks – and even this was about to change. On 21 September it was announced that they had both received Fed approval to become bank holding companies, giving up investment bank status. The significance of this was that it allowed them direct access to Fed lending, which was to give them a lifeline if necessary, and by being able to offer depositors FDIC insurance this would allow them to tap more sources of funding. This was a very significant event as it meant the end of the segregated business model that had been promoted by the Glass-Steagall Act. Ironically it seems increasingly likely that this Act may be revived in some form in the future to once again split the activities of commercial and investment banking. However, this change of status was prompted by expediency – it was yet another attempt to make the market more secure. It would be nice to be able to say that this worked and the market stabilized but that would be untrue. The next months saw more upheaval and massive investment in the market by the central banks as they lent funds and took equity stakes in some of the biggest bank names in the world, so changing the face of the industry.

It would have been hard to believe in September 2008 that the most hotly debated topic about banking just 18 months later would be the size of bankers' bonuses, and really this flatters to deceive. It can lead one to assume that having concerns about credit worthiness of the banks is a thing of the past, and it is not. Many of the central banks still have, or have only just closed, special liquidity programmes to deal with the Financial Crisis. We are a looking at a market where major corporate borrowers are still short of funds and are still reliant on significant funding from banks that already have substantial exposure to them. If we look at Europe we see a major crisis in the euro, with severe economic problems in Greece potentially threatening the very currency. Derivative markets are still expanding despite what has happened, and whilst some more controls have been introduced for the OTC derivatives market, such as an increasing use of central counterparties, highly leveraged risks are still being traded around the markets, as are the repackaged sub-prime mortgages, and they are still sitting on the balance sheets of banks. The situation has not gone away and there are many commentators who fear another banking crisis, but in the meantime we will worry about bankers' pay!

Appendix B
Northern Rock

Northern Rock was originally a building society in the UK formed by the merger of two 19th century building societies, the Northern Counties Permanent Building Society and the Rock Building Society in 1965. It then merged with a large of number of small regional societies until by 1997 it had integrated 53 of them, giving a broad, well-established customer base. As a building society its primary products were savings and mortgages. In the 1990s a number of building societies decided to demutualize to move further into the mainstream banking market and in 1997 Northern Rock became one of them. Whilst still remaining true to its building society roots by receiving bank authorization it also increased its product range. This, though, increased its reliance on market funding, which was to become a major part of its troubles 10 years later. Building societies have strict limits on how much funding they can raise in the markets, not being allowed to fund more than 50% of their lending with wholesale funds, the rest having to come from depositors' funds, and most building societies actually fund a substantially lower percentage on the wholesale markets. However as a bank Northern Rock was not covered by this rule and by 2007 they were funding 75% of their loans in this way, so completely changing their business model.

The summer of 2007 was when we first started to see the shortage of liquidity in the markets: the banks started to be more cautious of lending to one another as fears over the quality of assets sitting on banks' balance sheets started to build. In the UK's very competitive mortgage market there had been an increasing trend towards offering higher risk loans, mortgages with a higher loan to value ratio, and to less well qualified investors, in other words the sub-prime market. Northern Rock had entered this market but in fact most of their loans in this area were sold on to a mortgage company, SPML, owned by Lehman Brothers. Northern Rock actually carried very little sub-prime risk on its own books; its biggest problems came from funding. In June of 2007 they issued a profit warning which had a negative effect on the market lenders, who also saw them retreating and making themselves uncompetitive in the mortgage markets by increasing their interest rates, and so putting pressure on their business flows. The net result was the bank finding it harder to fund themselves both in the money markets and by securitizing their mortgage portfolio,[1] so cutting off their supply of both long and short-term funds. It does have to be said that a large part of this squeeze was actually driven by the market's fear for mortgage lenders in the US, and despite there being no direct link between Northern Rock and these banks the market was concerned that all the mortgage lenders in the UK were vulnerable to the same weaknesses as in the US. It is ironic that it was in this last trading statement before Northern Rock's crisis began, the one issued in June 2009 with the profit warning, that the bank outlined the plans it had begun to implement to pull away from the riskier business, but as we said the downside to this was giving up profit margins, and this appears to be what the market focused on.

Over the summer Northern Rock's shares were very actively traded, with the share price ultimately falling from around £12 at the beginning of the year to just over £6 in the middle of September before plunging to just under £2 by the end of the month. This had not all been a downward slope as there had been many rumours of potential takeovers with names such as Lloyds and HSBC being mentioned, but the overall trend was definitely down. It seemed as though there had been speculative short-selling in the stock, which in the aftermath was widely attributed to hedge funds, although it is unlikely that bank trading desks were not also involved in this. Along with this we had an anomalous situation in that whilst the market was selling the shares many research analysts were calling them as a good buy for investors. This is because the two sides were looking at different things: the analysts were looking at the fundamentals of the bank, its long-term prospects, position in the market etc., and with rumours of takeovers flying around it is not surprising that they should see value. The traders, on the other hand, were trading on a much shorter-term perspective. They were the ones who could see at first hand the tightening liquidity in the market and the way that market sentiment was turning against mortgage lenders. So whilst they might have agreed that the bank shares represented good overall value in practice they were more likely to sell than to buy. At the end of July they issued their interim trading report showing a 26.6% jump in underlying profits for the first half of the financial year, but repeating

---

[1] This means they would create a pool of mortgage loans they had made and use them as the assets behind an asset-backed security.

its profit warning and saying that they expected profits to rise for the following year by the lower end of their estimate which was 15–25%.

At the beginning of August the market funding situation worsened sharply, with the market effectively starting to dry up. If the large banks were becoming wary of lending to one another and were reducing their credit lines[2] it can hardly be a surprise that they started to refuse to lend to the second-tier banks, and so on 13 August Northern Rock went to the FSA and told them they were having liquidity problems that they saw rising to crisis level. Northern Rock shares were being aggressively hit (sold) in the market, and when questioned by the press about this they told them the markets were 'difficult for them', focusing ever more attention on their liquidity.

All of this led to the Bank of England's intervention on 13 September, when it had to publicly step in as lender of last resort, with the terms of the deal being announced in a trading statement issued at 7am on Friday 14 September, just in time for the opening of the markets – and the branches. As the details emerged so the money started leaving the bank with a well-publicized 'run on money'. Television in the UK was full of pictures of people queuing outside Northern Rock branches to withdraw their savings, a story that continued into Saturday and the beginning of the following week, prompting the government to announce it was guaranteeing all deposits in the bank. The effect of this was certainly to reverse this trend – and it caused a flood of savers to take their money from other banks and place them with Northern Rock. This created even more systemic problems for the sector as a whole so on 20 September the Bank of England had to amend these arrangements stating that their 100% guarantee applied only to deposits made before midnight on 19 September, but with a proviso that anybody reopening accounts that they had closed in the previous week would also be covered. To further aid matters they also announced a £10 billion cash injection into the wholesale money markets to try and ease the liquidity problems. This would prove to be the first of many measures as we saw in Appendix A.

There are two pieces of legislation in the UK which had significant impact on the Northern Rock situation. One is the Market Abuse Directive and the other the UK Takeover Code. This meant that over the next few months as negotiations took place to find a solution to the bank's problems – most probably a takeover – everything had to be done in the

---

[2] These credit lines dictate how much a bank is willing to lend to a counterparty with respect to their credit risk.

public eye with a high level of transparency and with careful consideration of the impact of any mergers on the competitive positioning of the bank. Over the next five months a buyer was actively sought. Whilst Lloyds had been the most likely candidate for the takeover they had dropped out of negotiations as they had funding issues of their own, leaving several other potential buyers including a couple of private equity firms, the UK-based J.C. Flowers and the US-based Cerberus, but ultimately there were two main suitors to emerge. One was a consortium led by Virgin Group including amongst its participants the American firm AIG, a hedge fund, Toscafund Asset Management, and an investment company with expertise in restructuring, WL Ross & Co. The second suitor was another UK private equity firm, Olivant, spearheaded by Luqman Arnold, a former head of Abbey National and so well experienced in running this type of bank with its business model dominated by its building society roots. Ultimately Olivant were not able to secure funding that met the government's requirements and so were obliged to pull out. Olivant pulled out of their bid on 5 February, and despite the Virgin consortium being the government's preferred bidder they could not make a financial bid that satisfied the government and so on 15 February the bank was nationalized. During this time the bank had experienced a lot of volatility as the market covered its trading positions, such as the shorts that we had suspected earlier in the middle of 2007, but there was also a lot of speculative buying of the stock by hedge funds leaving some with considerable holdings in the bank, holdings which had now been taken over by the government for no value.

From the very beginning it was said that this was a temporary measure but as we saw, the market crisis accelerated leaving the government more than two years on still owning Northern Rock. In April 2009 it announced that it expected to privatize part of the bank later that year. It was at this point that the idea of splitting the bank into two, a good bank and a bad bank, first emerged. This was to be a capital restructuring of the bank that would create two separate companies, one, Northern Rock plc (the good bank), would hold all customer savings and about £10 billion of mortgage accounts, along with some wholesale deposits. The bank would be licensed as a deposit-taker and mortgage provider, so pretty much continuing the basic business of Northern Rock before and since the crisis. The key difference, though, comes in the creation of the second, Northern Rock (Asset Management) plc (the bad bank). This company would be left holding the bulk of the residential mortgages, about £50 billion, along with the unsecured loans, the government loan and most of the wholesale funding and debt obligations. In other words this was the bank that would be left holding the so-called toxic assets. The second bank would only be authorized as a mortgage provider and would not be expected to offer any new mortgages. This plan had to seek EU approval, which was received in October 2009, and the restructuring came into place on 1 January 2010. It should be said, though, that at the time of the transfer 90% of the mortgage portfolio was actually fully performing and not in arrears so the asset quality had certainly not deteriorated substantially over the previous few years, which is ironic since this was the fear that had sparked the bank's problems in the first place. The government also made commitments to increase the size of their loan to the bank to finance their ongoing activities and to provide additional capital to Northern Rock (Asset Management), if required, to enable them to meet their capital requirements. So, going into 2010, the government now had two separate entities to sell to achieve their privatization goal. The good bank immediately started to attract interest with various potential buyers emerging from the moment the plan was announced. Amongst these was, again, Virgin Group, this time potentially working with the US private equity firm Blackstone. In the time since the first bid Virgin had bought a small British bank, Church House Trust Bank, which whilst not very active in the public market was nonetheless an authorized bank, and so this acquisition brought to the Virgin Group a banking licence and some infrastructure to carry them forward into the retail banking market. Taking over Northern Rock would give it an introduction into the mortgage market and so kick-start that part of their business. Other names that had been linked with Northern Rock included the UK supermarket, Tesco, although they ruled themselves out in October 2008, but several banks including National Australia Bank and Santander were reportedly still in the running following the legal restructure. As for the bad bank the government's intention is to sell it as well but this will not be happening in the short term. The first sale will be of the good bank which should probably not be too difficult although we should be wary of famous last words! Selling the second bank will be far more problematic and so it looks as though the UK government will not be free of nationalized banks for quite some time, irrespective of what they would prefer.

Appendix C
UK Financial Investments

As with pretty much all the other major economies the UK government found itself having to take unprecedented steps to protect the financial system following the events of 2008. Along with providing additional liquidity to the banking system as a whole the government also had to step in and recapitalize a small number of UK banks, leaving them as major shareholders. This created a problem for the government in terms of how they were going to manage these investments. If anyone had asked them even a year earlier if they had plans to nationalize any parts of the banking sector they would have laughed and yet this was the situation in which they found themselves, nationalizing and part-nationalizing by default rather than by choice.

Unlike some other countries the UK did not establish a separate agency to deal with additional funding for the UK banks. Instead it chose to raise the funds it needed by increasing its issuance of government debt, and for the Bank of England to continue to be the counterparty for trades with the market as in the normal way of business. The differences came in the scope of the deals as the government created additional borrowing facilities and then went on to pursue the policy of quantitative easing that we discussed in the chapter on Banking in the UK. Dealing with these new equity positions, though, was a different matter, and this is why the government felt it best to create an agency whose sole purpose was to do this, that agency being UKFI.

The creation of UKFI was announced in November 2008. The basic idea was to separate the two relationships that the government now had with banking, one being the classic relationship that we spoke about in the section on Commercial Banking, whereby the banks are used by governments, through the central banks, to implement monetary policy and raise funding, and in return they support the banking system, providing it with liquidity and standing as lender of last resort when required. This is a finely balanced relationship built up over time, and when the system is working well it meets the needs of both sides in an efficient manner. A lot of this efficiency comes from the closeness of the two sides. The Bank of England would maintain dialogue with the banks, telling them of their financial plans and working together to achieve these efficiently, and in return the Bank would be very sensitive to the needs of the market through these close contacts. On a typical day the Bank would be likely to keep pretty constant communication with the dealer market through its own internal dealing desks, and through these relationships the market experiences a good level of trust. This trust, though, could have easily been compromised by a second relationship if the bank represented the government's shareholdings of some of the very banks in the market with whom they dealt. The government invested in these banks with public money so, as we saw with the various investment companies we have discussed, it has a duty of care to manage these investments in the best interest of the stakeholders, bearing in mind the investment policy that would have to be set out to deal with this unexpected situation. If the Bank of England were to be in charge of managing these investments as it did other financial investments of the government, then clearly the UK Treasury could see that there was a large potential conflict of interest here that could impact not only on the investments themselves but on the whole integrity of the UK banking system. So it was decided that, in the best interests of all, the investments needed to be handled independently from the Bank of England.

When the management policy was set up for these investments it became clear that there were several key issues that needed to be carefully considered. This was an unplanned investment programme that needed exceptional funding from the debt market. This meant that the funding would need to be repaid and since there was no budget plan for this the obvious solution was to sell the investments and repay the debt. So from the beginning it was clear that these investments would need to be viewed as temporary for practical as well as political reasons. The government made it clear to all from the beginning that they were looking to divest their shareholdings as soon as practically achievable. In the chapter on Banking in the UK we spoke about the UK government's speedy acquisition and disposal of most of Dunfermline Building Society and Bradford & Bingley and probably in an ideal world this would have been the route for all of these bank investments but that was not to be. Instead the government was left with substantial holdings that they were planning to sell at some point in the future, and whilst sooner rather than later, this was an unknown date.

However selling these bank stakes is not that straightforward. The shares have to be sold at a price that gives some sense of value to the public. If they are sold too cheaply then the government is just locking the country into a loss on their investment. If they hold on until the positions are in profit then they are likely to be very long-term investors, and not in line with their stated policy. So, trying to determine a level that represents value is a difficult one. Difficult, too, is the issue of finding appropriate buyers. If the government went out and put all their shares on the market without thought as to who might be the buyers this would cause major instability. There are a lot of issues here about competition and public acceptance of the deal as well as pure price instability that will mean that the process of selling any of these assets is likely to involve a lot of negotiation. If all of the government's holdings of RBS were to be sold to Barclays (even assuming that they would be interested) this would create a major imbalance in the market distribution that might well be unacceptable to HSBC, giving one of their competitors too much exposure and market share and so diminishing HSBC's role in the markets. This is the sort of situation that happened in the US as a buyer was sought for Wachovia in 2008, the sixth largest bank in the US by assets at the time. This was particularly the case when it looked as though Citigroup would be the buyer, meaning that Citigroup, JPMorgan Chase and Bank of America would hold 30% of US banking deposits. Many were pleased when Wells Fargo came into the picture and ultimately ended up buying the bank because at least this did not increase the concentration of the Big Three. Another potential problem would be if the holding were to be sold to Mitsubishi UFJ (again without implying that they would be interested but just for argument's sake). Given the nationalist nature of the domestic commercial banking markets this sale might not be well received, and that is aside from any international political issues concerning Japanese restrictions on foreign ownership of Japanese banks and the need for reciprocity. So finding the buyer, or buyers, for these holdings will probably not happen overnight but will need to be carefully considered.

There is another sensitivity issue that the government had to bear in mind which is the risk that it may be seen as favouring these banks in their market operations. Obviously this would be anti-competitive and unacceptable. In fact in October 2008 Northern Rock, the wholly owned bank, was obliged to stop taking customer deposits as it had reached the caps on customer deposits that are imposed by European competition laws. This was because Northern Rock was the destination of a flight to safety as savers wanted to put their money in the safest haven in the market which had to be the bank owned by the government. So whilst this was not intentional it does show the difference in perspective that government ownership gives and how it can impact on market structure. So again it was hoped that the idea of removing control of these assets away from the Bank of England would help in distancing the market activities from this idea of conflict of interests.

UK Financial Investments Limited was set up as a private company with the UK Treasury as its only shareholder, and is therefore a government agency. It manages the government's shareholdings in RBS and Lloyds Banking Group, in which they have partial shareholdings, although in the case of RBS this is an overwhelming majority, and the parts of Bradford & Bingley not sold to Santander and the two parts of Northern Rock,[1] which are wholly owned. With the wholly owned entities there are also loans and guarantees that need to be managed, and this also falls within their remit. The agency is totally funded by the government and is not allowed to borrow money nor engage in any other activity in the financial markets beyond looking after these investments. The one overriding objective for the company is to create the strategy for disposal of the assets, but in the meantime they need to monitor the firms and try to create shareholder value. This has not necessarily been easy for them. Their mandate says they have to monitor the companies closely but proportionally to the government's shareholdings. So, in the case of RBS, given that the government holds a stake of 83% you would expect there to be a lot of close contact. Against this, though, they must also allow these partially owned banks to maintain their independent business models. They are not expected to intervene on a day-to-day basis any more than any other investor would be expected to do. They are expected to exercise their voting rights but core decision-making must lie with the management of the banks, including business planning and control of budgets. A good example of how this can become a difficult political issue for them was seen at the end of 2009 and the beginning of 2010 as banks began to talk about their bonus payouts for the year. Clearly these banks would come under a lot of public scrutiny, particularly when they announced their results, but the banking sector in general came in for a lot of criticism as many of the banks announced good results in investment banking and so correspondingly high bonus payments. A lot of this profit comes on the back of a market rally that was stimulated by government support both for the banks directly and in terms of the amounts of money they needed to raise to pay for the bailout

---

[1] See Appendix B: Northern Rock for an explanation of this.

of the financial system. To make the situation worse in many cases the liquidity crisis has caused some banks to restrict the availability of funds in the direct bank lending market for institutional borrowers, so forcing them into capital markets. All in all this helped create a bumper year for the investment banking divisions, with particularly good returns being achieved on the advisory side of the business. There were many calls for the UKFI to block these bonus payments in RBS, and so they found themselves in the situation of being called upon to intervene in the running of the bank. Under the terms of the bank receiving funds from the UK asset protection scheme the bonus pool required the consent of the UKFI but this placed them in an uncomfortable position. On the one hand they need to respect the integrity of the management of the bank and on the other they have a responsibility to the public who felt the payouts were unjustified, particularly in light of the bank posting overall losses of £3.6 billion. This perfectly highlights the conflict involved in this kind of part-nationalization deal and goes a long way to explaining why the sooner the assets are sold and UKFI is dissolved the better.

Appendix D
The European Investment Bank

The European Investment Bank (EIB) is one of the most high-profile of the supranational agencies. It was established in 1958 under the Treaty of Rome, the treaty that established the European Economic Community (EEC). Its shareholders are the Member States of the EU, with their share of the bank's capital being allocated according to their economic weight at the time of joining the union. As at the beginning of 2010 the countries listed in Table D.1 were the countries within the EU and therefore the shareholders of the EIB:

Table D.1   EU Country Members 2010

Member Countries of the EU 2010*	
Austria	Latvia
Belgium	Lithuania
Bulgaria	Luxembourg
Cyprus	Malta
Czech Republic	Netherlands
Denmark	Poland
Estonia	Portugal
Finland	Romania
France	Slovakia
Germany	Slovenia
Greece	Spain
Hungary	Sweden
Ireland	UK
Italy	

*There are also three more candidate countries, Turkey, Croatia and the Former Yugoslav Republic of Macedonia.

The four countries that account for the greatest amount of capital are France, Germany, Italy and the UK, each accounting for €37.578019 billion of the bank's total capital of €232 billion. This is important because this is how we measure the credit worthiness of the EIB when it comes to using the financial markets. Within the bank's statutes it can make loans up to 2.5 times its capital, so understanding the strength of this capital is an important part of understanding the bedrock on which the bank is built. These shareholders do have a very close connection with the agency since it is created with the purpose of acting as a development bank furthering the policies of the EU, so for many a vested interest. The overall management of the agency consists of a three-tier structure, as illustrated in Figure D.1:

Figure D.1   Management Structure

The Board of Governors consists of, normally, the Finance Ministers of the Member States, so this is a very high-level, political body. Their role is to oversee in the broadest sense, approving such things as lending policy and capital increases, but not getting involved in the approved functions of the bank. The Board of Directors, at present a group of 28, with one from each Member State and one from the European Commission, acts very much as a corporate Board of Directors would do. They again oversee borrowing and lending and ensure the bank is being managed and operated properly, but on a strategic level, leaving the hands-on element to the next tier down. This is the Management Committee which is the actual managing executive of the bank, tasked with ensuring good running of the day-to-day activities. Unlike the other bodies this is not a political representation of the shareholders, but instead the nine members of this committee are just responsible for running the firm. There is one proviso and that is that the President of this Committee will also be the Chairman of the Board of Directors to ensure the closeness of communication between the two. Beyond that appointments to this Committee will come from the bank. There is also an Audit Committee, reporting directly to the Board of Governors, whose role is to observe and verify that the bank is working within its statutes and guidelines. So this is the management structure within which the agency operates, and as we can see it is not surprisingly a mixture of political and business appointment.

The EIB group itself consists of two separate entities, one the bank, and the other the European Investment Fund (EIF). We will look at this second one a little later. The agency is a not-for-profit organization and its purpose is to invest in projects which, as they say, 'further the development of the European Union by making long-term finance available for sound investment'.[1] This brings up two important issues, first the need for the EIB to have access to long-term funding itself and, secondly, the goals of their investment in projects. The intention is for the agency to be self-funding so any projects in which it invests need to be considered economically viable in order to protect their investment. They are not there to provide bailout funds and have made this very clear over the past couple of years. Instead they are there to encourage economic development and there are three key ways in which they can offer support, by making direct loans, indirect loans and by leveraging off their own credit rating in giving guarantees.

Direct Loans

In order to be eligible for a direct loan from the EIB a project will have to be scrutinized using, not surprisingly, a formalized process, and the agency will then plan to follow the progress of the project through to its conclusion. These loans are intended to be given to larger projects, typically those with a cost of a minimum of €25 million, and the agency is willing to provide up to 50% financing for any one project. The borrowers that come to the EIB will be both private and public entities as two of the objectives of the bank are both to support the private sector and to provide for infrastructure development. These are not grants; unlike the World Bank the EIB does not make grants for projects, instead they make loans available which are commercial loans, albeit at good rates and with a streamlined fee structure, but the agency will expect repayment. This forms an important part of the EIB's own cash flows and is necessary to manage their own borrowings.

Indirect Loans

Another way in which they make funds available is to lend to banks to pass on to customers. They typically achieve this by giving lines of credit to banks to pass on to small and medium-sized firms (SMEs). The

---

[1] EIB website.

loans made under these indirect agreements are the responsibility of the bank; they decide who and how to lend, and the EIB is just giving them the liquidity. In Part II we took a look at Microfinance institutions and this is an area in which the EIB is becoming increasingly involved, on an indirect basis. They have already made a number of investments in Microfinance funds, in Africa, the Caribbean and the Pacific, and have intentions to increase this. These regions are not the dominant areas in which the bank commits funds, but again this form of lending fits in with an EU policy objective to help with the eradication of global poverty.

Guarantees

As well as lending funds the EIB can also help by providing guarantees to allow projects to borrow themselves at better rates. The EIB is a top-quality borrower rated triple A, so attaching a guarantee of this quality can make a very significant difference to attracting funds and the rates that will be paid. Obviously if the EIB offers this guarantee they are taking on the risk of default so again stringent controls need to be applied and reserves kept by the bank to cover this risk.

The bulk of the projects in which the EIB gets involved are, not surprisingly, within the Member States. In 2009 they lent €79.1 billion, €70.5 billion of which went to projects in the EU and the European Free Trade Association (EFTA).[2] Beyond this region they have also invested in neighbouring parts of Europe along with Africa, the Caribbean and the Pacific region, as we have already mentioned. Whilst the projects cover a wide range of interests, over the past five years the area that has received the most investment is transport.

EIF

The European Investment Fund was set up 1994 as a public-private enterprise. It was reorganized in 2000 leaving the shareholding as EIB with 62%, the European Commission with 29% and the remaining 9% in the hands of 30 European banks and financial institutions. This fund was set up to provide venture capital for smaller, higher risk borrowers. It does not lend directly but again uses the indirect model of investing in venture capital funds to pass on to the end borrowers. It also provides guarantees to reduce borrowing costs as we have seen with the EIB

---

[2] These are Iceland, Liechtenstein, Norway and Sweden.

itself. Effectively it is running a fund of funds with investments in venture capital and private equity. It will always take minority stakes but of large enough size to be significant. Unlike the main bank it does not have any debt on its balance sheet but is financed by its shareholders with a subscribed capital in 2010 of €2.865 billion. The areas in which the fund makes investment will be dictated by the policy of the EIB and the EU, with, for example, aiding early stage Research & Development being one of their prime targets at the moment. When a mandate is given the fund needs to uncover the best way in which to invest to promote this cause. So we can see that the EIF plays a very important investor role in this part of the market, often serving to underpin and stimulate interest in a specific area.

THE EIB AS A BORROWER IN THE MARKETS

The EIB is one of the most prolific borrowers in the financial markets, in fact it is often seen as the most frequent borrower in the international markets. In 2009 it set a target of raising €80 billion, a substantial increase from the €61.136 billion raised in 2008. This is not all new money being raised as there were scheduled redemptions of debt due, but nonetheless they were still looking to raise some €50 billion of new capital, as opposed to the net figure from 2008 of €23.933 billion. This was the level, though, that was again authorized for 2010. The bulk of this money is raised in the core currencies of euro, US dollar and British pound, but they will also use other currencies as opportunities arise, and in 2009 they used a total of 17 currencies. The reason for this is to cover the broadest range of potential investors and to take advantage of market situations, for example pockets of demand such as were seen in Australian dollars in 2009. In their core currencies they tend to issue very large deals, typically several billion of each currency, as they know there is a large appetite for this class of credit in these currencies. These are known as the benchmark issues as they mimic some of the features of issuance of government bonds, such as the EIB choosing to issue large enough size to try and ensure the deals are liquid, and using a range of maturities on a regular basis so that investors can always find, for example, a five-year bond in the market. They also monitor how their bonds are trading in the markets and try to ensure that there is good price transparency so that investors can keep an eye on changes in the value of their investments with ease. They feel that this helps to encourage investors to trust the EIB and so to keep buying their issues and thus to fund their projects. They also have a reputation for innovative use of the markets. Many of the bonds they issue will have different characteristics affecting how the interest is paid, for example linking the coupon payment rate to movements in another market index, or resetting on a periodic basis, and they also innovate in how they bring the deals to the market. In 2006 they introduced the EPOS (European Public Offering of Securities) structure which was a simultaneous launch across the EU using a group of strong retail banks to encourage retail placement of the securities. The return on this €1 billion bond was linked to inflation. In 2007 they launched EPOS II for €600 million. This bond is also known as the Climate Aware-ness Bond as its payment is linked to an index created specifically for the purpose called the FTSE4Good Environmental Leaders Europe 40 Index, the 40 largest companies that scored a high best practice rating (a rating of 5) in environmental practice. In other words companies striving to be environmentally friendly. Then to continue the theme the funds raised from this bond would only be used for environmental projects. This meant that investors would be buying a bond that was intended to give them a good return, and with something of a safety net in that the bond guaranteed to repay a minimum repayment of 105% of face value at maturity if the index did not reach a given level of return. So all in all this issue was not just targeting a broad geographic range of investors, through use of the EPOS structure again, but was also targeting socially responsible investing. Another interesting thing they did in 2009 was to issue a series of 'cooperative' bonds, issues that were only available at launch through a group of cooperative and popular banks, with the intention being that they would be able to place the paper with other similar institutions, a strategy that seemed to work very well. So we can see how innovative and broad-reaching they try to be whilst at all times aiming to meet their funding targets efficiently.

Whilst these issues are small in comparison with the straightforward core benchmark deals they are not small in their own right, and indeed the series of cooperative bonds raised €4.25 billion. An issue size of €1 billion is a good-sized deal in the financial markets. Not surprisingly the EIB has to pay close attention to the risks they take on using all these various forms of financing and they are therefore large users of financial derivatives, especially the swap structure[3] that allows them

---

[3] As we explained in the section on Supranationals an interest rate swap is a derivative contract where one party pays an interest rate on a notional amount to their counterparty in return for an

to manage and transform currency and interest rate risk. Whilst these instruments are intended to help the EIB to manage the market risks of their borrowings the use of them can increase the credit risk they have to the market and so they tend to apply stringent controls on their choices of counterparty and actively require additional controls such as obliging their counterparties to post collateral to cover potential losses. What may have seemed very stringent when the EIB first started requiring them have now become quite commonplace, particularly in the wake of the credit problems and failures from 2008.

THE EIB AS AN INVESTOR IN THE MARKETS

As at the end of 2008 the EIB held assets in money market and fixed income funds, as well as an alternative investment fund consisting of structured securities with returns linked to hedge funds. In total their holdings within the treasury department had a value of €29.2 billion,[4] divided between trading portfolios and portfolios of assets to be held to maturity, and across a range of products including money markets, fixed income, derivatives and structured securities. This is small compared to the €283 billion in debt securities that they had in issue at the time, but the income on these investments forms an important part of the financing strategy. In the chapter on Supranational Agencies we spoke about the investment strategy employed by some of these agencies, investing in slightly higher risk securities to achieve a spread above funding cost, and this strategy is carried out by the EIB. Whilst looking for a good return they are not willing to compromise too much on risk and so most of their investments beyond one year will be for very good quality credits, AA to AAA. It might seem that they are willing to take on a lower risk in the money markets as the bulk of their money market investment is with credits of single A, but actually this says a lot about the long-term risk of the banks in the market as a whole, as there are relatively few higher ranked banks. Also, a bank may have a single A rating from a long-term perspective but at the same time from a short-term perspective they may have a top-quality rating. This reflects the difference in risk depending on the length of the exposure. All in all the EIB takes a

interest payment made on another basis. The classic structure would be where one side pays a fixed interest rate and the other pays a floating one. The swap can also be across currencies, the same structure with one side paying an interest rate in one currency against receiving interest in a different one.

[4] EIF Annual Report.

conservative approach to both the assets they buy and the counterparties with whom they deal. Yet they are still able to generate returns above funding through their portfolios which contribute to the net profit they make on their overall funding cost against income on all investments.

The EIB is a good example of a supranational agency in terms of why it exists and also how it can use the financial markets. The triple A rating that the agency carries comes not from the business model but from the ownership. The fact that Germany, France, Italy and the UK are the biggest suppliers of capital says a lot about the firm foundations on which the agency is built. It is such a prolific borrower that people do have to pay close attention to its overall level of returns to ensure that the cost of this funding does not outstrip its revenue flows, but so far this seems not to be the case. However it should not surprise us that the EIB has to monitor very carefully the levels at which its debt is trading as this gives a good indication of how well its next issues will be received.

Appendix E
AIG

American Insurance Group is an insurance company that traces its roots back to the beginning of the 20th century in Shanghai, even though it is as a US-based insurer that it is primarily known. It hit the headlines in September 2008 when it received the first of a series of bailout payments from the Federal Reserve Bank (the Fed). This shocked the market as we had not expected to see the Fed bail out a non bank institution but such was AIG's involvement in the markets that the Fed felt that they had no choice. If they allowed this insurance company to fail its failure could bring down major banks worldwide so they felt obliged to step in to prevent this happening.

It is important to realize that the financial problems did not come from the insurance part of the business, which was and still is, in 2010, a solid, solvent insurer. Instead it was an area of the firm called AIG Financial Products (AIGFP) that brought the name to this position. AIGFP was set up in 1987 when Howard Sosin, a former college professor at Columbia University, and trader at Drexel Burnham, formed a joint venture with AIG, setting up this department within the firm, and bringing with him a team from his former employers. The intention behind the department was to concentrate on financial market transactions as a separate business from the core one of insurance. It built up a specialism in derivatives trading, based on mathematical models that they believed were a better way of evaluating these products than those commonly used in the markets. This is eerily reminiscent of people working at Enron who had the same idea! AIG was perfectly poised to take best advantage of these markets as banks are always on the lookout for non bank counterparties to whom they can pass risk. So much trading is done on the interbank market that managing bank counterparty risk is a major concern for the market. This was particularly true for the long-dated derivatives, products like interest rate swaps (IRS) and later credit default swaps (CDS). A CDS is a swap transaction where the CDS seller takes the risk of a credit defaulting in return for an annual payment, a percentage of the nominal amount of the deal. The buyer of the swap buys protection, the seller takes on the risk. For example if a swap buyer has a

$10 million corporate bond they could buy a $10 million CDS, for which they might pay 100bp (1%) of the nominal amount each year. This cost will obviously reduce the return they receive on the bond, but it mitigates the credit risk, as if the issuer of the bond defaults the seller of the CDS commits to making good this loss. The product has an uneven cash flow because as long as the credit does not default the only payment flow is from the CDS buyer to the seller, with the seller only making one payment and that happening only on default. They are also actively traded with movements in the price reflecting, broadly, the market's view on the probability of default and it was these very products that AIG believed they could price in a more efficient way. These derivatives could have maturities of anything from a year out to five or 10 years, or for the IRS even longer. So to have a top-quality, non bank name willing to step into the market was very well received. AIGFP also relied heavily on technology to monitor the movements in the market, looking to exploit any inefficiency. Sosin and AIG parted company in 1993 after the department suffered a loss of $100 million, which illustrates the size of risk they were taking. The two were then involved in a lengthy dispute about Sosin's severance settlement before he received a reported $150 million payout.

After Sosin's departure the department was given subsidiary status and far from reducing risk following these losses it continued to be run according to Sosin's models very successfully for the next 15 years, building up an international business. As the markets developed so did AIG, in particular increasing their CDS exposure to take on the risk of not just pure corporate credit but also taking on a lot of the sub-prime mortgage exposure that the banks were putting on their books. A key to AIGFP's success was its triple A rating, one shared by relatively few other market counterparties. Lesser counterparties were typically required to post collateral in a lot of their derivative deals to cover the counterparties against the credit risk. AIG, though, since it was a better counterparty than nearly everyone else they dealt with, managed to avoid doing this, claiming that they were the ones taking on the most credit risk, and thus whilst refusing to post collateral themselves demanding it from the bank counterparties. This was important since not having to provide collateral was very cost-efficient for them. It was fine until AIG lost its triple A rating in 2005, a critical event, but a situation made worse in 2008 when its rating fell below double A (AA). This was a key element in their subsequent liquidity crisis since at the time

AIG had about $400 billion of CDS exposure on its books and this fall in rating would mean that AIG would now have to post collateral. Not surprisingly AIG was involved in the asset-backed market, creating and buying asset-backed securities which as we have seen throughout this book have made a major contribution to the problems of financial institutions.

If we recall the market situation in September 2008, the sub-prime crisis, it is not hard to imagine the impact this would have on AIG's liquidity. They had already lost billions in writing down positions in CDS in the year to date, since many of the credits had lost value and so the prices of the CDS contracts they had written had risen, meaning that they were now receiving relatively too little for protecting the buyers against the credit risk. So if they were receiving 100bp on a contract and should in today's terms have been receiving 150bp then this becomes a 50bp mark to market loss. To make matters worse remember these are multiyear contracts, and so they were 'losing' not just 50bp this year but every year until the end of the deal, and whilst the situation could improve it could also get worse. This is why we have to again consider collateral. Since AIG now had to put up collateral against their positions to cover losses, this 50bp per annum fall in value would need to be represented by an increase in the collateral they posted against the positions. They had already raised $20 billion, and were known to still have liquidity problems. In a filing to the SEC in August AIG had estimated that a further one notch drop in ratings would force them to post extra collateral of $13.3 billion. Now not only were they having to post more collateral for their own fall in credit but they were also posting collateral against credits that were plummeting in value, with these values often being contributed by the counterparties with whom they had dealt, the banks. Some of these banks also quoted very conservative prices for deals for which they would be receiving collateral, to protect themselves. Furthermore the downgrade also triggered clauses in some contracts giving the counterparties the right to terminate the deals, meaning that losses that faced AIG were no longer just unrealized, paper losses, they would literally need to pay the differences in values to their counterparties, providing yet another potential drain on resources. So, AIGFP found itself in a situation where it was drastically short of liquidity and turned to the state for help. The Fed stepped in asking Goldman Sachs and JPMorgan Chase to make emergency loans to the firm, and hired Morgan Stanley to assist in determining a rescue strategy. The state of New York also stepped in allowing the firm to lend to itself, in other words to lend money from the core insurance business to this financial products subsidiary. Unfortunately this would prove not to be enough and on 16 September the Fed agreed to a secured loan of up to $85 billion in emergency funding in return for an equity stake of 79.9% in the firm.

Sadly this was not the end of the story as the losses of the firm continued to mount. AIG's full year loss in 2008 was $99 billion. The company embarked on a major restructuring programme involving selling parts of the business and other assets but they still required substantial state aid, including the establishment of two federal agencies, Maiden Lane II and III.[1] Maiden Lane II was set up on 10 November to purchase mortgage-backed securities from several of the insurance subsidiaries of AIG. These securities had a nominal value of $39.3 billion, and a market value of $20.8 billion. At the same time Maiden III was set up to buy Collateralized Debt Obligations (CDOs)[2] carrying AIG risk from some of their counterparties. Maiden III bought CDOs of a nominal value of $62.1 billion and for these securities and to terminate derivative contracts related to them they paid $26.8 billion. However they also allowed the counterparties to keep the collateral payments that had already been made against these deals, some $35 billion, and also had to make a payment to AIGFP of $2.6 billion for some contracts where the collateral value put up by AIG exceeded the fair value of the contracts. This meant that the counterparties received the full value of their exposure, thus taking no part in the failure of AIG. In total the cost of this bailout has exceeded $182 billion.

This bailout has caused a lot of controversy, not just over its size but over the very legitimacy of the Fed's intervention. A lot of negative feeling was stirred up when it was revealed that large bonuses were paid to AIGFP's executives after the bailout and in spite of the staggering losses we mentioned before. Then in November 2009 the Special Inspector General for the Troubled Asset Relief Program (SIGTARP),[3] published a report that levelled criticisms at how the Fed had dealt with this situation. In particular they raised the question of whether

---

[1] Maiden Lane I had been created to aid the merger of Bear Stearns and JPMorgan Chase.

[2] These are another form of asset-backed security in which AIG had securitized some of the risks it was carrying on its books. In their most vanilla form the collateral would have been debt but leading up to 2008 these products became increasingly complex with the collateral being in many different forms including CDS and other CDOs.

[3] TARP is the US programme set up to bail out financial institutions during the Financial Crisis.

Table E.1   AIG Counterparties

Bank of Montreal
Calyon
Deutsche Bank
Goldman Sachs
Merrill Lynch
Société Générale
UBS
Wachovia

the bailout had been over-generous to AIG's counterparties who had insisted that the failure of AIG would be catastrophic for them and had been influential in urging the Fed to take the measures it did. The report questions whether this was actually the case and also criticizes the Fed for not negotiating on the value of the assets they bought from these counterparties, with UBS cited as being the only bank willing to make concessions on this. These counterparties were the eight large financial institutions listed in Table E.1.

At first these names were not revealed for fear of the impact this would have on the market, but when they were finally published there was no noticeable impact.

All in all this has been the most contentious of the recent series of bailouts, notwithstanding the criticisms of banks that had taken bailout funds and then went on to produce large profits on the back of the market situation. However one important point to remember is that AIG was the largest insurance company in the world, by assets, and it was considered important to maintain the integrity of the insurance business for the benefit of the policyholders. A restructuring plan was put in progress to allow timely disposal of assets and for separation of key businesses. The company formed a General Insurance holding company, AIU, to be separate from AIG. They have also given a stake in their leading life insurance businesses, ALICO and AIA, in return for a reduction in the balance of their credit facility. These businesses are being positioned to be publicly sold off in 2010 or whenever the market would be appropriate. As for AIG Financial Products, gradually this is being wound down with offices outside of the US being closed and headcount gradually diminished. Trading positions were, on average, halved during 2009, and expected to further decrease in 2010. Hopefully, therefore, the insurance business should emerge from this situation as unscathed as possible, and a lot of care has been taken to try and ensure that the policyholders maintained faith with the brand. As to the impact of AIGFP on the market as a whole, that is much more difficult to ascertain. The scale of the losses and, ironically, the fact that they do not seem to have evolved from any wilful mismanagement is worrying for the markets. In many ways a scandal involving rogue traders would have been easier to accept than a scandal that highlights the risk in the very way in which the markets have allowed themselves to develop and the size of the exposures passed around between the market counterparties.

References

Aggregate Reserves of Depository Institutions and the Monetary Base, Federal Reserve Statistics Release, November 2009.

Cap Gemini 2009 World Wealth Report.

The Economic Significance of the Swiss Financial Centre, Swiss Bankers Association, November 2009.

European Banks Growing Bigger Sowing the Seeds of the Next Crisis, Bloomberg, December 2009.

The Financial Crisis in Japan in the 1990s: how the Bank of Japan responded and the lessons learnt, BIS, 2001.

Forbes 500, 2009.

The Future of Banking in America, FDIC Banking Review, Jan 2005.

Geld, Währung und Preisentwicklung: Der Niederrheinraum im europäischen Vergleich 1350–1800, R Metz, 1990.

Global Financial Stability Report, IMF, October 2009.

Global Pension Asset Study, Towers Watson, 2010.

The Global OTC Derivatives Market at end-June 1998, BIS.

The Global OTC Derivatives Market at end-June 1998, BIS.

Guidance to assess the importance of Financial Institutions, Markets and Instruments: Initial considerations Background Paper, October 2009, BIS, IMF and Secretariat of the Financial Stability Board, 2009.

IFSL Fund Management Brief, IFSL, 2009.

The International Private Banking Study 2009, Birchler, Cocca & Ettlin, Swiss Banking Institute, University of Zurich.

The Liechtenstein Banking Centre, Liechtenstein Bankers Association, 2009.

OTC Derivatives Market Activity in the first half of 1998, BIS.

OTC Derivatives Market Activity in the first half of 2008, BIS.

Reforming Financial Markets, HM Treasury, July 2009.

SIFMA US Key Statistics 2009.

Sovereign Wealth Funds – A Work Agenda, IMF, 2008The State of Public Finances: Outlook and Medium-Term Policies after the 2008 Crisis, IMF, 2009.

Summary of Fiscal Loan Fund Management Report, Ministry of Finance, 2009 White Paper on Local Public Finance, 2007, Ministry of Internal Affairs and Communications, 2009.

Index

Index compiled by Annette Musker